Education
and the **Arab**
World

Education and the Arab World

Challenges of the Next Millennium

 THE EMIRATES CENTER FOR STRATEGIC STUDIES AND RESEARCH

EDUCATION AND THE ARAB WORLD
Challenges of the Next Millennium

Published by
The Emirates Center for Strategic Studies and Research
PO Box 4567
Abu Dhabi
United Arab Emirates

e-mail: root@ecssr.ac.ae
http://www.ecssr.ac.ae

Distributed by
Ithaca Press, an imprint of Garnet Publishing Ltd
8 Southern Court
South Street
Reading
RG1 4QS

ISBN 0 86372 255 5

First Edition

British Library Cataloguing-in-Publication Data
A catalogue record for this book is available from the British Library

Printed in Lebanon

The Emirates Center for Strategic Studies and Research

The Emirates Center for Strategic Studies and Research (ECSSR) is an independent research institution dedicated to the promotion of professional studies and educational excellence in the UAE, the Gulf and the Arab world. Since its establishment in Abu Dhabi in 1994, ECSSR has served as a focal point for scholarship on political, economic and social matters. Indeed, ECSSR is at the forefront of analysis and commentary on Arab affairs.

The Center provides a forum for the scholarly exchange of ideas by hosting conferences and symposia, organizing workshops, sponsoring a lecture series, and publishing original and translated books and research papers. ECSSR also has an active fellowship and grant program for the writing of scholarly books and for the translation, into Arabic, of works relevant to the Center's mission. Moreover, ECSSR has a large library including rare and specialized holdings, and a state-of-the-art technology center, which has developed an award-winning website that is a unique and comprehensive source of information on the Gulf.

Through these and other activities, ECSSR aspires to engage in mutually beneficial professional endeavors with comparable institutions worldwide, and to contribute to the general educational and scientific development of the UAE.

Contents

SECTION 1
EDUCATION AND HUMAN RESOURCE DEVELOPMENT

SECTION 2
COMPARATIVE STUDIES IN EDUCATION

SECTION 3
EDUCATION IN THE GCC

Tables,
Figures and Diagrams

―――――――

These forces have a dynamic and interactive relationship with education. Educational change and reform require parallel and complementary changes and reform in other arenas.

Education and training do not stand alone. They are continuously influenced by social, political and economic changes. Education and educators at all levels work in a social context; they generally reflect the dominant views in their political environment. Nonetheless, educators and education have a reciprocal effect on the social, economic and political environment.

There are many important lessons for educators relating to these interconnections between education and other societal forces. One of these lessons is that planning for educational reform should be done only in relation to the social, political and economic realities of that time and place, and must be done so as to gain the interest and support of the relevant national or local leaders. Educational change should be carefully aligned with the best estimates of current and future societal needs. Educational change is a political process as well as a technical one.

A second important lesson is the need for greater communication between and collaboration by educators and educational planners with the leaders of other social sectors – including political leaders – and with parents and others in the communities that are served by educational institutions. These lessons suggest a realignment of most graduate school training programs for educational leaders toward more skills and knowledge about politics, negotiation and collaboration.

Finally, there is a clear lesson that if education is to contribute to both political and economic development, as well as to good citizenship, balanced development is needed. This means educational investments encompassing the expansion of education for very young children, the strengthening of elementary and secondary schooling, increased access to post-secondary college and technical study, higher quality graduate programs, and increased opportunities for education and training for adults throughout their lives. A balanced approach to educational investments means careful consideration of the needs of education in traditional institutions, training at or for the workplace and continuing education for adults. It is also important to balance the needs of the workplace with other civic, social and individual needs and interests.

2. Globalization is a fact and will have a major impact on education and training as well as on most other aspects of life on this planet
Nearly all the authors in this book write about globalization and its various effects on work, the workplace, training and education. Nearly all agree that globalization will require major changes and improvements in education in the next century.

Al-Sulayti tells us that the reality of globalization is seen as an opportunity and a blessing by many but as a destructive hurricane by others. Everyone needs to be concerned if globalization is allowed to become homogenization in which the lowest common denominators are facets of Western materialist culture, as exemplified by the hegemonic spread of Coca-Cola, McDonald's, rock music, violent or mindless movies and television programs, sex-drenched soap operas and hyper-malls. In all cultures and all countries, education at all levels, from pre-school through graduate school, can be a significant antidote to such hegemony.

Education can be designed to help individuals understand and appreciate their own culture, history and traditions, and to inculcate the ability to understand and assess others. Education can help both leaders and the rank and file of people across social and economic groups. Adnan Badran captures this point clearly:

> Education again has a major role in the preservation of the diversity of culture, language, traditions, values. Otherwise, a mono-culture and mono-language may become dominant, destroying the rich diversity of local cultures which were built through millions of years throughout the whole life of humanity.

Educational systems which properly use technology can help to connect their students to worldwide sources of information, ideas and help, and allow students to experience firsthand the interconnections between people everywhere.

It is not naïve to believe that education and training can help future leaders and ordinary citizens to understand that education can influence globalization and can help prepare individuals and communities for its consequences, at the same time helping to maximize the potential benefits of global forces while minimizing its negative potential, including deadening cultural homogenization.

One of the most critical implications of the agreement about globalization is to underscore the obsolescence and the inadequacy of so much current educational practice. The need for reform is clear.

3. Technology is an important tool for education and training, but is not a magic bullet with all of the cures for educational ills

Technology has had, and will continue to have, an enormous impact on national and international economies, on the workplace and needs for training and retraining, and on the acceleration of globalization. Technology in various forms is also having a discernible impact on some aspects of schooling and post-secondary education. But the significant impact of technology on teaching and learning, and on the relationships between learners and sources of knowledge, is just the beginning.

Norman Henchey reminds the reader that "information and communication technologies form an essential element of education: as a subject of learning (both skills and deeper significance); as a set of tools to acquire, process and communicate information; and as a system to expand access to learning resources, expertise and services."

Margaret Riel sketches the ways in which the many forms and uses of technology can enhance learning, pointing out that traditional educational practice no longer serves the needs of society so rich in information. Nor does it meet the needs of citizens who know how to use different resources and talents in concert to solve problems. Riel also points to the world-expanding potential of technology. She writes:

> Internet technology provides a rich format for the larger community to participate in the education of the next generation. Past technologies (print, photography, film and computers) have made it possible for many people to share their ideas with students without actually entering the school, but only in a one-way transmission mode of communication. With communication on the Internet, it is possible for students to interact with many more people . . . Transforming the classroom into a learning community makes it possible for many more people to be a part of the learning process . . .

But Riel also argues that in the new world of educational technology, skillful teachers are even more important than they were before.

The implications of the importance of technology in education in the future are many, including:

- the need to train and retrain teachers to use technology imaginatively
- the need to maintain the human relationships that are traditionally important in education against the possible de-humanizing impacts of some kinds of technology, and
- the need to guard against having technology widen rather than narrow the gaps between the haves and have-nots among countries and regions and within countries.

Perhaps the most important implication is the need to keep educational technology in perspective. In all of its manifestations, technology can be an important tool, but it is not a magic answer to all social and educational problems.

4. Poverty is the enemy of social and educational development and reform

There was a fourth potential agreement only touched upon in a few of the papers which needs much further elaboration by others if a more complete picture of the prospects for education and training in the twenty-first century is to be seen. Poverty has a profound, negative impact on individuals, families, communities, nations and the world.

Worldwide there is much talk about the gaps between the haves and have-nots and the effects of these gaps on education and national development. However, I have seen no evidence that there is any serious narrowing of the gaps.

Eighty percent of the people in the world live in underdeveloped countries. Most of these people are poor. Even in many countries in the developed world, the disparities between the poor and the rest of the population are large and, at least in the case of the United States (US), growing. These facts may seem of less importance in the United Arab Emirates (UAE) and other Gulf states, where affluence is the rule. But the enormous gaps between the haves and have-nots will threaten the progress and development in affluent societies just as surely as they do in the emerging and less-developed areas of the world. If nothing else, globalization breaks down the walls and fills in the moats that once were thought by some to have protected the affluent from the poor.

Problems of disease, environmental disasters, overpopulation, social ignorance and the instability of uneducated masses of people in any one place can affect all other people and countries. Globalization simply underscores John Donne's warning that no man is an island.

It is far beyond the scope and intent of this introduction to provide data or recommendations relevant to the effects of widespread poverty (between countries and regions and within them). But it is important to remember that poverty – and the social and economic costs that accompany it – will continue to have a serious effect on the contribution that education and training can make to both individual and national growth and development.

Those who advocate educational reform must recognize that substantial improvement in the educational progress and achievement of an individual living in poverty, of an impoverished community, or of a country with meager wealth and resources is not likely to occur without improvements in housing, health, job opportunities and freedom from crime and other anti-social behavior. The converse is also true. Improvements in all of the environmental conditions are not likely to occur without substantial improvements in education.

If our vision for the world of the twenty-first century emphasizes a reduction of war, strife and violence, increased positive relationships among all peoples, justice and fairness for all, and increased protection of the natural environment, the gaps between the haves and have-nots must be reduced. Educators ignore this reality at their own peril.

Major Issues

Beyond the broad agreements identified earlier, there are many issues that the nations of the world will face in the coming years. While some of these issues are addressed directly, some are only dealt with indirectly and many others not much at all.

At the close of the twentieth century, there is a great surge of activity worldwide to reform, renew or reinvent schools, and a distinctly smaller but still important wave of interest in changing post-secondary education and training. There has always been and will continue to be wide disagreements about the direction of reform. For example, what levels of education and forms of delivery (traditional and non-traditional) deserve the greatest investment? What should drive decisions about curriculum and methods: the needs and interests of individuals or those of the local community, or the larger national society?

In most educational debates today, questions about power and levels of decision-making are central. Should decisions about curriculum/

methodology, textbooks, teacher qualifications and assignments and school structure be made by the national government, regional or state governments, local communities, the school or the classroom? What influence in decision-making should be exercised by students, parents, teachers, community residents, employers or religious institutions?

At the school level, the focus in reform is often on technology: how it can help improve teaching; how more children can have access to computers; how inequities in technology access or skill can be ameliorated; and how teachers can be prepared to use new technology skillfully.

In many countries, the issues of inequities based on race, income, geography and gender in access to education and educational quality are being addressed, with considerable concern about how such inequities can inhibit global competitiveness or economic development. This concern leads to questions about which segments of the population should receive special attention or priority in educational investments – women, racial and ethnic minorities, the handicapped, gifted and talented students, immigrants or guest workers, the middle class or children of the elite.

Changes in work, the workplace itself and globalization demand changes in both education and training. Most countries face serious questions about how best to link school and work, and how to assure integrated planning for education and training. Both Masanori Hashimoto of Japan and Daphne Pan of Singapore stress the importance in their own countries of close school–work–training articulation. But most countries have fragmented planning and decision-making across education–business and school and work lines.

Privatization in education as well as in industry and social services is a major trend in many parts of the developed world, and most countries face political disagreements about the desirability and nature of such privatization. Many questions are debated about which levels and aspects of education can or should be privatized and about how both equity and quality can be assured when private forces are in charge. In some countries, privatization is related to the issue of secular/religious influence or control of education. This is a contentious issues in the US and in many Islamic countries.

Nearly everywhere, money is always the dominant issue in education – past, present and in the future. How much money is enough for the kind of education we need? What portion of a nation's gross national product (GNP) should be devoted to education and at what levels of the educational ladder? What kinds of cost benefit analysis are appropriate for assessing education?

The Kind of Education We Need

The trends, questions and issues listed earlier are mostly perennial ones. None is resolved satisfactorily in any conference or book. However, this volume offers many ideas that can be useful in thinking about the issues in the context of one's own circumstances and educational and social goals.

As the reader considers his or her circumstances and educational and social goals, I propose an overall question of great importance: What kind of education do we need as the world begins a new millennium?

I have reviewed and sought to understand the many diverse ideas and recommendations in these pages, but I shall attempt no summary or synthesis here. I will offer brief comments about six of my own personal answers to this question. These ideas, despite being rooted in my own culture-bound view, define the kind of education that can help to realize a broad, progressive vision of social, economic and political progress and national development in my own country and across the world.

Beyond Skills and Knowledge

We need education that offers all young people and adults solid academic skills and knowledge, and work-related experience and skills. But knowledge and technical skills are not enough.

Educators must recognize that academic achievement cannot be divorced from social, emotional, moral and physical development. Children and adult learners need personal and emotional nurturing and support as well as knowledge and discipline. Educational institutions at all levels can also have a positive impact on the moral and ethical development and on the reinforcement of spiritual values.

Education should contribute importantly to the development of good habits of health, nutrition and exercise, including the fostering of the recreational and sports interests of young people.

Several of the authors in this book discuss the importance of learning the skills and attitudes needed for collaboration. Robert Cornesky points out that team work and cooperative learning are key elements of the Total Quality Management (TQM) approach in business and educational organizations.

Hashimoto stresses the role that Japanese schools play in preparing students to work cooperatively in groups and establish productive relationships with co-workers.

In Geoff Spring's vision for the future, education is not simply about preparing people to work in a changing economy. He asserts that education is also about enlivening students' imaginations, preparing them for citizenship and equipping them with a sense of belonging to the community of which they are a part.

There is much experience and many models in several countries for educators to draw on if they want to infuse schools and post-secondary institutions with opportunities for the full, well-rounded development of young people. Good health, good character, good moral behavior, good emotional stability, good skills in working with others and good use of leisure time are all part of the human equation needed for strong educational systems in the century just ahead.

Educational Success for All

To be productive and competitive in a global and interdependent world, all countries should seek to have all children and youth achieve both academic and social success. Society has an obligation to foster equality of education opportunity and to attend to the interests of the powerless as well as the powerful.

Even in many developed, democratic countries, educational triage is widely practiced. This means that from 20 to 30 percent of the students are not expected to achieve much academic success in school. Much research shows that low expectations of students have a negative impact on their achievement. Such students often drop out, leaving school with minimal academic preparation, and are consigned to lives on the lowest rungs of the social and economic ladders. Often, their community and family backgrounds are accepted as the reasons for their lack of success. Low expectations are often attached to children who come from low-income communities or whose families are immigrants, members of a racial or ethnic minority group, or are socially marginalized.

A challenge for the next century is to have close to 100 percent of the children achieve at least satisfactory academic and social success in school. As Geoff Spring points out, losing a substantial percentage of the children to academic failure should no longer be acceptable for any nation that aspires to succeed in a globalized economy. In addition, countries which aspire to be democratic societies can hardly realize that goal if a third of their population lack the skills and motivation for positive citizenship.

Confronting the need for equality of opportunity requires effective educational interventions and substantial investments of resources strong enough to overcome historic inequities across lines of race, ethnicity, religion, native language, gender and social class. Obviously, special interventions are needed as well for children who are mentally and physically handicapped and for groups that are often marginalized, such as immigrants and guest workers.

A Central Role for Teachers

In the next century, teachers will be the primary determinant of the quality of education at all levels.

Riel sets the key theme for this point when she asserts that technology will increase, not decrease, the need for good teachers and skilled teaching. She argues further that we need to increase our investment in human resources and in the professional development of educators rather than in technological approaches such as "just-in-time learning," as useful a concept as that might be for some purposes.

Henchey reminds us that new kinds of teachers are needed for a reformed educational system in the future. Some teachers need to be models of artistic skill or maturity – some coaches and mentors and some designers of learning programs – while others need to be communicators – some managers of learning systems and some experts in different areas.

The point about the continuing and increased importance of teachers applies to all levels – from early childhood education through graduate school and into adult education. But societies generally do not offer equal status or compensation across these levels. College and university teachers in most countries enjoy relatively high status and moderate income and working conditions. But teachers at the primary and secondary school levels are almost universally on the lower rungs of white collar pay and status in society. Ironically, teachers of the youngest children – who are adored and treasured in nearly all cultures – typically receive the lowest pay and status.

If teachers are as important as most experts say they are, and as most students and parents believe, then a reformed educational system will need to find ways to recruit excellent people into teaching and provide them with reasonable pay, working conditions and recognition.

Improving the pre-service and in-service preparation of teachers, especially those in early childhood and the elementary and secondary levels, should also be an important component of any country's educational reform strategy.

Building a Civil Society

The quality of life in the next century will depend a great deal on the success of nations and communities to build and sustain civil societies. A civil society generally means a society or a country which meets its residents' basic needs for housing, nutrition, education, security from crime and violence, opportunities for stable family life, spiritual sustenance, an aesthetically satisfying environment, and opportunities for both work and play. But it means more than that. A civil society will also have these other characteristics: a fair judicial system, fair treatment for all by government and other institutions, opportunities for self-expression, established means and an inclination on the part of citizens to resolve disputes and conflicts without recourse to violence, physical safety, personal privacy, respect for racial, cultural, ethnic, religious and political diversity, and polite and considerate relationships within families and with others.

There are two basic building blocks needed before countries and communities can move toward creating a more civil society. The first is the development of a strong "third sector," of independent community organizations, which Jeremy Rifkin describes as ". . . the bonding force. The social glue that unites the diverse interests of the American people into a cohesive social identity." But the capacity to join in civic associations to help one another and the community is not limited to Americans. Jeremy Rifkin cites the economic importance of the "third sector" as a provider of jobs, training, continuing education for adults, social services of all kinds and as a producer of social capital.[1]

Clearly for the many countries of the world seeking to find a balance of power between the market and the government, strengthening the third sector of community organizations and agencies has realistic potential for increasing productivity, competitiveness and the nation's quality of life.

The second building block for a civil society is an educational system from pre-school through graduate school that is committed to building the civic life of the country. The educational system can, and should, endow its students with the attitudes and skills needed to contribute to the common good and to be active participants in civic life. One way to do this is to have students devote some of their educational time to voluntary community service. Another approach is to teach students to understand and value their own community's history, traditions and culture.

Family–Community–School Partnerships

Creating and sustaining significant educational improvement require the substantial involvement of families and the communities; schools cannot do the job of education alone.

Organizations of parents and community people who are involved in the schools are one important part of the "third sector." Such organizations are one way in which parents can influence school policies and practices and collaborate with educators. As I try to show in some detail in my own chapter later in this book, effective working partnerships between public schools and the families and communities they serve are necessary if the public school systems are to survive as we know them and to flourish into the next century. In most countries, educational reform will be difficult to achieve and sustain without the involvement and support of most parents and many forces in the community – that is, without real partnerships. Creating such partnerships will require courage and vision on the part of educational leaders; technology can play an important role in these efforts.

Geoff Spring and I both argue that partnerships between schools and parents need to be reinvigorated if students are to receive the best education and life chances. Spring points out that "students from homes where parents take an active interest in their schooling, where there are discussions about a wide range of subjects, where there are books and a culture of inquiry, have been clearly shown to do better academically than do students from homes where these advantages are absent."

Robert Cornesky broadens this point by arguing that in applying the ideas of TQM by having students, parents and employers help to shape educational goals and methods is one key to improvement either in business or in education.

I argue that a partnership of schools, families and communities requires reciprocity in exchange of services, information and influence. It also practices democratic procedures. Partnership should be the theme of school, family and community relationships in the century ahead.

Lifelong Learning

Education in the next century should be conceived as starting with infants and continuing throughout the senior years. Lifelong learning will be the hallmark of the most successful and productive societies.

Successful societies in the century ahead will be characterized by "learning communities," which means communities that offer diverse resources to education and support to all of their residents from infants through senior citizens. In a learning community, children and youths, along with their families, are surrounded by a network of agencies and institutions, including public schools, which continue to help individuals as they move through life.

Hashimoto reminds us that one of the keys to the success of the Japanese educational system is that the schools work hard to develop in young people "a propensity for lifelong learning." Henchey makes a similar point when writes that "[t]he attitudes and skills of *lifelong learning* are essential elements of preparation for life and work."

In most communities, lifelong learning can be best realized when both formal and informal learning opportunities are embedded in a variety of structures, including the home, the community institutions discussed above as a part of the third sector, schools and work.

Training for employees is one important component of lifelong learning. This responsibility can be shared by employers themselves through on-the-job training and educational institutions including technical institutes, universities, on-line courses, distance learning using radio and television and public schools in their role as community education centers. Good training programs offer signal benefits to employers and to the individuals.

Implications for the United Arab Emirates

The UAE has made great progress in education in less than three decades. Abdullah Mograby provides useful documentation of this progress. However, workforce quality is clearly not the only factor of importance. The development of human capital must also embrace fostering good citizens of high character who can work cooperatively with others at home and in the community as well as in the workplace. Education that contributes to the quality of life in the UAE, as in other countries, should equip its people to understand their country's cultural traditions and strengths and who, at the same time, can understand and deal with differences in tolerance and see themselves as citizens of an interconnected world.

Roger Benjamin recommends that the UAE undertake a comprehensive audit of their education and training assets in order to disclose gaps and misalignments. He asserts that in the merging global economy, the quality of a state's workforce (human capital) is the only asset that will count.

William F. Halloran, a specialist in higher education, urges the UAE and other countries of the Gulf ". . . to equip young people with the attitudes, knowledge and technical skills that will enable them to flourish as members of the family of nations in the twenty-first century."

There are other educational implications that may be derived from this volume by policy makers and educators as outlined below.

- Education in the early years (ages 0 to 8) deserves special priority and attention.
- Support and education for mothers and fathers can be an important part of strengthening early education programs.
- Teachers will be the key to improved education at every level. Training and retraining are needed in order to move away from an emphasis on rote-learning and classrooms stressing lecturing and recitation.
- New approaches recognizing differences in learning styles of children can make a big difference in student motivation and educational results.

- Opportunities to learn the skills and values of cooperation in school can be a good foundation to practice cooperation and teamwork in the workplace and in the community.
- Schools and universities can be asked to play an active role in helping to energize communities with new or revitalized civic organizations and activities.
- Increased opportunities for continuing education for adults can strengthen the networks of civil life so vital to building a civil society.
- Planning for all levels of education and training can be better articulated and coordinated.
- Employers (including both national and multinational firms) should be encouraged to offer high quality training opportunities on the job.
- Changes in education and training can contribute to diversifying the national economy as it moves away from the dominant oil industry in the years ahead.

Conclusion

This volume is essentially a mosaic of important and diverse ideas about education, economic development and technology. The chief value of the ideas and information offered is to stimulate readers – both educators and policy makers – to think more deeply and imaginatively about the kind of world they want to seek in the next century and beyond and then to develop a vision for the kind of educational system that can contribute strongly to achieving such a world.

I use the word "vision" deliberately. Vision implies a broad view and comprehensive goals. It requires going beyond the nuts and bolts of everyday educational planning. It requires a framework of values and principles. Visionary leadership means the practical and political skills to put the vision into practice and is what all societies will need in the coming century if we all are to avoid many of the tragic, cruel and bloody mistakes of the twentieth century.

In calling for vision I am not yearning for universal, worldwide agreement about the nature of society. Such an outcome is neither possible nor desirable. I see the diversity of cultures, languages, religions and educational approaches as a distinct advantage. Homogenization would leave us in an impoverished state and is really only achievable by authoritarian means.

Social institutions, including all variety of educational institutions, are and should be rooted in their distinctive cultures. Education must be aligned with the economic, political and cultural needs and realities of the society it serves. Educational policies, structures and methodologies should not be homogenized. But there are a few basic educational goals which can and should be universally sought: academic and social success for all children and adults in a society, education which fosters good character, morals and citizenship, education which fosters peaceful, non-violent and tolerant attitudes toward other people, religions, cultures and nations, and education which prepares individuals to live economically and socially productive lives.

While education should help each society build on its distinctive cultural, religious and political strengths, cross-fertilization is to be encouraged. In fact, cross-fertilization of ideas in education is almost inevitable because of the forces of globalization.

Research and examples from one country and culture are useful to those in other countries and cultures which are seeking to improve educational policies and practices. This is what I call the "more distant mirror" phenomenon. Looking at one's problems and alternative solutions at a distance seems to give policy makers, planners, administrators and researchers different ways of thinking about close-to-home problems. Research and successful practice in one country offer support for those who want to act to improve education in another.

Some anthropologists who have studied the process of cultural change point out that diffusion does not typically involve the replication in one society of some practice developed elsewhere. Rather, what is transposed is the basic idea, a model – one might even say a metaphor – which is then applied to the particular circumstances of the receiving society.

We should seize as many opportunities as we can in the years ahead to engage in cross-national and cross-cultural studies and conversation. That is one of the reasons why the ECSSR conference and this publication are so important.

It is encouraging to note that education and training have moved closer to the top of the political and economic agenda in most countries of the world, certainly higher than in the past. The importance of education for individual development, for economic growth, for national productivity and for strong civil societies is undeniable. The century ahead will bring a rare opportunity for educators to join with leaders of political, economic and religious institutions in realizing the potential that effective education has to help societies and humankind at large move toward a more peaceful and just life for all.

The Volume

This volume is divided into three main sections. The first section provides an overview of education and human resource development in the twenty-first century. William E. Becker synthesizes economists' views of how and in what form education and training influence economic growth. While the biggest social and private benefits of education are at the primary level of schooling, he argues that for education to matter, a country must have a population that has achieved more than the basic skill levels. His chapter is followed by Don Davies, who looks at education and society. Monther Sharè and Adnan Badran then explore the important issues of human capital development, providing policy makers with useful guidance regarding future decisions relating to investment in education and training. Margaret Riel argues that rather than being replaced by technology, educators are becoming even more important in the age of technology and that technology can be used to enhance rather than facilitate a student's learning. Robert Cornesky discusses how his concept of TQM, a philosophy that promotes an organization's mission, can be applied in education and training. Geoff Spring concludes the first section by discussing the make-up of future schools in a post-information age. He argues that the key challenge is for schools to adapt to the new environment and technologies while maintaining their traditional values and purposes of education.

The second section provides a comparative analysis, surveying education and its implementation in various international settings: Masanori Hashimoto illustrates the experiences in Japan, Daphne Pan draws on the Singaporean model and Norman Henchey considers education in Canada.

The final section reviews education in the Gulf, particularly the UAE. Hamad Ali Al-Sulayti draws some issues of concern for education and training in the Gulf Co-operation Council (GCC) countries. Abdullah Mograby looks at the challenges to and prospects for human resource development while Roger Benjamin looks at developing the UAE workforce for the future. William Halloran provides an account of the important experience of Zayed University in implementing an educational system that is in step with the changing technological environment. Jamal Al-Suwaidi closes the volume by providing a general overview on ways in which the UAE education system can improve.

Special thanks are given to Herro Mustafa and Susan Al-Baker of ECSSR who provided considerable guidance and editorial assistance throughout the production of this volume.

SECTION I

EDUCATION AND HUMAN RESOURCE DEVELOPMENT

1

The Role of Education and Training in Economic Development

William E. Becker

Economists and philosophers have debated the contribution of education to national welfare from the time of Adam Smith.[1] Donald McCloskey, for example, reports on an exchange between Nobel Laureates George Stigler and Milton Friedman in which Stigler argued that people will find their own self-interest with or without education, and that no amount of teaching would change that. But Friedman came to the defense of teaching and argued that while individuals pursue their self-interests, they are often ignorant and require education to see that something thought to be in their personal or national interest was not.[2]

Paul Douglas and then Theodore Schultz eschewed the philosophical debate about education and national welfare when they focused attention on the measurement of education's contribution to economic growth.[3] The 1960s' inquiries into the productivity effects of education by John Kendrick and Edward Denison inspired the more recent work of Angus Maddison and John Pencavel to identify the sources of economic growth within an input–output framework.[4] This growth accounting is based on the idea that countries are on the frontiers of their aggregate production functions and that factors of production are used to the point where the values of the marginal (private and social) products of each of the inputs equals their respective prices. The economist's job is to determine how much of the increase in a country's output is attributable to the accumulation of physical capital and the other factors of production. The residual (what is not explained by all the measured factors) is attributed to the country's knowledge base. Education is assumed to influence both this residual as well as the physical capital and labor inputs themselves.

References to education, training and technology appear in all explanations of aggregate production and per capita income levels. Growth theorists such as Robert Lucas and Paul Romer extended

Robert Solow's analysis of the influence of technology and education on economic growth by making technological innovations dependent on incentives.[5] Other economists, such as Theo Eicher, have added to this new endogenous growth literature by explicitly modeling the impact of education and human capital accumulation on economic growth.[6] Still other economists, such as William Baumol, discuss the role of education and training as a facilitator of international transfers of technologies from innovating countries to imitating countries.[7] Economists, such as Robert Barro and Xavier Sala-i-Martin and Lant Pritchett, hotly debate the nature of the educational input and its effect on economic growth.[8]

Gary Becker observed that educators generally resisted the early work on the economic effects of education; focusing on jobs and earnings was viewed as too narrow by the education practitioner.[9] Education specialists (and the policy centers that hire them, such as the Center for Educational Research and Innovation of the Organisation for Economic Co-operation and Development [OECD]) now talk about efficiency, cost and benefit, rates of return, credentialing and educational practice in making policy recommendations for public spending on education and training. In this policy analysis and advocacy for one type of education versus another, however, there is still little recognition of the economics literature and the implications of aggregate production function or growth accounting, the old exogenous and new endogenous growth theories and technology transfer.

This chapter provides a synthesis of economists' views of how and in what forms education and training influence economic growth. Attention is given to the definition of the education outputs and the implications of alternative measurements for assessing education's contribution to the economic growth of both developed and developing countries. Although intended to provide guidance to policy makers attempting to devise education policies aimed at complementing and advancing economic growth, it should also be of interest to anyone working in the area of training and education.

Differences in the pecuniary returns to primary, secondary and tertiary education and alternative forms of training are provided and considered for policy implementation. The premise is that private incentives induce students and their families to invest in education. The emphasis is on pecuniary returns to education; little attention is given to the cultural and institutional details that also influence both the individual's decision to invest and society's capacity to supply educational opportunities. Even with this limited scope, the picture that emerges is that the best policy for a country to pursue with regard to education is to recognize that there may not be a single best policy. Educational policy must depend on the education levels of the country; countries that have ignored education in the past have to start from the base they have, yet recognize that there may be no noticeable effect until a critical minimum has been achieved. For a more advanced country, unless the education stimulates and is complementary with innovation, it will sooner or later lead to diminishing marginal returns.

Education and Earnings

Educators and legislators in the US were shocked in the late 1970s by the assertion that many Americans may have been "overeducated," at least when viewed from the relatively low financial returns for higher education reported by Richard Freeman in his 1976 book, *The Overeducated American*. More recent evidence indicates that the difference between the earnings of secondary school degree holders and four-year tertiary degree holders increased rapidly during the 1980s throughout the world. Finis Welch's work with Kevin Murphy, for example, indicates that even after controlling for experience and restricting attention to only earnings, the difference in earnings between holders of higher tertiary degrees and high school degrees was larger at the end of the 1980s than at any time since World War II; after 11 or 15 years of job experience, the tertiary degree holder earned some 60 percent more than a high school graduate.[10]

The cause of the up-turn in earnings associated with education in the 1980s cannot rest on events in any one country because most countries to some extent experienced an increasing payoff to tertiary education. Although the supply of highly educated individuals increased worldwide, the needs of changing technology appear to have raised the demand for these highly educated individuals even further. High paying, low-skill jobs are on the decline in most developed countries. The rising tertiary earnings premium is thus the result of falling high school earnings as well as the rising tertiary earnings. John Bishop and others associate falling high school earnings in the US with a change in the composition of the labor force brought about by a decrease in unob-servable quality attributes of high school graduates. Indeed, high school graduates in the US are not as good as they once were.[11]

In Japan, high school is rewarded relatively more than it is in the US. The big payoff to high school graduation in Japan is the reason that high school students work so hard in Japan, according to Bishop. He claims that high school students in Japan know something upon graduation and they are rewarded for it. He and others argue for national tests to assess and evaluate individual students and the high schools they attend.

William E. Becker, William Greene and Sherwin Rosen argue that the attempt to assess the contribution of educational institutions based solely on changes in student test scores from the time of admission to graduation could be a misleading measure of the benefit to the individual and society because it ignores the financial returns that are associated with that knowledge.[12] For example, Eric Hanushek reports that for the 147 studies he considered, the instructional expenditure variables (teacher–student ratio, teacher education or teacher salaries) are unrelated to student performance.[13] Based on a literature review as well as their own work, David Card and Alan Krueger report that the pupil–teacher ratio is negatively related and teacher education is positively related to the financial returns for an additional year of schooling.[14] Calls for national standardized tests are simply missing the distinction between learning and the value of learning. Similarly, those who attempt to compare standardized test scores across countries are missing the importance of the rewards to test-score performance in those countries. To assess the value of education and what contributes to it, we must focus more on market-valued outcomes such as earnings and not standardized test scores.[15]

It is much easier to measure the pecuniary benefits that accrue to the student than those that accrue to society. To the extent that education makes individuals more productive, it benefits society. On the other hand, if education is serving only as a filter or screening device that merely identifies the brightest future employees, rather than imparting productive skills, there may be no net social benefit.[16] If labeling of students from bright to dull is the only function of education screening, there is little reason for government subsidies; the private gains justify self-financing.[17] Government subsidies would only add to the number of credentialed individuals, depreciating education's value to the individual.

The labor force in the United States has the world's highest proportion of university graduates (see Table 1:1) and yet the premium paid to these graduates is also among the highest (see Table 2:1). The screening argument suggests that as the proportion of university degrees increases, the university earnings premium should decrease. For the countries in Tables 1:1 and 2:1, there is only a slight within-sample negative correlation, which is statistically insignificant ($r = -0.079$, with a one-tail p-value of 0.38), suggesting no relationship between the proportion of people holding degrees in the labor markets and the earnings premium. Hence, education appears to be doing more than screening.

In post-World War II Britain, when its elite system of higher education was being expanded, Sir Kingsley Amis offered the dictum: "More will mean worse."[18] The lack of correlation between the proportion of university degrees in the labor markets and its earnings premium demonstrates that this need not be true.[19] Many of those who went to Britain's universities in the age of elite higher education were there as a birthright.

The mass higher education in the US has expanded greatly, with more than 100 great research universities and prestigious liberal arts colleges (see Table 3:1).[20] Beyond these institutions, there is a diverse range of tertiary institutions that deliver a varied education that fits the aptitudes of students at costs lower than those of the elite schools.[21] Yet standards have not been sacrificed. From 1986 to 1992, for example, the percentage of the 1,562 tertiary institutions that required or recommended high school mathematics for admission increased from 69 percent to 83 percent and the average number of high school units of mathematics required or recommended rose from 2.6 to 2.7. Furthermore, student mathematics skills, as measured by either the mean ACT or SAT (two twelfth-year standardized tests that college applicants take in the US), were unchanged in the late 1980s and early 1990s.[22]

Percentage Distribution of the Labor Force 25 to 64 Years of Age by the Highest Completed Level of Education (1995)

	Early childhood, primary and lower secondary education	Upper secondary education	Non-university tertiary education	University-level education	Total
North America					
Canada	19	29	32	19	100
United States	11	52	9	28	100
Pacific Area					
Australia	42	31	12	16	100
Korea	39	41	x	20	100
New Zealand	36	37	16	12	100
European Union					
Austria	24	66	2	7	100
Belgium	37	32	17	14	100
Denmark	33	44	7	16	100
Finland	30	47	10	13	100
France	25	54	9	12	100
Germany	12	62	11	15	100
Greece	52	26	8	15	100
Ireland	45	29	12	13	100

Italy	56	33	x	11	100
Luxembourg	63	21	x	16	100
Netherlands	31	43	a	27	100
Portugal	76	10	4	9	100
Spain	64	15	6	16	100
Sweden	24	47	14	15	100
United Kingdom	19	57	10	14	100
Other OECD Countries					
Czech Republic	12	76	x	12	100
Norway	15	53	12	20	100
Poland	21	64	4	12	100
Switzerland	15	61	14	10	100
Turkey	76	15	a	9	100
Country Mean	**35**	**42**	**10**	**15**	**100**

Notes: a = Data not applicable because the category does not apply.

x = Data included in another category/column of the table.

The figures in the Total column do not add to exactly 100% because the percentages have been rounded.

Source: Centre for Education Research and Innovation, *Education at a Glance: OECD Indicators* (Paris: OECD, 1997).

TABLE 2:1
Relative Earnings of Persons Aged 25 to 64 with Income from Employment
(income for upper secondary education = 100) by Level of Educational Attainment and Gender (1995)

	Below upper secondary education			Non-university tertiary education			University-level education		
	M+W	Men	Women	M+W	Men	Women	M+W	Men	Women
North America									
Canada	87	84	75	110	108	113	156	148	164
United States	68	67	62	119	118	126	174	167	176
Pacific Area									
Australia	89	105	87	111	118	105	142	161	139
New Zealand	82	82	79	106	98	102	165	163	146
European Union									
Denmark	83	86	85	104	108	110	133	139	130
Finland	93	91	93	126	127	126	187	190	174
France	80	86	78	128	132	137	175	183	168
Germany	78	88	82	111	107	116	163	158	154
Ireland*	85	77	62	123	121	123	183	171	187
Italy	77	74	74	x	x	x	134	142	120

Netherlands	77	85	68	124	126	131	162	153	158
Portugal	68	66	67	x	x	x	183	180	174
Sweden	89	88	87	109	111	112	151	154	144
United Kingdom	75	73	73	132	114	151	179	153	195
Other OECD countries									
Czech Republic	66	72	75	x	x	x	158	154	149
Norway	82	84	77	123	125	124	149	149	150
Switzerland	67	75	70	145	124	134	157	141	156
Country Mean	**79**	**81**	**76**	**119**	**117**	**122**	**162**	**159**	**158**

Note: *1993 data.

x = Data included in another category/column of the table.

Source: Centre for Education Research and Innovation, *Education at a Glance: OECD Indicators* (Paris: OECD, 1997).

TABLE 3:1
Classification of United States Tertiary Educational Institutions
(number of institutions/proportion of subtotal)

	1970	1976	1987	1994
Research	92	98	104	125
%	6.81	7.20	7.54	8.92
Doctorate	81	86	109	111
%	6.0	6.32	7.90	7.92
Master's	456	594	595	529
%	33.78	43.64	43.12	37.73
BS/BA	721	583	572	637
%	53.41	42.84	41.45	45.44
Subtotal	1,350	1,361	1,380	1,402
Associate	1,063	1,146	1,367	1,471
Total	**2,413**	**2,507**	**2,747**	**2,873**

Source: William E. Becker, "Teaching Economics to Undergraduates," *Journal of Economic Literature* vol. 35, no. 3 (September 1997): 1349.

Rates of Return

The earnings premium associated with tertiary education gives some idea of the value of education among countries. It is only one piece of a cost-benefit analysis. To assess the net value of completing any particular level of education, we need to know the differential benefits – private and social – that accrue over a lifetime and the cost of the education.

Economists calculate the net value of an investment in education and training in two basic ways (although there are many variations): the internal rate of return method and the earnings function regression approach.

The internal rate of return method requires detailed information on expected earnings at each future age for students completing various levels of education. The difference in the mean earnings at regular time intervals for those completing only primary school and those completing the secondary level is the expected earnings benefit of completing the secondary level. The costs are the earnings foregone while in school, and any directly assessed schooling expenses paid by the student and his or her family. The private rate of return should be calculated from after tax earnings plus other non-monetary and personal costs incurred. The social rate of return should be calculated from gross earnings plus other monetary and non-monetary benefits and externalities to society and all the costs incurred by society.[23] In actual calculations, however, differences in before and after tax earnings and non-monetary benefits accruing to the individual and society are ignored. The actual direct costs of school paid by the individual are also often ignored with the assumption that any earnings while in school equal direct costs paid. To the extent that schooling is subsidized, the cost to society will exceed the private costs. The internal rate of return to education is the rate of interest that makes the present value of the expected future differential benefits equal to the cost of the additional education.[24]

Internal rates of return can be calculated for any investment, be it education or shares of Microsoft stock. The decision rule is to pursue investments with higher internal rates of return. For example, if one can borrow money at 10 percent interest, then ignoring risk, any investment with an internal rate of return above 10 percent is worth undertaking.

Calculating the internal rate of return from actual data on earnings stratified by age and schooling level is tedious and demanding in terms of data. As a substitute, researchers have turned to estimating the marginal private return to schooling directly from age-earning profiles. This involves the estimation of a regression equation in which the dependent variable is a measure of earnings and the explanatory variables include completed years of schooling (or level of schooling) and other variables believed to influence an individual's earnings. As with the internal rate of return method, direct schooling costs are ignored. Typical age-earnings scatterplots to which earnings functions are fit can be seen in Figure 1:1, where Anil Deolalikar has stratified age-earning data by schooling in Indonesia.[25] Age-earnings scatterplots typically show a high diversity in earnings at older ages, as seen in Figure 1:1. The semi-logarithmic earnings equation introduced by Jacob Mincer is used to control for this heteroscedasticity (larger errors in predicting higher earnings).[26] In this specification, the dependent variable is the natural log of earnings but the explanatory variables are not transformed; thus, the name "semi-log." Mincerian earnings functions use individual earnings data (Y), years of schooling (S), years of labor market experience (X) and other attributes believed to influence earnings. A typical sample regression equation for predicting the natural logarithm of earnings (lnY) is then of the form:

1. $\hat{\ln Y} = b_0 + b_1 S + b_2 X + b_3 X^2 + \ldots$

The population return to education is estimated by $\delta \ln Y / \delta S = \delta Y / Y \delta S = b_1$ whereas the population return to experience is estimated by $\delta \ln Y / \delta X = b_2 + 2 b_3 X$, assuming Y, S and X are continuous.

For discrete changes in schooling, most economists interpret the return to a year of schooling as:

2. $b_1 = \dfrac{\ln Y_h - \ln Y_{h-s}}{h - (h-s)} = \dfrac{1}{s} \left[\dfrac{Y_h - Y_{h-s}}{Y_{h-s}} \right]$

Thus, the coefficient b_1 multiplied by 100 is said to be equal to the percentage change in Y for a small change in years of schooling from (h - s) years to h years. But this is only an approximation. For a one year change, where s = 1, we have:

3. $b_1 = \ln Y_h - \ln Y_{h-1} = \ln \left[\dfrac{Y_h}{Y_{h-1}} \right]$ and exp (b) = $Y_h / Y_{h-1} = 1 + c$

FIGURE 1:1

Male and Female Age–Earnings Profiles by Schooling Type

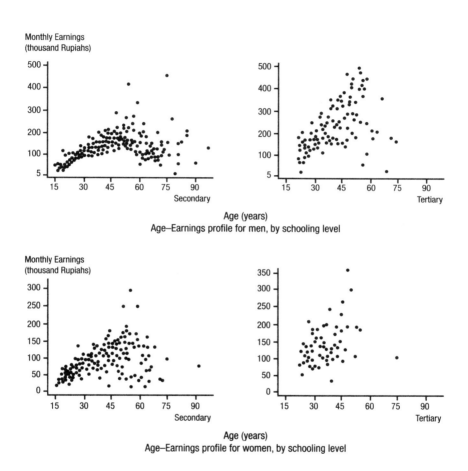

Age (years)
Age–Earnings profile for men, by schooling level

Age (years)
Age–Earnings profile for women, by schooling level

Source: Anil Deolalikar, "Gender Differences in the Returns to Schooling and in School Enrollment Rates in Indonesia," *Journal of Human Resources* vol. 28, no. 4 (Fall 1993): 920–21, as reprinted in William E. Becker, *Statistics for Business and Economics Using Microsoft Excel 97* (Bloomington: S.R.B. Publishing, 1997), 463.

but c is defined by:

4. $Y_h = (1 + c)Y_{h-1}$

The exponent of b_1 is equal to $1 + c$ but c is only approximately equal to b_1 [i.e. $\ln(1 + c) - c = b_1$] for small values of c. This is not always the case. For instance, Table 4:1 provides the means of the regression coefficients on years of schooling in a semi-log earnings function in which the logarithm of earnings is a function of years of schooling, years of experience and years of experience squared.[27] The coefficient 13.4 percent figure for Sub-Saharan Africa represents a 14.3 percent rate of return to an additional year of education.[28]

TABLE 4:1
The Coefficient on Years of Schooling: Mincerian Rate of Return
(regional average)

Country	Rate of return to		
	Years of schooling	Coefficient (percent)	Years of schooling
Sub-Saharan Africa	5.9	13.4	14.3
Asia*	8.4	9.6	10.0
Europe/Middle East/North Africa*	8.5	8.2	8.5
Latin America/Caribbean	7.9	12.4	13.2
OECD	10.9	6.8	7.0
World	8.4	10.1	10.6

Note: *Non-OECD.
Source: Years of schooling and coefficients from George Psacharopoulos, "Returns to Investment in Education: A Global Update," *World Development* vol. 22, no. 9 (1994): 1329.

Although the World Bank has supported studies of education involving both internal rate of return and earnings function estimation, George Psacharopoulos, its leading advocate of internal rate of return studies, argues that the "discounting of actual net age-earnings profiles (to obtain the internal rate of return) is the most appropriate . . . because it takes into account the most important part of the early earnings history of the individual (when foregone earnings are zero)."[29] Table 5:1 provides

Psacharopoulos' world patterns in internal rates of return to levels of education. Private internal rates of returns are higher than social returns because of the subsidies to education. The social internal rate of return reflects the total cost to society whereas the private rate only captures the cost to the individual being educated. Among the three levels of education, primary education provides the highest social net value in all regions of the world. The lowest social rate of return is to tertiary education in OECD countries. Even for tertiary education, however, the 8.7 percent rate is not low, suggesting that there has not been an "overinvestment in education."

TABLE 5:1
Returns to Investments in Education by Level (Percentage)
Full Method, Latest Year, Regional Averages

Country	Social			Private		
	Prim.	Sec.	Higher	Prim.	Sec.	Higher
Sub-Saharan Africa	24.3	18.2	11.2	41.3	26.6	27.8
Asia*	19.9	13.3	11.7	39.0	18.9	19.9
Europe/Middle East/North Africa*	15.5	11.2	10.6	17.4	15.9	21.7
Latin America/Caribbean	17.9	12.8	12.3	26.2	16.8	19.7
OECD	14.4	10.2	8.7	21.7	12.4	12.3
World	18.4	13.1	10.9	29.1	18.1	20.3

Note: *Non-OECD
Source: George Psacharopoulos, "Returns to Investment in Education: A Global Update," *World Development* vol. 22, no. 9 (1994): 1328.

To a large extent, primary schooling has a high social rate of return because it is inexpensive; young students give up little if any earning potential to attend school. Higher education is expensive; thus, its social rate of return is pulled down. Vocational education is more expensive with a lower social internal rate of return (10.6 percent) than the more general secondary schooling because the cost of vocational instruction is higher than the cost of general instruction. What is often overlooked, however, is that technical and vocational training can be highly complementary to general secondary education. Psacharopoulos and Velez found a strong positive interaction between training and years of formal education in determining earnings, with significant effects after a worker has eight years of formal education.[30]

Higher education faculties (or disciplines of study) also show a large variation in returns (see Table 6:1). Curiously, higher education in agriculture has a relatively low social rate of return but is generally viewed as desirable by politicians. Worldwide, lawyers are viewed with disdain by the general public; yet, legal studies have a relatively high social rate of return. A comparison of rates of return can tax intuition and preconceived notions of socially valuable education. Keep in mind, however, that the rates of return in Table 6:1 ignore non-pecuniary benefits and externalities.[31]

TABLE 6:1
Returns to Higher Education by Faculty
(Percentages)

Subject	Social	Private
Agriculture	7.6	15.0
Soc. Sciences, Art and Human.	9.1	14.6
Economics & Business	12.0	17.7
Engineering	10.9	19.0
Law	12.7	16.8
Medicine	10.0	17.7
Physics	1.8	13.7
Sciences	8.9	17.0

Source: George Psacharopoulos, "Returns to Investment in Education: A Global Update," *World Development* vol. 22, no. 9 (1994): 1330.

Acceptance of internal rate of return estimates and the idea that the primary beneficiaries of higher education are the individual students have given rise to the argument that most of the cost of this education should be borne by the individual student. A movement in this direction is underway in the US where university tuition and fees have been rising faster than general price inflation while government subsidies have been falling. In both private and public universities, students pay a substantial part of the cost of a bachelor's (tertiary) degree in the US; Britain and Australia are following suit. Starting in September 1998, for example, most British students will have to pay newly enacted fees (£1,000 sterling or US$1,700) in order to pursue a higher education. In Australia, universities are now free to give up a portion of the government subsidies to accept a small percentage of full fee-paying students who would otherwise not be accepted.

Comparisons of the social and private rates of returns to education and comparison of these rates with those of other investment alternatives are tricky if general prices are not constant. They may also be difficult to interpret between countries if one economy is enjoying major technological change while the other is not.

Since educational expenses are measured in monetary terms, they are sensitive to the economic conditions of the country in which the education takes place. Educational costs tend to rise quickly with the wealth of the country. They also tend to rise more rapidly than the general rate of inflation within the country. As long as the delivery of education is human capital intensive (requiring classroom instructors and other human personnel), technological developments in physical capital occurring elsewhere in the economy will be difficult to implement in education. Baumol, Blackman and Wolff argue that technological advances drive down relative prices in the sectors where these advances can be implemented.[32] In these innovating sectors, wages can rise even though product prices and the cost per unit of output are falling. Because the cost of labor tends to move uniformly with average productivity across the economy, the cost per unit of output and the relative price of the output will rise in the sectors that cannot implement the new technologies. Thus, the apparent rates of return to education may fall as its price (tuition and fees) rises even though the driving cost increases had little to do with the quality of education or its actual contribution to the overall growth process.

As pointed out by Baumol et al., the "cost disease phenomenon" is insensitive to the contribution that education is making to the innovations taking place in the other sectors. Ironically, the education industry, and higher education in particular, may be the least able to implement the technology that it is helping to create and disseminate. The research and development aspect of higher education, as well as the general instruction and service functions of lower levels, contain factors that are not amenable to technological improvements.

Education and Growth Accounting

Education rate of return studies miss the externalities (i.e. better health care, more informed voters, better consumer choice etc.) associated with education while suffering from Baumol's cost disease. Individual rate of return studies say nothing about the spillover effect of education on aggregate economic activity. Allegedly, education does more than contribute to an individual's earning potential; it is the engine of growth – so the argument goes.

Accounting for growth in gross domestic product provides an alternative to rate of return studies. Growth accounting is based on the concept of an aggregate production function that links output to various forms of inputs. Patterned after the early work by Kendrick and Denison, most studies of the contribution of education to aggregate economic growth start with a production function in which the total economy's output of goods and services, O (measured by gross domestic product), is produced on a fixed amount of land by the inputs of labor, L (measured by total person hours worked), and physical capital, K (measured by inventories of machines and equipment).[33] In functional notation,

5. $O = f(L, K)$

Maddison states that "the oldest index of productivity growth is that for labor productivity, Π," which he defined as the difference between the compound rate of increase in output, $\dot{O}$, and the rate of increase in labor, $\dot{L}$:

6. $\Pi (L) = \dot{O} - \dot{L}$

where the dots over the variables indicate percentage changes.[34] Similarly, productivity growth associated with increases in capital is defined by:

7. $\Pi (K) = \dot{O} - \dot{K}$

These measures of productivity do not show the same patterns over time. Labor productivity tends not to fluctuate with the business cycle while indices of capital productivity tend to move with the business cycle, being negative in recessions. Allowing for these changes in both labor and capital productivity gives rise to the total factor productivity (TFP) approach:

$$8. \quad \dot{\Pi}(L, K) = \dot{O} - \alpha\dot{L} - (1 - \alpha)\dot{K}$$

where α is the fraction of national income paid to labor, which under the assumptions of perfect competition and constant returns to scale is constrained to equal one minus the factor share going to capital. The early work of Douglas (1948), for example, placed α at 0.75. [35]

Because the total factor approach accounted for less than half of the US growth, researchers introduced the "augmented" and "supplementary" factor approaches to take account of improvements in educational attainment and other factors such as changes in the age–sex composition of labor and changes in economic structures. Again, in the notation of Maddison:

$$9. \quad \dot{\Pi}(L^*, K^*, S) = \dot{O} - \alpha\dot{L}^* - (1 - \alpha)\dot{K}^* - \dot{S}$$

where S stands for factors other than augmented labor, L^* and capital, K^*, that are believed to influence growth. Dots over the variables again indicate percentage changes and the asterisks indicate multiple component terms. Maddison identifies nine structural changes that are reflected in S; augmented capital K^* includes adjustments for new technologies and depreciation. For labor, L^* stands for two components of labor – the number of workers times their average hours of work and the number of years of schooling completed by the labor force.

John Pencavel demonstrates how the contribution of the different levels of schooling (primary, secondary and higher education) can be derived from aggregate measures of the schooling contribution. [36] Working with Maddison's indices of average years of schooling of the populations in the US, UK, Japan, France and The Netherlands, with Maddison's measure of the contribution to output growth of schooling in those six countries and with Maddison's estimate of α equal to 0.7, Pencavel calculated higher education's contribution to output growth for the three periods shown in Table 7:1. [37]

Growth in Schooling and its Contribution to the Growth in Output, 1913–84

	USA	UK	Japan	Germany	France	Netherlands
1913–50						
1. Percent growth in educational index	0.59	0.47	0.87	0.35	0.51	0.38
2. Percent higher education's contribution to (1)	8.69	1.53	3.88	2.55	2.92	11.13
3. Percent growth in output (GDP)	2.78	1.29	2.24	1.30	1.06	2.43
4. Schooling's contribution to output growth (%)	14.78	25.49	27.04	19.00	33.88	11.03
5. Higher education's contribution to output growth (%)	1.29	0.39	1.05	0.48	0.99	1.23
1950–73						
1. Percent growth in educational index	0.58	0.29	0.74	0.28	0.52	0.62
2. Percent higher education's contribution to (1)	23.88	16.42	11.08	7.41	22.20	7.70

3. Percent growth in output (GDP)	4.70	5.13	5.92	9.37	3.02	3.72
4. Schooling's contribution to output growth (%)	9.17	7.08	3.26	5.54	6.61	10.87
5. Higher education's contribution to output growth (%)	0.71	1.57	0.24	0.61	1.08	2.60
1973–84						
1. Percent growth in educational index	0.78	0.86	0.14	0.63	0.46	0.78
2. Percent higher education's contribution to (1)	17.05	38.21	71.19	21.16	28.57	62.41
3. Percent growth in output (GDP)	1.58	2.18	1.68	3.78	1.06	2.32
4. Schooling's contribution to output growth (%)	34.61	27.53	5.90	11.71	30.23	23.41
5. Higher education's contribution to output growth (%)	5.90	10.52	4.20	2.48	8.64	14.61

Source: John Pencavel, "Higher Education, Productivity, and Earnings: A Review," *Journal of Economic Education* vol. 22, no. 4 (Fall 1991): 336.

A comparison of the fifth lines for each of these time periods shows that the contribution of higher education to economic growth in the US has always been relatively large and it has increased dramatically in this century (rising from 1.29 percent in the 1913–50 period to 14.61 percent in the 1973–84 period) while the contribution of schooling generally rose less dramatically (rising from 14.78 percent to 23.41 percent). On the other hand, the contribution of higher education to output growth in Japan has been small for the entire period. The contribution of education to economic growth is highly variable across countries, with education in Japan and Germany showing little contribution to growth whereas the effect of education in the other countries has been substantial.

There is no fixed pattern among countries for the level and type of education that contributes most to growth in output. In the US, there is a relatively smooth transfer of people and ideas from top-flight private universities like MIT and public universities like the University of Michigan, which is not the case in Japan. *The Economist* (October 4, 1997) warns, however, that "it is the ability of American universities to spawn patents and entrepreneurs, rather than to collect Nobel prizes, that excites onlookers most." Unfortunately, we do not know if it is the basic research associated with the Nobel prize and/or the applied-research–associated entrepreneurial activity that gives higher education its biggest impact on aggregate production.

Although growth accounting methods shed some light on the relationship between schooling and economic growth, there are persistent questions in political debates and among growth theorists as to whether and how the infrastructure of public education actually contributes to economic growth. Growth accounting methods may not be appropriate for assessing the contribution of intermediate inputs in production. Education is embodied in the primary input of labor (and physical capital); it uses resources that enhance labor even though this resource use is not directly observable in the goods and services produced. Thus, an adjustment for alternative uses to which these resources could have been put should be made in accounting for the determinants of growth. This requires consideration of the endogenous nature associated with resource use.

Education both influences and is influenced by economic development. What is missing from growth accounting is a positive adjustment for the contribution that education makes through the mix of other intermediate inputs and the diffusion of ideas. As stated by Barro and Sala-i-Martin, growth accounting provides mechanical decomposition of the growth of aggregate output into the growth of an array of inputs and total factor product but it cannot provide a theory of growth because it does not include the fundamental decision theory that drives the allocation of the inputs.[38]

Aggregate Cross-Country Growth Regressions

Aggregate growth rates differ greatly among countries over time. Recent efforts to explain these differences have brought attention to the role of school attainment. The traditional regression analysis aimed at explaining aggregate output growth has some measure of school attainment (proportion of the labor force with a given level of schooling, average schooling level of the labor force, or proportion of age group enrolled, for example) serving as the human capital measure that enters the production function as an ordinary covariate.[39] The newer alternative approach is to model technological progress, or the growth of total factor productivity, as a function of the level of education.[40] This new endogenous growth literature has also seen the construction of "human capital" indices, which generally are combinations of school attainment and life expectancy measures.[41] Regression equations have been estimated to explain the growth in real per capita GDP with educational attainment, human capital accumulation and other control variables. Instead of using individual data as in Equation 1 of this chapter, aggregate country data are used.

Arguably, the most well known of this work is that of Barro and his co-authors. Barro and Sala-i-Martin find that the school-attainment variables that tend to be related significantly to subsequent aggregate growth are average years of mean secondary and higher schooling for both men and women but the male effect is positive whereas the female effect is negative.[42] They speculate that this puzzling negative effect is brought about by a large spread between male and female attainment reflecting "backwardness." Fewer females attaining the higher level of education is associated with underdeveloped countries and hence with higher growth potential through the convergence mechanism.[43]

Barro's and Sala-i-Martin's human capital measure enters as an interaction variable with a logarithmic transformation of GDP. The estimated coefficient for this interaction term is significantly negative, as expected from the convergence mechanism. That is, the negative coefficient means that the aggregate growth rate is more sensitive to the starting or initial value of GDP when overall human capital – the total effect from educational attainment and life expectancy – is higher. In addition, the more government spending on education (and by implication the higher its quality), the greater the aggregate growth rate. In short, education matters.

In spite of numerous criticisms of both the data set constructed by Barro and his co-authors and their econometric methods, empirical work continues to show that education matters. One notable exception to this finding is the work of Lant Pritchett for the World Bank. Pritchett finds the effects of growth in "educational capital" on growth of GDP per worker are consistently small and negative but statistically significant.[44] His measure of educational capital, however, is peculiar.

Pritchett starts with a Mincerian earnings function but instead of the observations being individuals, as in Equations 1 through 4 of this chapter, the units of observations are countries:

10. $\ln(Y_N) = \ln(Y_0) + rN$

where Y_N and Y_0 are wage earnings with N years of schooling on zero years of schooling, and r is the wage increment to a year of schooling. The value of the stock of educational capital at any time t is the present value of the wage premium for N years of schooling:

11. $HK(t) = \sum^T \rho^t (Y_N - Y_0)$

where ρ^t is the discount factor $(1 - \text{discount rate})^{-t}$. Pritchett recognizes the problem in specifying the discount rate. He makes his measure of educational capital $HK(t)$ peculiar, however, by setting $Y_0 = 1$, and confessed that he "dropped out the growth of the $\ln(Y_0)$ term because [he] didn't know what to do with it. This seems wrong." Pritchett appears to recognize that his theoretical concept of "educational capital" does not have a correct empirical estimator; this does not stop him from continuing. He defines the rate of growth of educational capital to be $\Delta hk(t)$, where Δ signifies time rate of change and lower case hk indicates the logarithmic transformation:

12. $\Delta hk(t) = \Delta ln(exp^{rN(t)} - 1)$

Pritchett ignores the fact that $\hat{ln Y} \neq \hat{ln} Y$ and $ln[E(Y)] \neq E[ln(Y)]$, which is not trivial as William E. Becker and Robert Toutkoushian demonstrate for highly skewed distributions of earnings.[45] In short, that which is measured by Pritchett's index of educational capital lacks validity; it need not be measuring what he claims.[46]

Education, Innovation and Diffusion

Paul Romer defines innovation or technological change as an improvement in the instructions for mixing raw materials. He argues that advances in technology are the primary source of economic growth because the creation of new instructions can occur without bound and these instructions can be used over and over again at next to no additional cost. They are non-rival, meaning one person's use of the instructions does not rival or preclude its use by another.[47]

Although improvements in the instructions by which resources are mixed can occur by chance, Romer argues that innovation is the result of intentional actions taken by people who respond to market incentives. For an innovation to be profitable, the owner must be able to exclude or prevent others from using it freely. Growth requires the input of an excludable but non-rival good.

In assessing the manner in which human capital enters the production function, Romer makes a distinction between different forms of education and training:

> It is clear that something like knowledge, understanding, or science has grown per capita and shows every prospect of continuing to do so . . . that unbounded growth is possible is an indication that this input is a very different kind of intangible from cognitive skill or memory related to the performance of a task. The feature that makes cognitive skill and memory easy to include in economic models is the one that makes them bounded. They are inextricably tied to a particular individual.[48]

To Romer, the early years of schooling produce only basic skills (reading, writing and arithmetic) that are tied to the individual. Such human capital is a rival input because the person who possesses this ability cannot be in more than one place at the same time, nor can this person solve many problems at once. This ability is also bounded by the population; it is embedded in physical objects. It cannot account for unbounded growth in per capita output for its accumulation must involve diminishing returns.[49] In contrast, a new design, piece of software, or mathematical model is non-rival. Once the design, software and model have been created, they can be used as often as desired by as many people as would like at little to no cost. They are not closely tied to any physical object. Education that contributes to the creation of these new ways of mixing raw materials can lead to unbounded growth. But the rivalrous skills of reading, writing and arithmetic as taught in primary education are not sufficient for unbounded growth.[50]

Baumol, Blackman and Wolff provide supporting empirical evidence for the importance of education and the indispensability of secondary education for economic growth.[51] Citing several studies, including his own, McMahon concludes that until recently, expansion of enrollments at the secondary level as well as quality investments at the secondary level and the higher levels played a central role in the development of East Asia.[52] Primary education is not enough for a nation to advance its use of modern technology. Higher education is clearly important for reasons advanced by Romer. But extensive involvement in basic research and development (R&D) is expensive and may only be achievable by the wealthiest of nations. It is much less expensive to import and adopt technology than to create it; modern technology is easily copied. For a country to imitate the innovations of another, only a small group of highly educated persons, with advanced and specialized university educations, may be needed but a large number of technicians with the reasoning skills usually associated with secondary education are essential.

Additional support for the importance of high levels of education can be found in Donal O'Neill who found that changes in production technology that shift demand toward skilled labor, leading to higher returns to higher education, will tend to favor the developed countries relative to the less developed countries (LDCs), resulting in absolute divergence in output.[53] As noted by O'Neill, Barro and Lee's data show average years of schooling increased by almost 60 percent among the LDCs between 1960 and 1985, but by 1985 the average was still only 3.37 years of schooling.[54] Average education levels grew more slowly among developed countries (40 percent) but in 1985 it was eight years.

Changes in technology that raise the marginal product of skilled labor lead to product growth for the developed countries that have the stock of skilled labor. Having an educated labor force is required to capitalize on technological change taking place throughout the world.

Conclusion

The pecuniary returns to education as well as the cost-adjusted rates of return to education show that biggest social and private benefits of education are at the primary levels of schooling, regardless of country. On the other hand, the basic reading, writing and arithmetic skills of a primary education are not sufficient to advance innovation or even imitation; higher levels of general education are required, and possibly in conjunction with vocational training, if developing countries are going to be able to implement the technologies of the "growth club" countries.

Growth accounting shows us that there is no unique way in which education enters the aggregate production function. The contribution of various forms of education to economic growth depends on the country considered and the definition of the "human capital" measure employed. Measures of years of schooling completed by the workforce and enrollment rates have been shown to be important in explanations of economic growth. However, the rate of growth in these measures of schooling may not be as important as the level.

To take advantage of rapidly changing technology, countries must have a sufficiently high level of educational base to imitate and implement that which the leading countries are creating. All forms of education may not be equally important in moving a developing country toward membership in the growth club. Test score comparisons will not shed light on the desired forms of education. Theoretical considerations tell us that for unbounded growth, the education output must be non-rival; again, the basic skills of reading, writing and arithmetic of primary education are not sufficient. For education to matter, a country must have a population that has achieved more than the basic skill levels. It may also need institutions of higher learning to take part in or at least imitate technological advances occurring throughout the world.

Underdeveloped countries must first raise their education base to reflect more closely that of the leaders. They need not invest heavily in advanced education if they can send their more able students to the expensive higher education institutions of the innovators. Underdeveloped countries can take advantage of the subsidies provided to their students by the developed countries. For example, in the US, all students share in the environment and resources of the major public and private universities that are receiving large federal and state grants. Yet foreign students do not pay the taxes that make these grants possible; they pay only tuition that does not reflect the full cost of the instruction.[55] To the extent that tuition and the cost of higher education differ in the host country, the country of the guest student is receiving a subsidy when that student returns (assuming the student can and does return to a position in which they can and do use that which they have acquired).

Developing nations have no choice but to raise their educational base. The challenge, however, is not to create institutions of higher learning that compete with those of the developed nations. Students can be sent out of the country for a higher education that is subsidized by the host. The challenge is to get the expatriate students back in their home countries working with those who have the secondary school level skills needed to imitate and implement the technologies being created by the innovating countries.

2

Partnership:
A Theme for Education and Communities
in the Twenty-First Century

Don Davies

Foreword

My interests and talents are definitely toward the practical rather than theoretical side of the educational world – including educational policies and politics. Consequently, this chapter presents a practical commentary on aspects of the topic with a variety of suggestions and recommendations, based on my own experience and through the lenses of my own culture. As Jerome Bruner has pointed out, "to know is to interpret, and interpretation is through the filter of culture."[1]

This chapter is an *interpretation* and a personal statement. Since I use the term the twenty-first century in the title, I must point out that I am not a futurist and have little faith in predictions. The one thing we can be certain about is that uncertainty is the rule.

With these preliminary comments, I want now to make specific the central messages of this chapter. Schools and other educational institutions from pre-school centers through to universities and graduate schools are interrelated, interdependent components of a dynamic, highly complex societal system. For the next century, societies must reform and reconstruct educational systems which are more equal, more individualized and more humane, as well as more effective. Reform is needed if education is to contribute strongly to society's ability to cope with rapid change and with the challenges that the next century will bring.

The most effective relationships between education and society will be partnerships or collaborative connections between educational institutions and the families and communities they serve. Parents should be partners with schools in the education of children.

Conceptual Framework

These central messages are grounded in the concept that families, schools and communities – as the most immediate and engaging units of society – have overlapping spheres of influence and responsibility for the upbringing and education of children. The theoretical basis for this concept was developed over many years by Joyce Epstein of The Johns Hopkins University and then adapted and applied in many of the studies of the Center on Families, Communities, Schools and Children's Learning, which I co-directed with Dr. Epstein.[2]

This concept sees the connections among schools, families and community agencies and institutions of all kinds as a set of overlapping spheres of influence. This is in sharp contrast to the traditional views of many sociologists and educational scholars who emphasize the separateness of institutions and their roles in children's development.

In this framework, the family is the primary institution within which children are nurtured, shaped and readied for an independent role in life. Regardless of their size or composition, families have the primary obligations for the protection, health and education of their own children. Societies should hold families accountable for meeting their obligations. But they often need help. While some must struggle more than others, nearly all of today's families at one time or another need support from the community and from the schools.

The obligations of schools for the education and socialization of the community's young are central. Schools must be held accountable for meeting these obligations, but they cannot do their jobs alone. They need the help and support of families and of the community and its agencies and institutions, including religious institutions.

Communities have obligations to provide a safe and orderly environment in which families and children can satisfy their basic needs and in which schools can thrive. The community – through its government, public and private institutions, religious and civic organizations employers, and cultural and social agencies – offers its citizens protection, work, recreation, and health and social services as well as an environment in which a healthy civic culture can exist. The community, in all of its parts, must be held accountable by the residents meeting its obligations for children and their families.

But communities need the help of productive educational institutions and citizens who contribute to the common good as responsible parents and well-educated, democratic people.

This overlapping spheres model integrates the educational insights of scholars who have developed the idea of families as educators, including Hope Leichter and the emphasis on shared responsibility developed by David Seeley and Don Davies. It is also a part of a long tradition of sociological and psychological research on school and family environments by James Coleman, Epstein and many others.[3]

Thoughts on Terminology

In this chapter, the term "society" means the large collectivity of people which traditionally organizes itself into a nation-state. The society forms institutions – governments, and public and private agencies and mechanisms, including educational agencies of many kinds – to manage and conduct its affairs.

A society is also composed of smaller entities known as communities and families. Communities are both geographic – cities, towns, villages and parts of cities – and collections of people with shared interests or characteristics such as religion or ethnicity. In this chapter, I will use the term "community" primarily in the geographic sense. Families are the smallest and most important societal unit, but they take very diverse forms in different settings and cultures.

Scholars argue about the meaning of two interrelated terms and concepts, society and community. Ferdinand Tonnies and Emile Durkheim debated the issue many years ago. Tonnies argued for the concept of *Gemeinschaft,* a close-to-home geographic area which provides society with its natural social orientation. This idea of community is opposed to the larger, looser society or *Gesellschaft,* a much larger aggregation resulting from the artificial actions of the state. Durkheim argued that the larger social agglomeration often referred to as society was as natural as the smaller aggregates.[4]

William Schambra uses the term "community" but differentiates between the great national communities and communities of "the small platoons," meaning local communities of family, religious institutions and voluntary associations.[5] The term "third sector" is used by Jeremy

Rifkin and many other writers today to describe the non-governmental and non-business elements of these local communities.

In many ways, the arguments about terminology and the virtues and deficits of large societies versus small communities are artificial and academic. In practice, people organize themselves both nationally and locally, and devise means to control and influence schools and other educational institutions. They organize through governments, public agencies and private mechanisms. The national, regional and local units or entities of a society are interconnected and new technology reduces the distances among them.

Both large and small aggregations (i.e. societies, communities and families) and public and private mechanisms are necessary and will certainly persist through the century ahead. But it seems inevitable that there will be continuing debate and conflict in nearly all countries about the balance of power and influence between the local and national levels and between public and private forces as regards educational policies and practices. It seems to me that the third sector is likely to grow in importance and influence in the century ahead, even in those countries where this sector is relatively undeveloped. Educators and political leaders should devote more time, energy and resources to supporting the parent and citizen organizations which form such a key part of the third sector.

The Challenges Ahead

Education in all countries and cultures will both help to shape society and to be shaped by it. Education and society inevitably have an interactive relationship. This relationship will be based on each society's goals and values.

Education is a more powerful instrument to maintain the status quo than it is to be an agent of change. It is stronger as a reflector than as a shaper. Educators often claim too much for the potential of education, neglecting the fact that education is but one element among many social, economic, political, religious, military and geographic factors.

We often like to forget that society can use schools and other educational media for hostile and inhumane purposes. Schooling in Nazi Germany and Stalinist Soviet Union are two vivid examples. Societies can also use education either to build bridges for diverse communities within the society or to erect higher fences.

Society, through governments and other institutions, can influence and shape the traditional and formal institutions of education, but institutions such as schools and universities are not easy to change. I recently heard a comment by Seymour Pappert, the eminent MIT scientist and educational innovator. He said that if a visitor from the early nineteenth century time-traveled to a hospital or bank of today, he or she would be completely bewildered, hardly recognizing anything. But, a time traveler to a late twentieth century school would feel right at home, as not much has changed.

I would like to be able to talk about "world society" – but I think that the next century may be too soon to make that idealistic, global concept possible. Perhaps sometime in the next millennium we will have moved closer to that vision. However, at present there is no such thing as world society. There are societies, embedded in nation-states, dotted with smaller communities. There are cultures and societies within nation-states and cutting across them. There are political and/or religious alliances such as the Arab League or the European Community. There are international organizations such as the Arab League Educational, Cultural and Scientific Organization (ALECSO), the United Nations Education, Science and Cultural Organization (UNESCO) and the United Nations (UN). The trend toward globalization is a reality.

The ease of worldwide communication – such as the Internet, e-mail, fax machines and satellite television – radically diminishes the isolation of many people, nations and cultures from one another. Many do not like this development and are fearful of homogenization, loss of cultural values, and particularly of growing American cultural influence through music, television, clothing and the spread of the English language. The military and economic dominance of my country fuels these fears, and with considerable justification.

It seems likely that the struggle between global forces and local interests will be both an educational and political challenge in an increasingly interdependent and interconnected world. The tensions caused by this struggle are reflected in many of the chapters in this volume.

Multiple Challenges

There is vastly more conflict and disagreement worldwide about both goals and means than there is consensus, but there are some broad challenges that can enlist the interest of educators and other leaders across cultures and national boundaries – challenges that have worldwide implications. Here are six such challenges, chosen from a long list of possibilities.

Rapid Change

An overriding challenge in the coming century will be adapting to continuing, rapid social, economic, political and technological change. The pace of change we have seen in this century is not likely to slow, and will continue to put increasing stress on individuals and institutions. The skill and knowledge needed to cope with rapid change are necessary not only for elite leadership of society but also for the public at large. The need for education beyond the academic and intellectual is also salient to this challenge.

Psychological and emotional stress sometimes has disastrous effects. Rapid change certainly contributes to such stress for many people. Finding effective ways to help people deal with change to minimize stress is an enormous challenge to educators, psychologists, medical professionals and religious leaders. The answers will not come in the typical school textbook or school curriculum. But, education, if it is based on the partnership concept, has the potential to help societies face this challenge. Sophisticated personal skills and sensitivity will be vitally important for dealing with the stresses of rapid change.

Cultural Conflict

In the next century, we will continue to be challenged to reduce the religious, racial, ethnic, cultural and national conflicts that plague our planet from Northern Ireland, to the Basque country in Spain, to the Balkans, the Middle East, Rwanda, Sri Lanka and others. The twentieth century was probably the bloodiest and most conflict-ridden in recorded history. We have seen unprecedented levels of war, genocide and killing. Our newspapers and television bring home horrible reminders every day that these kinds of hatreds and violence are increasing rather than decreasing.

Learning to live together in reasonable harmony, with less war, violence, conflict and terrorism, is one aspiration that unites most of mankind across existing boundaries and cultures – except perhaps a relatively small minority of zealots who will never be satisfied unless the whole world believes and acts as they do.

Understanding and dealing with questions of identity will be crucial. There are built-in conflicts between religious and secular values and between nationalist and ethnic or religious affiliations. These are probably more difficult to settle than conflicts between countries. How much organized education in the schools and universities can contribute positively to reducing some of these conflicts will depend largely on the political will of societal leaders to have educators and education involved seriously and positively in these issues. But without educational interventions there is little hope that the levels of conflict will be reduced. Military strategies alone will never be sufficient.

Education, both formal and informal, from the earliest years through adulthood has a role to play in equipping individuals with the knowledge, skills and attitudes needed for more humane, collaborative, peaceful and conflict-resolving behavior. Effective education must reach all segments of society in a way that engages them personally, as changes in attitude and compassion are needed if this challenge is to be met.

A solid and balanced knowledge of history, widely shared across society and not limited to scholars, is another part of the strategy for reducing bloodshed and violence. But, if history is mostly propaganda, it will not play a properly constructive educational role. How to deal with history in education is almost always determined by the political leaders of a society. Enlightened political leadership is badly needed.

Teachers from pre-school on should be seen as agents of inter-cultural understanding and of democracy. As Stephen Stoer points out, this means a heightened democracy, "whose development in (and through) education depends substantially on the principle of equality of opportunity for success in schooling, which in turns depends on the development of inter/multicultural (anti-racist) understanding, attitudes and behavior on the part of teachers."[6]

The mass media have an enormous impact on attitudes on diversity, violence and super-nationalism. That impact can be either positive or negative. Educators need to worry about the increasing levels of sex, violence and crime that are depicted in American movies, popular music, television and magazines. These need to be counteracted in whatever ways we can by more positive educational interventions. Partnerships should be a theme in these efforts.

The family is the place to start. Choices about media are made there. Education for tolerance, understanding among peoples who are different and choices for non-violent solutions to problems begin in the family, which is surely the most powerful shaper of attitudes on these matters. This close-to-home education is by example as well as by talk and starts when children are infants.

Gaps between the Haves and Have-Nots

A related challenge ahead is to find realistic ways of reducing the huge gaps between the haves and have-nots of the world. These gaps exists within cities, and between cities and rural areas, within countries, between countries, and between and among the regions of the world – the classic north–south divide. And as we all know, increasing prosperity does not assure more equitable distribution of resources. The gaps are not just economic. Differences in "social capital," including access to information and the new technology, are equally important.

The US offers vivid and embarrassing examples of the gaps. The US has the second highest economic output per person of the 18 most industrialized Western nations and has the most affluent children (based on numbers of children compared to the total population), but it has more poor children and these children are poorer than in most of the other Western countries. More than one in five children live in poverty.

The US has the widest gap between rich and poor families, and the gap has increased in recent years. The country offers fewer and less generous social programs for families and children than any of the other 17 countries.[7]

On the positive side, American public schools and universities have made an important contribution to helping expand economic opportunities and social mobility beyond the privileged groups, breaking down racial barriers, and increasing, to some extent, economic stability by contributing to the development of a more broadly based and better-educated work force. On the negative side, huge gaps still exist between the educational resources available and educational success rates between low-income and working-class children and adults and the more affluent segments of our society. These gaps must be closed if America's ideals of democracy and equality are to be realized more fully.

Other countries face similar gaps. Worldwide we face huge disparities in development, wealth and power between the affluent developed world and much of Africa, Latin America, the Middle East and some of Asia. Narrowing the gaps in educational access, opportunities and achievement has to be one part of efforts to meet this challenge.

Educational interventions are of central importance to meeting this challenge. Educational systems must prepare young people with the skills and attitudes needed for productive work and for the rapid changes that affect many occupations. Education must provide advanced technological and academic skills needed by many in developing countries seeking to move away from subsistence agriculture. Education rooted in the partnership concept can help to equip the citizenry to make wise decisions about savings and spending, investing in education and protecting one's health – including family planning and drug and alcohol abuse.

But, educational efforts to reduce the gaps must be based on a belief that all children – across lines of race, class and income – can learn and achieve success in school. Educational and social resources must be allocated consistent with this belief.

Protecting the Environment

Another challenge that can unite many of us across existing boundaries is that of reducing the destruction of our natural environment. But we saw in the 1997 summit meeting on global warming how difficult it is to get agreements that satisfy both the environmentalists and business interests and the economically powerful countries and the developing world.

The challenge is to find the balance between economic development and protection of the environment. We need to apply what we already know about how to continue economic development, handle our growing population, maintain the lifestyles we desire and still preserve and sustain the ecology we all share. Much new research is needed on this issue, but so is substantially increased education in schools, communities and universities.

Knowledge is the key to expanding our options in finding workable approaches to preserving our environment – knowledge that is thoughtfully and consistently applied. Education has much to contribute to helping individuals and societies become better guardians of the natural world. Attitudes as well as academic knowledge are keys to learning how better to manage the environment world. Since individual behavior is a major contributor to environmental success or failure, education which affects people's lives in their families and communities is of central importance. Conservation and environmental sensitivity can begin in individual families and communities, and can be reflected in schools and classrooms. Environmental projects in schools and universities offer good opportunities for partnerships with communities and families.

Catching up with Science and Technology

Society will be challenged to find ways for our human and social under-standing and organization to catch up with our scientific and technological breakthroughs. One of the curses of both science and social science in our present century – which has seen the extraordinary flowering of both – has been to exalt production of new knowledge and technology over its positive, humane and equitable uses.

Education at all levels is essential to provide the skills, attitudes and motivation needed to strengthen social organizations and to decrease the gap between researchers and practitioners in education and many other social service fields.

The training of social scientists of many varieties needs to be given equal priority to the training of scientists, mathematicians and engineers. Skilled research-based expertise and wisdom are needed to create social organizations at the same level of sophistication as our scientific organizations.

Integrity

Perhaps the most difficult challenge for the coming century is much less tangible. It is putting integrity ahead of aggrandizement, character ahead of greed. Integrity includes everyday honesty, reliability in meeting one's commitments, moral behavior, a willingness to live and act consistently with one's principles and consideration of the effects of one's actions on others. It was Francis Bacon in the sixteenth century who urged Mankind to put integrity ahead of personal or collective profit or aggrandizement. Societies have largely ignored this advice.

Our capitalist world's "bottom line" has become an all-powerful mantra in a century in which huge material and economic advances have gone side by side with incredible slaughter, conflict, hunger, human misery and often uncontrolled individual and national greed.

An American religious leader captured this challenge succinctly:

> Education stands in danger of seeing people only as tools for economic progress, unless it is accompanied by a vision of individuals as creative, responsible, spiritual and society as a matrix within which general fulfillment is the goal for all.[8]

Robert Kennedy captured this challenge eloquently in 1967 when he wrote:

> We will find neither national purpose nor personal satisfaction in a mere continuation of economic progress, in an endless amassing of worldly goods. We cannot measure national spirit by the Dow Jones Average . . . The gross national product does not allow for the health of our families, the quality of our education or the joy of their play. It does not include the beauty of our poetry or the strength of our marriages, the intelligence of our public debate, or the integrity of public officials.[9]

For this less tangible challenge, educators need to muster their expertise to find educational interventions powerful enough to make a difference. The most effective interventions will be based on partnerships between schools, families and communities.

Meeting the Challenges

To meet these and other challenges, world societies need to reinvigorate institutions and governments and strengthen community life. Education is one of the ways to do this. Partnership should be a major theme of education at every level.

An important first step will be for governments to provide the money and facilities necessary for a public education system which serves children from early childhood into adulthood and the senior years. The centerpiece of a reformed and expanded public educational system should be strong elementary and secondary schools. This is a costly demand, as it means paying salaries high enough to attract and hold as teachers men and women who have first-rate intellectual and social abilities, against the competition of attractive high-status occupations such as law, medicine and engineering. It also means training school teachers and administrators effectively and paying the high price for providing technology to schools, which is at roughly the same level as demanded by banking and business institutions.

What Kind of Education Will Society Need in the Twenty-First Century?

To meet the challenges, education at all levels must have a powerful influence on students; it must be effective. An effective education for societies to meet the challenges ahead should have three main themes. These themes, as relevant for the coming years as they have been for the past, can be captured in three verbs: to equalize, to individualize, to humanize.

To Equalize

An important societal goal is to create an educational system that is effective for all students, including those who are disadvantaged economically, by low social status or in other important ways, and to help all students meet high standards of academic achievement. Governments as agencies of society have a special obligation to foster equality of opportunity in education and to attend the interests of the powerless as well as the powerful.

To Individualize

Educators at all levels have an obligation to plan curriculum and programs which can make the best of the many differences in the ways that children and students of all ages learn and in the many differences in their interests, talents, motivations and cultures. One of the primary obligations of society is to support educational interventions that are attuned to the interests and needs of the diverse individuals who comprise that society. To do this, new approaches to curriculum and teaching are badly needed.

To Humanize

Educators must recognize that academic achievement and intellectual activity in education cannot be divorced from social, emotional and moral development. Children and adult learners need personal and emotional nurturing and support as well as knowledge and discipline. Learners are not simply intellectual vessels to be filled by academic instruction. One of the primary goals of education in shaping society is to foster the development of the human potential of all individuals in that society. One of the great needs in the coming century will be to counteract the depersonalization of society which threatens all of our institutions.

Dr. Abdul Halimi Ahmad of Malaysia underlined this point when he said recently:

> . . . as we speak of education, industrialization and progress we should also focus on the growing need of humanity to preserve spiritual and moral values. We need the "total human being." Not robots or machines. Islam focuses on the total happiness of mankind and the welfare of society. This is what our educational system should aim at.[10]

Strategies for the Next Century

What must education and educators do in order to help society meet the challenges in the century about to begin? What must the leaders of society do to shape education so that it will contribute strongly to meeting these challenges? Here are five strategies that might be useful for educators, families and policy makers to consider.

Create Learning Communities: School is Not Enough

Schools should be seen as the heart of sound educational system. But school is not enough. My vision of education for the twenty-first century is lifelong learning embracing both formal and non-formal approaches.

Central Role for Public Schools

Informal education began when our species still lived in trees and caves, while formal schooling worldwide is a product of the last 150 to 200 years. In many societies, there were special types of schools much earlier. For example, in the early part of this millennium, Koranic schools developed as an early form of adult education to teach the Koran, reading, writing and arithmetic. Some specialists consider these among the first formal educational systems sponsored by the state.[11]

In most of the world until very late in this millennium, formal schooling was limited largely to the elite and mostly to males. In the US, for example, it was not until the middle of the nineteenth century that elementary schools were developed for the common people. The American common school was rooted in Protestantism, capitalism and republicanism (small "r" meaning the belief in representative government through carefully controlled electoral politics). By the end of the nineteenth century, political stability and the Americanization and enculturation of millions of immigrants from both Europe and Asia became the dominant purposes of a rapidly growing school system. Opportunities were gradually extended to girls, and in limited and poorly funded ways to the newly freed slaves.[12]

By the 1960s and 1970s, public schools had expanded and had made progress toward extending opportunities across lines of race, gender and income, serving about 90 percent of all children from ages 5 through 17, with most of the others enrolled in private and religious schools. Mass education through schools was based on a commitment to educate all our citizens at public expense and was America's greatest social invention. The schools have made possible the transfer of knowledge and social and intellectual skills beyond the small affluent elites to the masses.

Successes in public education include the development of an extensive and quite accessible system of public higher education – including community colleges, vocational education linked closely to business and industry and educational access and services for all children who are physically or mentally disabled.

The public school system is *the* critical component for constructing the kind of functioning, democratic communities necessary for a healthy society. As historian Ira Harkavy points out, "If the public school system works badly, American society *must* work badly."[13]

Despite the achievements, there were and still are many shortcomings and problems. Chief among these serious problems are the big differences in funding, program quality and student achievement between schools serving middle-class and affluent families and those serving the working class and poor. Most commentators would also agree that our schools have not kept pace with changing social and economic conditions, with research about learning, and the need for more consistent and higher academic content and achievement. Our school systems need major reform and renewal.

There are some commentators and critics of schools – especially some of those who are captivated by the possibilities of advanced electronic technology – who say that rather than reform the schools, we should help them fade away. I disagree. I believe that the institution of the public school can and should continue to play a vital role for society. It is an institutional invention that has worked very well for us, despite all of its flaws, and should *not* be abandoned, but be renewed and reinvigorated.

Across most of the rest of the world in this century, schools have been an essential element in a rapidly industrializing, urbanizing, technologically advancing and increasingly interdependent world. There is dramatic evidence of this in the UAE. Growth in less than 40 years from one school to more than 1,100 schools and more than a half million students is striking.

The Arab world and the US, despite all their differences and disagreements, share a strong commitment to learning and education, going back to the beginnings of Islam and, in the case of the US, to the era of the Enlightenment in Europe in the eighteenth century. A statement by Massialis and Jarrar asserts that education has been the most potent force in this century for the Arab world for supporting political independence, rebuilding human resources, reconstructing society and establishing national identities.[14]

Children spend less than 20 percent of their lives in school during their years of childhood and adolescence. That is a very important 20 percent, but society's shaping of education should also seek to make maximum use of the potential positive influences of all other educational forces. Society's planners and decision makers should think of education as a process that begins at birth and proceeds through the final stages of life.

Learning Communities
John Abbott makes the central point that, "[s]uccessful societies in the twenty-first century will have learning communities that are in-line with the needs of a continually changing economic and social environment."[15]

He defines learning communities as:

> . . . communities that use all of their resources – physical and intellectual; formal and informal; in school and outside of school, within an agenda that recognizes every individual's potential to grow and be involved with others.[16]

Education in ancient Greece reflected this concept as it took place through the *Paidea* – the educational matrix created by the whole Athenian culture, in which the community and all of its developers guaranteed learning resources for the individual. Partnership, even though that term was not used, was the theme. In a twenty-first century learning community, children and youth will be surrounded by a multitude of supportive networks and institutions, and these supportive networks will continue to help individuals as they move through life.

This concept of education as a seamless web may seem obvious or even trite but, in most countries today, education is dealt with in fragmented fashion by planners and policy makers. Planning and management of schools are often separate from that of young children, of adults and of old people. Bureaucratic fragmentation means that decisions about higher education are often made without much reference to what comes before. Informal and non-traditional educational agencies operate on the periphery with little communication with, or connection to, the schools. The third sector of community in many countries is underdeveloped. Private and public schools, at least in my country, compete for students. Public universities compete with public schools for financial support.

Studies show that in the US, most public schools continue to keep community agencies and institutions at arm's length, fearing interference and competition for resources. Adult or community education programs are often supported minimally and considered of only marginal importance. A few schools – possibly one in ten – have made great progress is establishing collaborative relationships with community agencies and parents and are demonstrating that important benefits accrue to all of the partners.

Characteristics of the Learning Community
The kind of comprehensive educational system which twenty-first century societies need will exhibit many of the following characteristics.

- All residents will have access to education from the earliest years through old age, not dependent on their wealth or social status.
- Both large and small businesses will become partners with individual schools and school districts, offering expertise, consultant help, volunteers, equipment and money. Schools and employers will join in coordinated internship and apprenticeship projects to facilitate the transition from school to work, using students' vocational interests to spur their academic interest and success and try to give young people a head-start on successful work careers.
- Schools and community organizations and agencies will take seriously their educational responsibilities for both children and adults. Schools will offer community education programs which keep the buildings and facilities open for extended hours, on weekends and during vacation times, and offer parent education courses as well as academic, vocational, self-improvement, and recreation courses and activities for all community residents.
- Many schools will have partnerships with local agencies to provide health and social services to children and their families, both on and near schools themselves and through referrals. This concept of school-linked services is of special importance in urban schools which recognize that the unmet health and social needs of their students and families are reducing children's chances of academic success.
- Nearly all schools and school districts will have volunteer programs which offer training and support to individuals who want to offer time and expertise to the schools. Volunteer activities include tutoring individuals and groups of students, helping teachers in the classroom, assisting in lunchrooms and on playgrounds, providing business expertise to administrators, coordinating programs for parents, and giving talks and demonstrations to students.
- In nearly every city and town, high school and university students will engage in community service programs, working as volunteers in a variety of settings, sometimes receiving academic credit.
- Employers and educational institutions offer multiple opportunities for workers at all levels to learn new skills for their present work and to re-train for new jobs requiring new skills. In the US in the years ahead most adults will change jobs and careers two or more times, so the need for re-training opportunities is important.

The hope is that the public will enjoy the benefits of the expanded learning community and will come to be willing to provide the needed financial resources to make it possible. Governments will begin to recognize the practical and economic importance of having learning communities and will provide supportive policies and funding.

For these characteristics of the learning community to be realized, much attention must be given to building stronger communities.

Building Strong Communities

Just as strong families are the building blocks of strong communities, strong local communities are the foundations of a strong society. Building effective and productive local communities is the first requirement of creating the kind of "civil society" that we should strive for in the twenty-first century. A civil society is one in which all of its members can meet their basic needs for health, housing, nutrition, education, security from crime and violence, opportunities for stable family life, spiritual sustenance, an aesthetically satisfying environment, and opportunities for both work and play.

Civil societies will be different in different cultures and different parts of the world. But there are some hallmarks which cross many cultural and political boundaries. These include access to a fair judicial system; fair treatment for all by government and other institutions; opportunities for self-expression; established means and an inclination on the part of citizens to resolve disputes and conflicts without recourse to violence; physical safety; personal privacy; respect for racial, cultural, ethnic, religious and political diversity; and polite and considerate relationships within families and with others. Civility and human relationships will be the rule, not the exception in the civil society.

Such societies and their communities will assure that all people can meet their basic needs for health, housing, nutrition, education, security from crime and violence, opportunities for stable family life, spiritual sustenance, an aesthetically satisfying environment and opportunities for both work and play. They will also have an abundant supply of what James Coleman calls "social capital," which refers to features of social organization such as networks, values, norms of behavior, trust that facilitate cooperation and coordination for mutual benefit.[17]

Some Arab scholars are also writing and thinking about the civil society idea. For example, Saad Eddin Ibrahim has recently asserted that participatory political systems have proven to be most effective in the peaceful management of social cleavages in general and in ethnic conflicts in particular. He points out the values of "criss-crossing modern associational networks." He suggests that a civil society would include political parties, trade unions, professional associations, as well as NGOs at the community and national levels. He is quick to point out the dangers of these approaches, including instability and separatist tendencies in multi-ethnic societies.[23]

Closer collaboration between schools, families and communities is one strategy that can be helpful in societies seeking to balance secular and religious interests. In many parts of the world, there is serious conflict between secular and religious influences in schools. The resolution of these conflicts does not seem likely apart from the strategies of school–family–community partnership, which will be discussed in a later section.

Community Schools

Community schools can be another part of a strategy for building stronger communities. As American schools became more professionalized and more centralized in the first half of this century, they often became more isolated from their communities. Schools in many rural and urban settings lost their power and value they once had as community resources. Many people felt a loss of personal connection to their neighbors and neighborhoods.

In the 1940s and 1950s in the US, a movement known as "community education" was begun to address this situation by opening schools for use by the community and by young people after school hours, on weekends and in the summer. The plan was first seen as a way of combating juvenile delinquency and boredom, but it was soon expanded into a way to serve the educational and recreational interests of people of all ages in the community and to bring people together to work on common problems.

Thousands of community schools were opened in the US, many of them as a part of public school systems. In many places, the term "community school" was replaced by a broader title, "community education." Many offered primarily recreational activities for young people and adults and traditional adult education courses such as foreign languages, arts and crafts, typing and computer skills, and some ventured into helping to organize community people to take on community problems such as drug abuse or crime. During recent decades, the community school movement appeared to fade somewhat, but there appears to be a resurgence of interest in the waning years of the twentieth century.

The community education idea has spread throughout the world. Today, there is considerable activity and interest in community education in both developed and less-developed countries. The programs take many different forms but usually involve low-cost, grass-roots efforts to expand educational opportunities for adults and make educational opportunity more widely accessible in economically disadvantaged rural and urban communities. Literacy training, parent education, and education about improving health and nutrition are common emphases in less-developed countries. Some of these efforts are publicly supported, but many are sponsored by NGOs using funds from international organizations and philanthropic foundations.

Community education in the US and in many other countries still remains a peripheral component of the educational system, seldom receiving much funding. But the idea makes sense as a way for many public schools to utilize their facilities and expertise to serve adults as well as children on a more extended basis than the usual hours and days of required schooling. Community schools, adapted to changing community needs, can be one important part of a strategy to build stronger communities in the century ahead.

Education and Economic Development

Educational interventions, both formal and non-traditional, should be a significant part of any comprehensive economic development program. Often in this century they have not been. New roads are built or new technology introduced with inadequate attention to preparing people at the community level with the knowledge and skill they need to utilize the new offerings. Education is clearly not sufficient to produce economic development, but it should be seen as one important ingredient.

Societies concerned about building stronger communities should not overlook the contribution that schools can make to their local communities, if they are revitalized and accept their reciprocal relationship to society. This reciprocal relationship means more than the community contributing to the child and to the school. It must also mean that the school contributes to the economic and social development of the community. A true partnership involves an exchange of resources.

Some examples from the US of school resources that can be exchanged with the community are:

- use of facilities such as buildings, playgrounds, libraries, swimming pools and meeting rooms
- use of materials and equipment such as computers and audio–visual equipment
- purchases of materials, commodities and services by schools from local providers
- hiring practices of school employees which give preference to local residents
- teachers and other school specialists offering their skills and knowledge to community organizations and activities beyond the school, and
- the energy and idealism of young people themselves, who can participate in service to the community, as interns and workers in community enterprises.[24]

Economic productivity requires opportunities for continuous job training and education for adults, effective transitions from school to work for young people, informed consumers, constructive citizens and adults who can handle the stresses of modern life and rapid change. It also requires opening opportunities for continuing education to those who are often excluded now by social class, race, physical handicaps or limited language ability. These needs will place great demands on existing educational systems, and require much more coordination and collaboration among agencies and institutions than exists at present.

Economic development should be defined as including the development of the social capital of everyone in the community, especially those who are marginalized because of race, social status or other factors. Social capital, as discussed briefly above, according to Putnam, is coming to be seen as a vital ingredient in economic development around the world. He points out that studies of the rapidly growing economies of East Asia almost always emphasize the importance of dense social networks, sometimes called "network capitalism."[25]

Schools can make a powerful contribution to building or rebuilding the social capital available to the families and schools they serve. This is one of the reasons that partnerships between schools, families and communities is of such great significance to building strong communities and to school reform.

Partnership Between School, Family and Community

Collaboration or partnership between schools, families and communities is a significant strategy that can help schools and society jointly meet the challenges in the next century. Partnerships will be one important element in a network of community organizations and institutions vital to building a civil society. Schools are a good laboratory in which the reciprocal relationship between society and education can be forged.

There are multiple benefits to schools and communities that establish partnerships.[26] Children's chances for success in school and life are likely to be improved. Their parents and other family members can also gain skills, knowledge and confidence that will help them in rearing children, improving their economic condition and being good citizens. When families are informed about how the teacher and the school are supporting the child's efforts to learn, family expectations for the child's success go up. Teachers and schools are also helped. When families see that teachers communicate frequently and positively with them, they give higher ratings to the teachers and to the schools. Families are more likely to understand the goals of the teacher and the school and to be more supportive of proposed changes.

This kind of extensive school reform requires family and community support. Without such support, at least in the US, schools' efforts to set higher standards, restructure schedules, rules and procedures, introduce different curriculum or teaching methods and link with other community agencies and institutions are not likely to succeed. Families and community residents and agencies who see themselves as partners with the schools are more likely to support educators' efforts to gain increased financial support. Those that feel excluded are likely to be suspicious, resistant and find ways to undermine the proposed changes.[27]

Community agencies and institutions also can benefit when they collaborate effectively with schools. They can reach more of their constituents, increase public support for their work, sometimes realize cost-savings, and gain access to school facilities and expertise.

Good partnerships can be formed in all kinds of schools, from pre-school through high school. They can work in all kinds of communities – urban, suburban and rural – regardless of level of affluence or racial, ethnic or religious composition. Successful partnerships will exhibit as much variety as the local conditions that spawn them. Partnerships work best when they recognize differences among families, communities, cultures, states and regions.

There are three principles that should underlie school, family and community partnerships in the century ahead.

- Reciprocity: Successful school partnerships in the century ahead will be based on reciprocity. This principle means that all the key parts of the child's world – school, family and community – have both unique and overlapping responsibilities and authority for children's learning and development, consistent with the conceptual framework outlined earlier. Reciprocity means clear relationships and mutual obligations between schools, families, and community agencies and organizations. All the parts of the child's world need to come to accept their mutual and separate obligations, and to recognize that partnership means sharing power and responsibility.

- Democratic Principles: Developing effective partnerships requires attention to some of the essential elements of the democratic process. These elements include recognizing different interests, respecting all participants regardless of color, religion or educational status and respecting minority viewpoints. In addition, conflict resolution, mediation, negotiation and compromise are necessary aspects of this process. Schools can make a substantial contribution to the education of children and the community when they practice democratic principles, as these are defined and practiced differently across cultures, families and communities. Effective democratic decision-making, in my view of the world, includes all families and all sectors of the community, across lines of race, language, social class, income and other factors. Democracy in practice is more than a set of rules and laws. It reflects a way of thinking that encourages diversity of opinion and giving all participants an opportunity to have their voice heard.

- Diverse Opportunities: Effective programs of school–family–community collaboration provide a varied menu of opportunities, geared to the diverse needs of families and their children, and to the particular conditions of each school and school district. The typology developed by Joyce Epstein of The Johns Hopkins University can illustrate what partnerships can look like. There are six basic categories of partnership activities.

Typology of School–Family–Community Collaboration

TYPE 1: BASIC OBLIGATIONS OF FAMILIES

Schools help families to meet their basic obligations to provide for children's health and safety, developing parenting skills and child-rearing approaches that prepare children for school and that maintain healthy child development across grades. Good examples of this type are parent education and home visiting programs designed to assist families with information and support about education, training for work or health problems.

TYPE 2: BASIC OBLIGATIONS OF SCHOOLS FOR COMMUNICATION

Schools are responsible for communicating with families about school programs and children's progress and for encouraging two-way communication between home and school. Communications include the notices, phone calls, visits, report cards and conferences that most schools provide as well as more innovative ways to promote two-way home-school communication such as the use of the Internet or e-mail boxes for parents and teachers. Some schools use community agencies and organizations as a means of reaching parents about schools.

TYPE 3: INVOLVEMENT AT SCHOOL

Parents and other volunteers assist educators and children in the school. Parents and other family members serve as volunteers, tutors, mentors or aides in classrooms, on the playground, on field trips or in the school office. They also support the school by attending student performances and other school events. They speak in classes and offer demonstrations of their own skills, such as arts, crafts and cooking.

TYPE 4: INVOLVEMENT IN LEARNING ACTIVITIES AT HOME

Teachers request and guide parents to monitor and assist their own children at home. Schools enable families to understand how to help their own children at home by providing information on academic and other skills, with directions on how to monitor, discuss and help with homework and on how to reinforce needed skills.

Type 5: Involvement in Decision-making, Governance and Advocacy
Parents and others in the community play decision-making and/or advisory roles in the school. Examples are parent associations, advisory councils and policy boards, school site management teams or other committees and community organizations. Parents also become activists in independent advocacy groups in the community. Schools assist family members to be leaders and representatives by training them in decision-making skills and by including parents as true, not token, contributors to school decisions, and by providing information to community advocacy groups so they may knowledgeably address issues of school improvement.

Type 6: Collaboration and Exchange with Community Organizations
Schools collaborate with agencies, businesses, cultural organizations, libraries, universities, health agencies and other groups to share responsibility for children's education and future success. Collaboration includes school programs that provide or coordinate child and family access to community and support services, such as before and after-school care, health services, cultural events, partnerships with businesses and cultural institutions. Schools also provide expertise and services to community agencies and institutions.[28]

Practical Guidelines
Here are a few practical guidelines for the development of school–family–community partnerships.

- Every aspect of the school building is open, helpful and friendly to parents.
- Communication with parents, whether about school policies and programs or about their own children are frequent, clear and two-way. Educational jargon is avoided.
- Parents are treated by teachers as collaborators, not just as clients in the educational process. Parents' knowledge, expertise and resources are valued as essential to their child's success in school.
- The school recognizes its responsibility to forge a partnership with all families in the school, not simply those who are most easily available.

- The school principal and other administrators actively express in words and deeds the philosophy of partnership with families.
- The school encourages volunteer support and help from all parents by providing a wide variety of volunteer options, including those that can be done from home and during non-work hours.
- The school provides opportunities for parents to meet their own needs for information, advice and peer support.
- Parents' views and expertise are sought in developing policies and solving school-wide problems; in many schools they are given important decision-making responsibilities.
- Schools recognize that they can best help parents provide a home environment conducive to children's learning if they facilitate their access to basic and supportive services.[29]

To implement these concepts requires vigorous and sustained reaching out by educators. Teachers and administrators need to be trained and oriented to the idea, given support and guidance on trying different approaches and rewarded for their efforts. Decades of tradition must be overcome. Educators need to see that their professional expertise and status will be enhanced and not undermined if they work with families and communities as partners rather than as passive clients.

Government policies at national and local levels must also be modified to encourage partnerships and to provide financial resources needed for implementing good partnership programs. In the century ahead, family, community and school partnerships should become a part of the normal way that schools go about their business, not a peripheral or trivial series of events.

Applying New Approaches to Learning

I believe that the education societies need in the coming century will not be achievable if we continue to use nineteenth-century approaches to teaching and learning. If a society wishes to use education powerfully to help it meet its challenges, it needs to create educational institutions which ground their work in new approaches to learning. Fortunately, there is a rich legacy of knowledge about learning that the twentieth century offers to planners, policy makers and educators. For example, recent studies of the brain offer exciting insights into how learning can be enhanced. Multidisciplinary researchers using advanced computer technology have tracked how the brain actually functions and have shown that learner motivation and interest increase the number of brain cells that are activated.[30]

This knowledge simply confirms what we have known for centuries about the connection between learner interest and motivation and student learning. This idea supports the appeal to individualize and humanize education.

Here are a few of the additional legacies about learning from this century that can be drawn upon as we begin a new one.

Starting Early

The importance of early learning has been tested and demonstrated in many diverse studies. We know how important the early years are for later learning and development. We know, for example, that language development and word recognition begin in the early weeks of infancy. We know that the first four years are crucial to the development of a human being's intellectual capacity and personality.

There are many important practical implications of what we have learned about the importance of the early years to learning. One is that we should invest much more heavily in parent education, helping both mothers and fathers understand how they can facilitate the learning of their own children through language stimulation, reading to their children, encouragement of collaborative activity, and through attention to children's health and nutritional needs. Parenting is a product of biological necessity, but human beings are not born with the knowledge, skills or confidence they need to be good parents.

A second implication is that societies wishing to reform education for the next century should dramatically increase their investments in the education of young children. We need the best trained and qualified teachers for the youngest children just the reverse of the way it is in most places in the world today – investments and status in education grow with the age of the student. Through the developed world, early childhood and day care workers are poorly paid, relative to other occupations, and often not well trained. Increasing a society's investment in early childhood education and involving many more children in these efforts is probably the single most important investment that can be made in a country wishing substantially to improve its educational system.

Multiple Intelligences

Harvard University's Howard Gardner has challenged the unitary concept of intelligence that dominated education for centuries. He has identified seven distinct types of intelligence. He believes that these are genetically influenced but can be enhanced through practice and learning. He has described the characteristics of children and adults for each of the types.

LINGUISTIC

Children with this kind of intelligence enjoy writing, reading, telling stories or doing crossword puzzles.

LOGICAL-MATHEMATICAL

Children with lots of logical intelligence are interested in patterns, categories and relationships. They are drawn to arithmetic problems, strategy games and experiments.

SENSORY-KINESTHETIC

Children with this kind of intelligence process knowledge through bodily sensations. They are often athletic, dancers, or good at crafts such as sewing or woodworking.

SPATIAL

These children think in images and pictures. They may be fascinated with mazes or jigsaw puzzles, or spend free time drawing, building with Lego or daydreaming.

MUSICAL

Musical children often sing or drum to themselves. They are usually quite aware of sounds that others may miss. They are often discriminating listeners.

INTERPERSONAL

Children who are leaders among their peers, who are good at communicating and who seem to understand others' feelings and motives possess interpersonal intelligence.

INTRAPERSONAL

Children with this kind of intelligence are often shy. They are very aware of their own feelings and are self-motivated.[31]

This diversity of learning styles has powerful implications for education at all levels, and reinforces the importance of individualizing and humanizing education. Achieving diversity of educational approaches to match differing learning styles will be made easier because of the new technology we already have and which is still being developed. The computer, computer-based learning and the Internet put individualization of teaching and learning within the reach of educators and families everywhere.

Gardner also calls for "humanizing intelligence," declaring:

> The human being is more than his or her intellectual powers. Perhaps more crucial than intelligence in the human firmament are motivation, personality, emotions and will. If we are ever to obtain a comprehensive and integrated picture of human beings, we need to meld our insights about cognition with comparable insights in respect of these other aspects of human beings.[32]

Teachers of children and adults will need to be equipped with the necessary know-how and skill to use the new knowledge about multiple intelligences and how technology can help to foster learning for children with different learning styles. Teacher trainers in university graduate schools will need to re-tool themselves in order to train teachers and other educators. New approaches to teaching and learning suggested by the work on multiple intelligences must be carefully explained to families and communities, as well as to teachers. Partnership will be the key to change here as in other aspects of education.

Cultural Influences on Learning

Students' learning is affected not only by their differences in learning styles but also by their cultural differences. Jerome Bruner has asserted that knowledge should be recognized as a product of culture rather than freestanding ideas or facts. He maintains that knowledge is interpretation, and that it is entwined with who we are and our world view. He maintains that interpretation can be taught "with the same rigor that characterizes the teaching of scientific method."[33]

This perspective suggests a new way of thinking about curriculum and teaching in schools and universities and institutions serving adults in which educators attend to the personal or human needs of students of all ages. Here once again, humanizing and individualizing education seem relevant.

The cultural differences between the Anglo-Saxon and the Islamic societies illuminate this point. In Islam, the community, religion and obligations are preeminent, while in the Anglo-Saxon world, emphasis is on the individual and individual rights. Such differences have strong influence on how educational institutions approach students and on how students learn. These differences suggest that the partnership concept in the two cultures will be implemented differently.

Learning as a Social and Collaborative Activity
Scientists in many fields – including mathematics, biology, physics, psychology and computer technology – are making discoveries that demonstrate the dynamic relationships among the elements in the natural world. Interconnection is the theme. The educational implications of these challenges to the Newtonian world dominated by analysis is to point to the need for human beings to synthesize, see connections and collaborate with others.[34]

The needs of the emerging knowledge-based, post-industrial world suggest that students require the basic academic skills but also personal competencies. The British Education Trust described these requirements as including:

> . . . the abilities to be self-starters, quick-thinking, problem-solving, risk-taking individuals who can operate in collaborative situations . . . The process of learning has passed from a simple self-organization to a collaborative, social, problem-solving activity much dependent on talk, practical involvement and experimentation.[35]

Much traditional classroom practice is not compatible with this idea.

Between three and six years of age, young children have a natural predisposition to be cooperative and enjoy collaborative play and learning. Positive experiences along these lines can lay the groundwork for learning and practicing the skills of collaboration later on.

The need for collaboration is hardly a new idea. There is a Chinese proverb from the previous millennium about heaven and hell which makes the point quite well:

> Hell is a large room full of starving people, with great caldrons of sweet-smelling, bubbling stew in the middle. But the people have

such long chopsticks that however they hold them they can't get the food into their mouths. Heaven is exactly the same room, same food, same hungry people, same chopsticks . . . but everyone is feeding each other.[36]

If societies wish to stress partnership and such related skills as negotiation and conflict resolution, there are many educational interventions that have been tested and can be used. However, many educators still need to be convinced that this is a legitimate field of work and belongs in the curriculum along with traditional subject matters.

Learning to Learn

I heard a high school student say a few years ago, "I can learn all the facts the school can hand out, but what I need help on is how to deal with the unexpected in the future when the teacher isn't around to tell me what to do." Psychologists give this the fancy label *metacognition* – the ability to think about your own thinking and the development of skills that are genuinely transferable and not tied to a single body of knowledge, and so can be applied in different settings. This kind of learning is crucial in a time of rapid change.

In his work with the British Education Trust 2000, John Abbott stresses the concept of "weaning." He says that formal schooling should start a process through which pupils are weaned from their teachers and institutions and are helped to learn adaptability and flexibility. He writes:

> Schools and parents have to start a dynamic process through which young people are progressively weaned from their dependence on teachers and institutions and given confidence to manage their own learning, collaborating with colleagues as appropriate, and using a range of resources and learning situations.[37]

Communities also have a responsibility in the process that Abbott describes. They can present multiple opportunities to provide service to others in the community, through which they can gain the satisfaction of helping others while developing their own independence and self-confidence.

In these few paragraphs I have only scratched the surface of the vast and complex field of learning. But it is clear that moving in the direction suggested by these lessons about new approaches to learning will require serious changes in how most families, communities and schools contribute to the learning and development of children. It is not likely that such changes can be implemented successfully without using partnerships as a key theme.

Applying as Well as Producing Knowledge

Back in the late sixteenth century, Francis Bacon told us that research must entail both the production and the use of knowledge. He called for the planned, dynamic, integrated production and use of knowledge for specified ends in view. He forecast that if production were isolated or separated from use, the results would not be beneficial and rejected the ancient Greek belief that pure theory was superior and applied practice inferior. Unfortunately, societies have not heeded this advice to any great extent.

There is no question that knowledge production and science and technology have dramatically outrun social development and organization. An American historian, Ira Harkavy, has reminded us that, "what is most useful in practice is most correct in theory. What is most significant in theory is that [which] most improves practice."[38]

The knowledge already exists to invigorate our institutions and social organizations in order to equip societies to deal with change and with the complex challenges we will face. Advances in knowledge of science, mathematics, the social sciences, psychology, communications theory and medicine have been astounding. More research is needed, of course, but a primary need now is to learn how to use knowledge and the fruits of research to modify individual and institutional practices. Unhappily, most researchers are better producers than appliers; most intellectuals and specialists are better at identifying problems than at knowing how to solve them.

In the twenty-first century, much attention should be given to strategies to help people at all levels of sophistication make use of that which is already known and that which will be discovered in the years ahead. This is clearly an educational task of special importance.

Societies will need to use their educational systems to focus on the positive applications of knowledge with as much vigor as they now stress the production of new knowledge.

American education is full of examples of good research or important new theory that is not applied in schools and classrooms, or applied inadequately by teachers and school administrators who were not given the training and support to understand, accept and apply the new ideas in practice. Researchers and practitioners in American education live in different worlds, talk different languages and are often very critical of each other.

Social scientists and educational researchers usually conduct studies themselves with little or no involvement of the practitioners. The results, if they have implications for action, are not conveyed in language which is user-friendly for practitioners, and the implications are seldom fleshed out so as to be clear to those who might apply them, such as teachers, nurses or social workers.

Action Research as a Methodology

Improved methodologies are also needed. Action research is one tool that can be used to reconnect knowledge and its use, and at the same time link schools and universities with the wider society. Action research has been shown to facilitate reflection and action based on that reflection by practitioners and hence can help to bridge the gap between theory and research-based knowledge on the one hand and practice on the other.

Most approaches to action research stress a collaborative relationships between academics, practitioners and community people. Mutual learning is the objective as are both production and use of knowledge. The approach makes possible access by researchers and scholars to the world of the practitioner that is not easy to achieve with traditional models of research conducted solely by outsiders.

There are several kinds of action research that have been tested with good results. In one type, professional researchers conduct the research themselves but only after practitioners identify and define problems to be studied. In another approach, the intent is improved practice through action. Academics collaborate with practitioners in identifying problems to be studied, in designing of studies, and then in interpreting the results for application to practice.

In another variety, participatory action research, researchers, practitioners and those affected by the problems under study – parents or community residents for example – become partners in deciding what is to be studied, collaboratively design a study, gather data, interpret the findings and then develop and implement action plans based on the results.

In my own work with the Center on Families, Communities, Schools and Children's Learning we developed and applied an approach in schools which we call parent–teacher action research. This is a concept and methodology that combine knowledge production and knowledge use. My colleague, Ameetha Palanki, has described how parent–teacher action research provides opportunities for reflection and interaction by bringing together teachers and parents to exchange and synthesize the knowledge that each possesses.[39]

This approach has been tested by schools both in the US and in several other countries in projects sponsored by our center. In these projects, the school forms a small team of volunteer teachers, family members, community representatives and students, along with the principal, to assess school and community strengths and priorities or to investigate a troubling problem or issue.

The team talks to teachers, families and community agencies and residents through various means including focus groups, interviews and surveys. They analyze the results and decide on one or two priority objectives which can be addressed through family or community collaboration. The team works with others in the school or community to plan and carry out one or more interventions or projects aimed at the objective. The team then studies and evaluates what happens. Some examples of interventions in Center on Families projects were home visits, parent–teacher conferences, family centers and mentoring programs.

One of the main results in some projects was that families and teachers learned to work together to solve problems that were meaningful to the children and families in that school and to communicate with and trust, each other. It is also a process that invites participation of families in making decisions about their own children as well as the school as a whole.[40]

One of the benefits of this kind of action research is that teachers and other school practitioners become researchers themselves; they own the process and the results. Research and researchers become less esoteric and removed. Knowledge is applied not just accumulated. The process of applying in practice what has been learned through action research can become an everyday and natural activity.

University–Community Partnerships Collaboration
Another approach to making better connections between knowledge and its application in practice is to strengthen the relationships between schools and universities.

Universities and schools are a part of the same complex societal system. They have mutual obligations, but they too often ignore each other. Academics in universities and related research centers can make a significant contribution to professional practitioners in education and other community-serving fields, and to children and adults served by those professional practitioners. These contributions include offering their expertise to practitioners and the community in collaborative ways, providing training, making information understandable and accessible and, importantly, assisting and encouraging non-academics to use the results of the new knowledge.

In past few years, some American universities have taken their societal obligations seriously and have developed collaborative relationships with schools and school systems. But the traditions of our academic world are hard to change, and most higher institutions keep schools and the community at arm's length except on ceremonial occasions.

The academic reward system heavily emphasizes research and publication in scholarly journals and not the uses and applications of knowledge or collaborative approaches to studying problems such as action research.

Partnerships between schools and communities with institutions of higher education are good examples of the kind of collaboration needed to face the challenges of the coming century.

Conclusion

One hundred years ago, the great American philosopher John Dewey wrote *School and Society*, and asserted that for social progress to occur relatively smoothly as science develops and societies evolve economically, educational systems must evolve appropriately.[41]

It is clear that real wealth creation – the creation of both economic and social capital – in the hundred years ahead will be dependent on the production, dissemination and application of knowledge. This means the societies of the world will need to push hard to reinvigorate or reform their educational systems, at all levels.

This chapter proposes themes and strategies that might be useful to educators and policy makers thinking about how educational systems should evolve in order to meet better the challenges of the twenty-first century.

Educators must be optimists – and I am one, even though cynicism is always fashionable in academia. My optimism about the next century is built on the hope that a stronger, more positive reciprocal relationship between society at large and its communities and educational institutions will be forged, and that we will learn to use the positive potential of education for good and humane purposes.

My special concern is that we can harness the potential of education to develop new generations that can escape the legacies of violence, war, hatred of people who have different color, ethnicity, race or religion that the twentieth century has left for the coming hundred years. I think that educational systems that succeed in equalizing, individualizing and humanizing their efforts will help to meet this challenge and the others that we face.

John Dewey would approve this call for raising new generations who can better control hatred, fear and violence, as he made a similar one a hundred years ago. He would also approve of the appeal for inventing workable ways in which the responsibility for the learning and development of all children and adults can be more widely shared through partnerships across all of the components of society.

Dewey would not be satisfied with the progress that has been made in the last century, and neither am I, but he would be hopeful, as I am, that in the next century we will move more rapidly toward better educational opportunities for all and a more peaceful and harmonious world.[42]

3

Investment in Human Capital: A Cost-Benefit Approach

Monther Sharè

Introduction

The costs and benefits of education are at the heart of the economics of education, which is a fairly new branch of economics but not without historical roots that extend back to the classical school. Since the late 1950s, there has been momentous development in the field, which stimulated interest not only among economists but also among educators, social scientists, politicians and others.

At the earlier stages, economists' interest was centered on the relationships between education and the economy. Since then, interest increasingly widened to cover such subjects as the role of education in economic growth, returns to investment in education (both social and private), the role of educated workers in economic development, forecasts of manpower requirements, costs and benefits of education, cost-effectiveness in education, efficiency of labor, financing education and the impact of education on income distribution.[1]

The major concern of this chapter is to introduce a lucid, concise and not-too-mathematical presentation of the cost-benefit approach to investment in human capital. Such presentation would provide policy makers with useful guidance regarding future decisions relating to investment in education and training. It could also be equally useful in guiding private decision makers in this field. This chapter does not relate to a particular country, but whenever an example is useful, the empirical experience of Jordan, among other countries, will be used.

Human Capital Theory

Recognition of the need to evaluate the economic value of man can be traced back to very early economic thought. In 1776, Adam Smith considered the skills of the workers to be the predominant force for economic progress. Recognizing the analogy between investment in physical capital and human capital, Smith suggested that the educated worker is similar to an expensive machine:

> A man educated at the expense of much labor and time to any of those employments, which require extraordinary dexterity and skill, may be compared to one of those expensive machines. The work, which he learns to perform, it must be expected, over and above the usual wages of common labor, will replace in him the whole expense of his education, with at least the ordinary profits of an equally valuable capital . . . The deference between the wages of skilled labor and those of common labor is founded upon this principle.[2]

A century later, Alfred Marshall also considered education as an investment in people and pointed out its analogy to investment in machines:

> The worker sells his work, but he himself remains his own property, those who bear the expenses of rearing and educating him receive but very little of the price that is paid for his services in later years.[3]

Marshall proceeded to emphasize the importance of the education of parents as they form a group in the society which commands the means of production and:

> . . . exert themselves much to select the best careers for their sons and the best training for those careers; and they are generally willing and able to incur a considerable expense for this purpose. The professional classes especially, while generally eager to save some capital for their children, are even more on the alert for opportunities of investing it in them.[4]

However, the universal acceptance of education as an investment in human capital and its analogy to physical capital investment did not result in any serious application of the techniques of investment appraisal to expenditure on education until the 1960s, when Schultz estimated the stock of human capital in the US for the period 1900–1957;[5] the contribution of education to economic growth was also measured by Schultz and Denison.[6] The works of the early 1960s triggered rapid development and research into investment in education.[7]

It is now universally accepted that human capital refers to those individual skills, talents, capacities and elements of knowledge that improve the individual's contribution to the production of goods and services.[8] Human capital manifests itself in higher labor productivity, and hence income, for the individual worker, and a higher national product, if the worker is paid according to marginal revenue product.[9] Variations in worker incomes imply that labor must be heterogeneous, thus income variations are only a reflection of the difference in human capital. In the neoclassical marginal productivity theory, labor was assumed homogeneous in those aspects that yield a labor supply curve. Differences were assumed away in the initial presentation of the marginal productivity theory of wage determination. What was ignored becomes the cornerstone for the human capital analysis of individual income differences. Heterogeneity of the labor force with differences in human capital forms the core of the human capital analysis.[10]

Investment in Human Capital

Investment means deferring current consumption in order to receive some future return. The motivation to accumulate human capital is the prospect of a higher earning capacity. This is the financial return that justifies investment in human capital whether by individuals, employers or society.

Investment in oneself, according to economists, is the result of rational optimizing decisions (by individuals or their parents) made on the basis of estimates of the probable present value of alternative lifetime income streams.

Investment in human capital involves formal education, on-the-job (OTJ) training and informal types of investment that augment human capital. Such investment, however, raises certain issues that are not present with investment in physical capital. There is a consumption part of education, which can be distinguished from the investment part. Yet, there no clear-cut lines that separate the two.[11]

Education and Earnings: The Benefits of Education

Determination of the effect of education on lifetime income (earnings) requires details of earnings related to age and years of schooling (educational level) involving a representative sample of workers of different ages and occupations. Such a cross-sectional approach allows the construction of age–education–earnings profiles.[12]

A considerable amount of the applied work in the economics of education focused on estimating a version of the following equation in order to construct the age–education–earnings profiles:[13]

$$Y_i = \alpha + \beta S_i + X_i \, \delta + ui$$

where Y measures income, earning or wage; S is measure of schooling; X is a set of other variables assumed to affect earnings, and u is a disturbance term.

Well-behaved age-earnings profiles are expected to exhibit the following characteristics.

- Earnings are highly correlated with education; they rise at each age with successive levels of education and they do not cross.
- All profiles rise with age to a single peak and then fall until the age of retirement.
- The higher the educational level, the steeper the profiles.
- The higher the educational level, the further in time is the peak earnings point.

Figures 1:3, 2:3 and 3:3 show three examples of age–education–earnings profiles for Jordan, the US, the UK, Mexico and India at different points in time.

Some of the researchers dwelling on the returns to education ascribe to the claimant that earning profiles often neglect several elements that affect earnings other than education, and hence overestimate the returns. While others stress that education delivers other financial and non-pecuniary benefits which are not included in earnings data, thus profiles underestimate the impact of education. Among the factors that might affect returns either way are ability, socio-economic background, motivation, parental background, fringe benefits, health status and even an element of luck.

For practical purposes, and statistical limitations, only a modest subset of variables is typically included.[14] Much of the empirical work during the last 30 years has been aimed at improving the specification of the earnings function through various sophisticated models.[15]

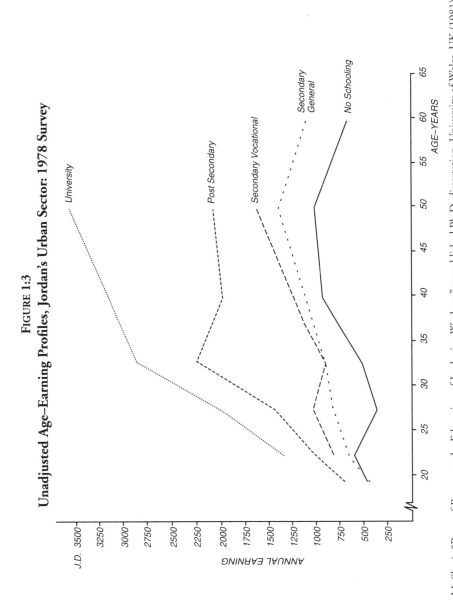

FIGURE 1:3

Unadjusted Age–Earning Profiles, Jordan's Urban Sector: 1978 Survey

University

Post Secondary

Secondary Vocational

Secondary General

No Schooling

ANNUAL EARNING

J.D. 3500
3250
3000
2750
2500
2250
2000
1750
1500
1250
1000
750
500
250

AGE–YEARS

20 25 30 35 40 45 50 55 60 65

Source: M. Sharè, "Rates of Return to the Education of Jordanian Workers," unpublished Ph.D. dissertation, University of Wales, UK (1981), 129

FIGURE 2.3
Age–Earning Profiles in Four Countries

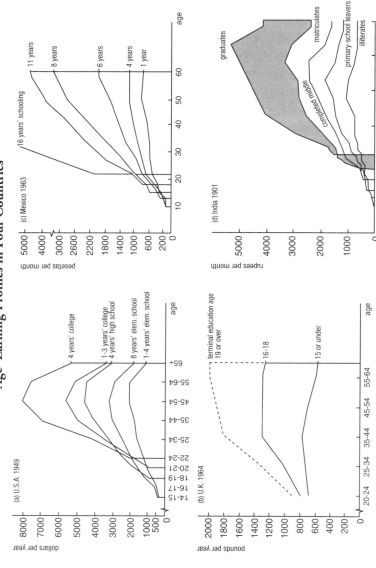

Note: In the U.K. diagram, the sample sizes for each age cohort for the TEA group 19 or over are too small to provide reliable results.

Source: From several sources in M. Blaug, *An Introduction to the Economics of Education* (Harmondsworth: Penguin Books, 1976).

The Costs of Education

For the calculation of the rates of return to investment in education, earnings must be compared with the relevant costs at each level of education. Estimation of the costs will differ between private and public viewpoints. Calculation of social cost (public cost) of education is crucial for governmental policy decisions on capital outlays. On the other hand, the costs borne by the individual (private) are important for the investment decision by the individual (or his/her guardian, parents or otherwise).

Social Costs

Social costs of education comprise all expenditures on current activities such as teachers and other personnel salaries during the current period as well as capital expenditures. A measure of foregone output of students (while in school instead of work) must also be included.[16]

It is important to note that annual capital cost of educational institutions must be calculated, for this is the economic cost pertinent to the current period. Therefore, total capital outlays on educational institutions must first be broken down by type according to economic life, and then the annual capital cost for each item will be calculated using the capital recovery factor for the assumed interest rate and economic life of the capital cost item.

The capital recovery factor can be determined for discrete payments and discrete compounding using the following formula:[17]

$$A = P \left[\frac{i(1 + i)^n}{(1 + i)^n - 1} \right] = P\,(A/p, i, n)$$

where A = the annual capital cost of the item; P = the capital outlay at the initial period, and i = the interest rate.

For example, if college building costs US$2 million, with an expected economic life of 60 years, and at an interest rate of 6 percent, then the annual cost loaded to each year would be:

A = US$2 million X capital recovery factor

A = US$2 million X 0.0619
A = US$123,800

The same method would be used for each item having economic life exceeding one year.

Private Costs

The costs incurred by the individuals (private) include fees minus scholarships, expenditure on books and relevant materials, and foregone earnings during the schooling period.

Rates of Return to Education

In determining the significance of a productive resource, economists look first and foremost at its price. If this resource is capital, they look at its rate of return.[18] But the question now is, whose investment are we considering? And hence, whose decision? Individual or public?

Individuals invest in their own human capital, and by so doing they abstain from current consumption and invest a sum of money, must probably not their own, looking for future benefits in the form of increased earnings, better job prospects, social status and many other benefits. When contemplating investment alternatives, the individual is presumed to be following rules of rational decision-making. This means the individual will invest so long as the expected stream of returns from the investment exceeds the costs incurred by making the investment.

On the other hand, the government is the largest investor in human capital formation. Not only does the government (any government) invest its resources in education at the school level, it also expends substantial amounts of money on higher education as well as vocational education. It also invests in various training programs.[19]

Governments do mobilize public expenditure toward investment in human capital because the price system would not produce a sufficient level of investment in that field. This is so for several reasons. First, externalities are inherent characteristics of education, which means that even a competitive price system could not be expected to come up with prices that reflect true relative scarcities of resources.[20] Thus considering educational investments solely on the basis of private costs and returns would neglect the social returns produced by such investment. Second, the private market is permeated with imperfections. It is often the case that poorer students are discriminated against in loans to finance education, a matter that extenuates an already unequal income distribution.

Third, the high degree of risk and uncertainty associated with human capital investments means that there would be under-investment if investment were left solely to the private market. Socializing risk and uncertainty (through public investment) removes some of these factors from the private market decision an individual would have to make.

The forms of investment in human capital undertaken by the government are an important issue because different segments of society have different interests. The most accepted human capital investment is that of universal primary and secondary education. Education beyond high school has been treated as a mixed private and public responsibility.

Next, we shed light on the discounting process on the basis of which rates of return to educational investments may be calculated, whether private or social.

Discounted Returns

The returns (benefits) from an investment in human capital will accrue over an extended period of time, perhaps an entire lifetime. Therefore the stream of returns to the investment must be computed over time. Thus, if a principal is invested in human capital, which will yield stream of returns over some period of time, the problem is to evaluate the worth of those returns. The procedure for making such a calculation is the same as the one that would be used if the money were put into an alternative investment that would yield the same returns.

The investor in human capital will seek to maximize the present value of the principal invested in human capital acquisition. The formula for doing this is:

$$PVR \overset{n}{\underset{t=0}{=}} \sum \frac{Rt}{(1 + i)^t}$$

The goal will be to maximize the present value (PVR) from some expected stream of returns (R), over (t) years, discounted by the interest rate (i), allowance must be made to risk and uncertainty as in the following equation:

$$PVR = \sum_{t=0}^{n} \frac{(P)(Rt)}{(1 + i)^t} \qquad = \sum_{t=0}^{n} \frac{(P)(Rt)}{(1 + i + u)^t}$$

Discounted Costs

There are costs that must be taken into account in the individual's investment decision. The discounted present value of the costs will be:

$$PVC = \sum_{t=0}^{n} \frac{Ct}{(1 + i)^t}$$

Adding risk and uncertainty:

$$PVC = \sum_{t=0}^{n} \frac{(P)(Ct)}{(1 + i + u)^t}$$

Taking account of the costs as well as the returns maximizes the net present value of an investment in human capital. Formally, net present value is represented as the difference between returns and costs:

$$NPV = \sum_{t=0}^{n} \frac{(Rt)}{(1 + i)t} - \sum_{t=0}^{n} \frac{Ct}{(1 + i)^t}$$

Adding risk and uncertainty:

$$NPV = \sum_{t=0}^{n} \left[\frac{(Pr)(Rt)}{(1 + i + u)^t} \right] - \sum_{t=0}^{n} \left[\frac{(Pc)(Ct)}{(1 + i + u)^t} \right]$$

The decision to invest in human capital should follow the decision rule implied by the maximization of net present value. Investment should occur as long as the expected returns exceed the expected costs, discounted to take account of the future and adjusted for risk and uncertainty.

To clarify this further, we follow the example used by Psacharopoulos.[21] Assume that a project called university education will be considered for investment. The costs during four years of study consist of direct costs

(Cu) and foregone earnings (Ws), while the benefits reflect the wage differentials between that of a university graduate (Wu) and a secondary school graduate (Ws). Assuming that a university graduate will have a working life of 43 years after graduation, the rate of return to the investment in university education compared to secondary school education may be found by solving the following equation for (r):

$$\sum_{t=-3}^{0} \frac{(P)(Cu + Ws)_t}{(1 + r + u)^t} - \sum_{t=1}^{43} \frac{(P)(Wu-Ws)^t}{(1 + r + u)^t} = 0$$

All costs of this educational project are accumulated forward to the year (0) and all returns are discounted back to the same year. Figure 3:3 shows a graphical illustration of such calculation. The same procedure is applicable to produce various rates of return associated with different educational levels.

FIGURE 3:3
A Cost-Benefit Comparison

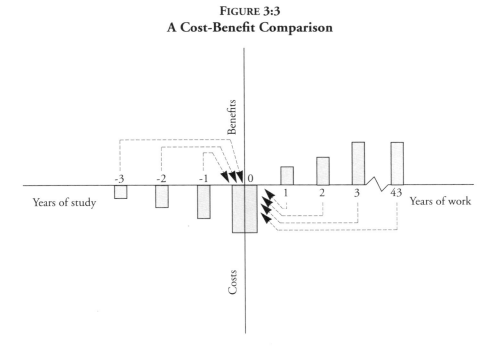

Source: George Pascharopoulos, *Returns to Education: An International Comparison* (Amsterdam: Elsevier Scientific Publishing Co., 1973), 21.

The difference between private and social rates of return lies in the data used for calculation. The private rate compares the costs of education borne by an individual with the returns that accrued to the same individual. Therefore earnings will be net of taxes and costs will be only those paid by the individual. For the social rates of return to education, earnings will be inclusive of taxes and the costs will include all economic costs of educational institutions as mentioned earlier. As a general rule, social rates will always be lower than private rates. Table 1:3 shows private and social rates of return to three educational levels for selected countries.

Private rates presented in Table 1:3 exceed the social rates for all countries representing different stages of development and wealth. However, an implicit assumption underlining the cross-country comparison of rates of return to education is the emigration of educated workers expected if the domestic private returns to certain levels of education are significantly below those prevailing abroad. In the case of Jordan, for example, it is evident from Table 1:3 that higher rates of return for Jordanian migrant workers in Kuwait attracted further migration in the 1970s, not only to Kuwait but also to the GCC countries in general.

We have no information on rates of return to education in the UAE. Yet the increase of immigrant workers, from 84.6 percent of the total labor force in 1975 to 89.1 percent in 1990 is a clear indication of extremely rewarding rates of return, or at least higher incomes, to the immigrant education compared to the rates of return prevailing in their home countries.[22]

Human Capital Investment (Training)

As aptly put by Jacob Mincer, "formal school instruction is neither an exclusive nor a sufficient method of training the labor force."[23] Occupational skills are usually acquired after joining the workforce and often occur over a prolonged period of time. This process now known as OTJ training.

Firms, as well as governmental organizations, do invest in human capital through OTJ training. Such training may be specialized as formal training or informal training (learning by doing). As the process of OTJ training is presumed to improve future productivity, it must be emphasized

TABLE 1:3
Social and Private Rates of Return by Educational Level for Selected Countries (Percentage)

Country	Year	Social			Private		
		Primary	Secondary	Higher	Primary	Secondary	Higher
Brazil	1962	10.7	17.2	14.5	11.3	21.4	38.1
Colombia	1966	40.0	24.0	8.0	50.0	32.0	15.5
Ghana	1967	18.0	13.0	16.5	24.5	17.0	37.0
Great Britain	1966	–	3.6	8.2	–	6.2	12.0
India	1960	20.0	16.8	12.7	24.7	19.2	14.3
Japan	1961	–	5.0	6.0	–	6.0	9.0
Jordan	1978						
Urban		29.5	-ve	21.5	52.4	-ve	27.0
Vocational		–	6.9	–	–	7.2	–
Public Sector		8.1	9.8	13.1	13.3	10.7	15.4
In Kuwait		–	–	–	40.6	11.8	28.2
Kenya	1968	21.7	19.2	8.8	32.7	30.0	27.4
Mexico	1963	25.0	17.0	23.0	32.0	23.0	29.0
Nigeria	1966	23.0	12.8	17.0	30.0	14.0	34.0
Norway	1966	–	7.2	7.5	–	7.4	7.7
Philippines	1966	7.0	21.0	11.0	7.5	28.0	12.5
Puerto Rico	1959	17.1	21.7	16.5	100.0	23.4	27.9
Sweden	1967	–	10.5	9.2	–	–	10.3
Thailand	1970	30.5	13.0	11.0	56.0	14.5	14.0
Venezuela	1957	82.0	17.0	23.0	–	18.0	27.0
United States	1959	17.8	14.0	9.7	155.1	19.5	13.6

Sources: For Jordan, M. Share, 'Rates of Return to the Education of Jordanian Workers' (unpublished PhD dissertation, University of Wales, 1981); data for other countries from G. Psacharopoulos, *Returns to Education: An International Comparison* (Amsterdam: Elsevier Scientific Publishing Co., 1973).

that such an improvement can only be realized at a cost, for otherwise there would be an overwhelming demand for training.[24] The nature of training costs vary with the type of training. However, they may include materials used up in the production process, the wages of instructors conducting the training, wasted production time of the trainee or output reduced during his training.

The employer that invests in the human capital of his employees has no guarantee that he will be able to reap the benefits from the improvement of the workers' human capital. This problem arises because, on the one hand, the employer does not own the individual worker, and on the other hand, OTJ training offered to the worker may be of the general type which raises the marginal product of the worker not only to his firm but to other firms as well.[25] Thus, the returns to the firm's investment in its workers' human capital must be captured through the provision of sufficient incentives for the worker to remain in the firm. This is why firms tend to hoard labor in which they had invested substantial human capital during the early stages of a recession and will dismiss such labor with great reluctance. By laying off workers in whom substantial training has been invested, the employer stands to lose the potential returns from his investment.

The returns from a firm's investment in human capital occur for two reasons. First, labor's marginal product should be increased by the investment in human capital. Second, the employer's physical capital should become more productive because of the complementarities that exist between investments in human and physical capital.

The firm, in deciding how much to invest in the human capital of its employees, will follow the familiar decision rule of investing as long as the expected returns from the investment exceed expected costs. The returns take the form of increased productivity. Suppose that the value of the marginal product of a worker before training (VMPP^b), increased to (VMPP^a) after training, and suppose that training is completed in one period at a cost (C) to the firm, then the firm's investment will be worth while if the discounted present value of the returns to training exceeds the cost of training as follows:

$$C < \sum_{i=1}^{n} \frac{VMPP_i^a - VMPP_i^b}{(1 + r)^i}$$

Firms tend to invest more in human capital that involves specific training, simply because the returns to such investment are more readily captured. This is particularly true for lower-skilled blue-collar and white-collar workers for whom there is substantial turnover. The higher up the skill and occupation ladder one moves, the more likely it is that there will be general training. For precisely this reason, governments have moved into the training and human capital formation process, because there are externalities to the education and training expenditure.

Empirical Evidence

In two surveys of the impact of training, Charles Brown and Robert Lalonde produced some interesting results for the US.[26] Despite difficulties in measuring informal OTJ training in terms of time or money spent, Brown determined that about 10 percent of those employed have participated in formal OTJ training while another 15 percent indicated receiving informal OTJ training. Another interesting observation was that public-sector employees received more formal training over time. It was also fascinating to discover that the more-educated workers get more training than the less educated. Brown recommends evading direct subsidization of informal training because of the difficulty in monitoring such training.

Lalonde's survey of public training programs since the late 1950s shows that public sector investment in training can generate substantial earnings gains for some participants, resulting from higher post-program employment rate in general. He also concludes that the large gains often associated with investments in inexpensive services such as job search assistance suggest that diminishing returns may plague investments in more expensive services such as classroom training and OTJ training.

In the case of Jordan, data and research on training whether formal or informal, are sparser. Al-Ali calculated a 13.67 percent internal rate of return on secondary education trainees in the public sector during the period 1970–75.[27] Sharè calculated 6.9 percent and 7.2 percent social and private rates of return respectively to the vocational trainees in 1978.[28] A more recent study reveals a social rate of return to community colleges graduates as low as 3.5 percent.[29] At first glance, it seems as if rates of return to training in Jordan are steadily declining. However, the observed differences are due to differences in the underlying assumptions and methodological approaches of those studies.

Conclusion

It is important to underline some policy considerations regarding finance and quality of education. Primary and secondary school enrollments have expanded rapidly in the past three decades. Higher education was not lagging far behind for the obvious financial and non-financial rewards involved. Yet, in developing countries, resources are spread thin to accommodate the pressure for expansion at the tertiary level of education.

Availing poorer students of higher education opportunities, while maintaining quality of education and containing public expenditure at some acceptable level present a conventional problem that needs unconventional measures to surmount. One may, without commitment at this stage, suggest further research into such fields as cost-effectiveness, cost recovery, students loan schemes and their potential role in financing higher education without compromising quality. For how money is spent is a more significant question than how much money is spent.

4

Human Capital and Quality Management: Strategies for an Era of Globalization

Adnan Badran

Introduction

In confronting the challenges of the unknown world, education provides the basics needed for problem-solving. Education provides a wealth of knowledge and skills capital which power the wheels of development; it produces the entrepreneurs and provides employment opportunities. Education is also indispensable to the development of a democratic society based on freedom and social justice, minimizing exclusion and marginalization, oppression and ignorance.

What type of education is envisaged for the twenty-first century? It is only a number of days before a new chapter in the history of humanity will begin. Education is an ongoing process of improving knowledge and skills, but it is also an evolutionary process which should be flexible in order to meet the emerging needs of society – local, regional or global.

Emerging future trends of globalization clearly show a move toward interdependence in which corporate has no distinctive nationality and every country has a business "outreach."

The competitive edge will be the determining factor for staying alive in the global market economy. Thus, the rule of the new game is to be efficient and innovative. Indeed, these requirements cannot be achieved except by preparing competitive human resources to meet the emerging needs of globality.

Fashioning the Future

There is a constant need to review priorities and comparative advantages, and to recheck relevant data and information in light of the incessant changes in economics and society – demographic contours, literacy profiles, occupational matrices, migration pattern, volumes of trades and international transactions, ongoing policies, and relevant and active training and research. When a society enters a development era, many of them suffer from severe paucity of data and information and non-availability of trained "natives" to undertake new responsibilities. Imported expertise for the initial phase fills the gap so that an initial blueprint can be developed. But it is crucial that the education system in the country responds quickly to changes and builds an endogenous capacity to steer human resources toward new opportunities.

Capacity-building

Endogenous sustainable development is possible only when capacity-building is achieved at the national level. An adequate infrastructure for education including training and research for industrial production, and adequate indigenous-trained capacity (teachers, researchers, technicians, engineers, bureaucrats and managers) are a prerequisite for endogenous development. Through education and training, challenges of the pattern of total dependence on expatriates may evolve. At the same time, it is important to prevent the emergence of a north and south divide within the country, which ultimately produces inequity and unequal opportunity. This, in turn, would result in widening the gap within the same society and leads to social instability, violence and apartheid poverty. Therefore, long-term processes, as well as structural adjustment policies, are required to increase equal opportunities; slower growth of employment means that more and more qualified people will be competing for jobs that require fewer skills and offer lower wages. In addition, migration to urban areas may lead to urban explosion. Already, 43 percent of a world population of 5.8 billion live in urban areas which may accentuate the social dislocation, disorganization and environmental pollution.

Tensions Brought by Globalization

Worldwide economic, scientific, cultural and political interdependence dictated by free trade of economic and financial markets, and by the global information and communications revolution are taking root. Without doubt, the emergence of this new world phenomenon will shape our life styles, behavior, concepts and deep-rooted traditions. Although it is difficult to apprehend or predict, it will create many uncertainties for future generations.

This means that the terms of national economic policies will be dictated by external forces, as characterized by steadily shifting mass capitals from one financial center to another at high speed, in accordance with interest rates and speculative forecasts. World growth will be export-driven, where exports of goods and services account for 20 percent of all economies, a volume that is steadily growing.

This new world economic order will put more pressure on education reforms. However, too many reforms can be detrimental to the educational process, because it does not allow the system time to absorb the changes and to deliver accordingly. Education is a long-term investment and its results cannot be obtained instantly. Otherwise disorientation of the system will lead to a delivery of confused graduates.

Another stress of globalization may lead to a conflict between the preservation of local roots while at the same time becoming universal. Education again has a major role to play in the preservation of the diversity of culture, language, traditions and values. Otherwise, a mono-culture and mono-language may become predominant, destroying the rich diversity of local cultures which were built through millions of years of evolution throughout the history of humanity.

Globalization may leave a large proportion of the world marginalized. More than two billion people on the planet still have no access to electricity, mostly in the rural areas of developing countries. Again, a conflict may rise among info-rich and info-poor, not only among countries but even within. This will pose another challenge in equal access to education among the different social groups: those who have access to multimedia and networks and innovative education, and those who will be blacked-out.

With the speed of globalization, short-term planning and gains may become a predominant policy which could overtax the long-term planning in education. As a result, much of education may be undertaken privately by corporate entities, through commercial "virtual" universities or through special well-tailored "sandwich" courses for career development. Continuous education (i.e. life-long) will be carried out privately to accommodate what dose of training is required for a specific job or for a shift in assignment. Public universities with a rigid curricula may lose ground in this race for short-term policies dictated by the ever-changing market forces.

With globalization, the phenomena of brain-drain and brain-gain will no longer exist. The delivery of education in terms of quality of human resources, who are trained locally, will compete for employment in the global market. So planners of education at the local level must act locally and think globally to seize the greatest portion of the global human capital. Human capital will cross borders to follow business opportunities anywhere in the world, and citizenship will give away to excellence and efficiency. The mobility of mass capital resources will follow global forces of competition for efficiency. The most important criteria for transnational corporations in considering a country or a region for investment will be the development level of the economic infrastructure and the quality of human capital for high-tech industries and low-cost, vocationally skilled human capital for labor-intensive industries.

With new communication technologies, distance and space are shrinking. Sites of manufacturing are increasingly independent of geographic distance and have no nationality. Capital will not only search for fresh markets but will also incorporate new groups in these global assembly lines. One part of a product may be manufactured in Dubai, another in Singapore, and a third in Japan before the final assembly in India. Cost-benefit analysis will determine who does what, locally and regionally, for the global assembly lines. Also, in order to remain competitive in the global economy, labor-intensive manufacturing will shift for profit-gains from the industrialized world into the developing world – e.g. in textiles and leathers, where women will become the larger portion of the workforce. While brain-intensive high-tech industries require a minimum of labor force, they will be promoted in the industrialized countries, where the capacity and infrastructure for producing the knowledge and technology through scientific research and development exist, and where frontier areas of science and technology are evolved through strong infrastructure in terms of a critical mass of scientists, highly equipped laboratories, strong support in the way of technical services, ideal environments for research, good incubation and business park facilities for the conversion of applied knowledge to technologies, strong financing facilities, and adequate patent and intellectual rights protection.

With globalization, we do expect a division of labor between the industrialized and the developing worlds. It is therefore for education and science in developing countries to determine how the forces which are dictating this division could be shifted gradually from north to south to develop a more equitable world for sharing knowledge and resources. Let us remember that division of labor has never been static, but changes according to emerging inputs for production efficiency, trade networks and market forces.

The tension of globality may create conflict between material and spiritual. How can ethics, values and traditions be maintained in a world driven by a consumer market-economy? Again, education must respond in building a pluralistic society based on justice, human rights and respect for the convictions of various groups so that minds and spirits will be lifted to the plane of the universal and in some measure to transcend themselves.[1] Development is more complicated than economists think. Developmental models have to take into consideration the values and cultural fabric of the society; otherwise, development may become a human adventure. So appraising the value of education and its standards to meet the needs of society requires a re-thinking of education strategies at all levels and a concrete plan of action based on emerging conditions to create new paradigms for the next millennium.

Challenges and Opportunities

Globalization is now more than a catchword. It is a reality which emerged after the end of the Cold War. It is characterized by fast-moving knowledge-driven information technologies and networks which have the potential to change every classroom practice. The impact of the use of computers and communication technologies will not be limited to the learning process (teachers and students), but will change the whole institutional infrastructure and pattern of behavior within education systems. We are passing through a transformation era in building human capital which is unparalleled in human history. Education faces the daunting challenge of preparing individuals for the information-age society to be able to:

- manage an avalanche of information
- prepare the most efficient human capital for the brain-intensive marketplace

- prepare flexible human resources to meet the uncertainties of a global economy, and
- innovate to keep up with a high-speed, knowledge-driven, competitive economy in the workplace.

In addition, education must:

- respond to social needs of "rights to education"
- provide "education for all"
- deal with limited resources (physical and financial)
- promote the development of citizenship, and
- maintain ethical and cultural value systems.

The rigid boundaries separating the various disciplines of science will soften to give way to a new breed of transdisciplinary and interdisciplinary scientific fields to address the emerging needs of new materials, communications and environmental issues and problems facing society in the next millennium. Therefore, education – and, in particular, higher education – must change to meet new requirements in the preparation of a new breed of human capital.

Knowledge theory moves quickly to scientific application for advancing competition in the marketplace but can only be absorbed and utilized commercially by a strong knowledge-based society. This again puts pressure on the education system to advocate a wide system of science literacy for the public at large. It is not sufficient to eradicate illiteracy, as declared by UNESCO, UNICEF, UNDP and the World Bank at the Jomtien Conference of 1990. Rather, it is imperative to introduce a strong component in science and technical literacy so that the whole of society becomes a science-literate population, able to cope with the knowledge-driven new world of the next millennium.

Globules of market-free economics underway around the world will gradually bring interdependence with free mobility and materials within the agglomerate, where a new culture will be born. This may lead to a loose confederated governance *sine qua non* building interests of the population sharing a new modality of geography and demography. Multi-dimensional education will enable people to become aware of themselves and their environment, and play a role in the community at large. Sharing knowledge, and knowing how to live with other people and share skills, constitute a new dimension of creativity. It combines non-formal with formal learning and the acquisition of new competencies; it also brings the joy of working together in the most complex social relationships within a new socio-cultural human dimension.

Human Capital for the Information Age

Schools and universities must change to meet the challenges of a knowledge-based economy in the information age. New skills are needed for the emerging information-age workplace. If students are to become intelligent users of technology and information, they should also learn how to be creative and innovative. They should be involved in problem-solving and research, and should be able to tackle case studies and understand how to analyze data and draw an intelligent conclusion. Students and researchers should know how to use new technologies and information from new sources and effectively disseminate their ideas. Equity and excellence should remain priorities in any new policy of education.

Learning in the twenty-first century requires:

- new curricula integrated with a strong component of interactive multi-media
- interactive multi-media written by leading international scholars, and produced by the best software and publishing houses
- levels of communication and computing technology suited to every level of student to energize creativity, inquiry, research and new skills
- a complete change of textbooks, to be replaced by a mix of hard-cover books and wide versions of instructional software, PCs, laptops, compact disk-read-only memory (CD-ROM), educational TV, video, interactive radio, cable and satellite educational communication
- new roles for teachers and new training (in-service and out-service) to build and share knowledge; teachers should change from lecturers to technology users, mentors, researchers, knowledge producers and life-long learners
- the strong involvement of the "home" school with the help of parents and multi-media of learning

- the involvement of the community and the neighborhood
- the involvement of the business community, in offering opportunities for training in a business-like environment, so it becomes involved in preparing future human capital for the competitive workplace
- a new version of student evaluation, assessment and aptitudes for the information age
- diversity of education away from the traditional lines which were borne after the industrial revolution toward an innovative, interdisciplinary approach, to develop new abilities and intelligence, and
- the ability to explore and represent knowledge, dynamically, in various forms.

Networking at the school level to provide connectivity and interactivity is crucial in the new learning process. User-groups and collaborators searching for information will open new avenues of thinking ahead and becoming independent in self-learning. The new setting-up of the classroom and the school, its materials and teaching aids will be dictated by learning for the information age.

From Basic Education to University to Life-Long Education

New Modality in Basic Education

The education system must be re-arranged to expand without any limitations on students' potential to advance. Various pathways have to be provided in which students can excel as opposed to being forced upon them. There should be possibilities of transfer to promote individual talents. Many failures and drop-outs are due to the inability of education to discover the hidden talents of individuals.

The spark of education starts at pre-schooling and primary schooling levels. This is where attitudes (concepts and behavior) develop, and this is where the pupil motivation toward acquiring knowledge skills is developed.

Recent findings in neurophysiology have revealed how the acquiring and learning process takes place in the brain and shows, step by step, how the most complicated human computer of the brain works in info-processing, storage of data and retrieval of data. The old theories of education on learning are becoming obsolete.

All languages should be taught at pre-school and primary school levels to build the micro-chips of the brain by acquiring and not learning. Three and four foreign languages could be acquired by the child in early childhood together with the native language. This will expand vocabulary and open memory to new horizons. Motivation to science and mathematics also takes place during early childhood. Introducing technology will make the educational model more efficient, equitable and cost-effective, and develop restructuring of mode of inquiry and problem-solving.

Globalization which is characterized by knowledge-based economy requires a new modality of basic education resulting in new human capital strong in languages, with the ability to speak globally, and strong on science and mathematics in order to search, research and create knowledge and absorb information to apply usefully, and to transform the future society into a science-literate one able to cope with the high-tech complexities of the twenty-first century. Globalization of technology requires skills in communicating, calculating, making intelligent decisions and innovating. Computers in terms of hardware and software should accompany the learners from their childhood throughout their entire life. This is how to build information technology and management of information as an inherent component of the individual brain. Information technology is the force that revolutionizes business, streamlines governments and evolutionizes operations. We must realize that to move to a high-tech society in the next millennium, we must start restructuring our schools from low-tech to high-tech. This obviously requires a new vision for the re-training of teachers so that we can improve the education of students.

Basic Education is a Basic Human Need

World primary education rose from 250 million children in 1960 to more than 1 billion in 1996. Literacy tripled during the same period to over 2.7 billion. However, the world still suffers from 860 million illiterates today, mostly women. Illiteracy exists in developing countries, mostly in the rural areas, where marginalization and exclusion from mainstream education take place. Basic education is a human right and essential for the development of society toward empowerment, justice and democracy. Basic education is an important tool in overcoming the "knowledge deficit" between the developed and developing worlds. It will insure unity of humankind. Governments have the obligation to give priority to basic education for all citizens, free of charge. Education should receive 6 percent of every country's GDP and basic education should have overall priority. Schools providing basic education should be within the neighborhood, well equipped, particularly with well-designed information technology, should have the best trained teachers, and have good infrastructure and modern facilities for learning and exercising extramural activities. Pupil guidance and individual attention to overcome the child's difficulties should be provided. Children should have access to plays, movies, art, field trips to factories, and should be introduced to the beauty of nature to enhance the concept of environmental education and sustainable development. Children should also be exposed to the diversity of cultures, values and traditions, so that they grow up in harmony with, and with appreciation for, other cultures in the global village concept of the twenty-first century.

Private schools for both pre-school and primary school should be encouraged and should be widely available but overall control by the state to ensure minimum quality should be assured. There are three models of financing basic education.

1. Public schooling financed totally by the state (e.g. from tax revenues).
2. Mixed public/private, where public schools financed by the state are also given extra finance from the municipality and civil groups to improve the quality of teachers (increase of public salaries) and the quality of learning infrastructure and physical facilities.
3. Fully private, financed by private enterprise (profit-making), or financed by foundation and civic groups (non-profit). These schools could either be controlled by the state to insure the minimum, but free to add over the minimal requirements, or be completely free of the control of the state.

With the advancement of globalization, the trend of the future will be more toward private schooling certified by the state. This will allow competition for quality and it will respond more quickly to the emerging needs for change. Nonetheless, public schools will be maintained to ensure equity.

Secondary Education: The Crossroads for Tertiary Development

On the one hand, secondary education is considered the gateway of preparing students for life; on the other, it has been accused of failing to prepare adolescents for higher education or the world of work. What type of secondary education is needed in terms of performance, productivity and competitiveness in a knowledge-based economy?

Traditional secondary schooling must change quickly, and technology is a key component in the process. Currently, secondary education is the fastest growing sector of formal education. Also, secondary education has the highest drop-out rate. Use of technologies to improve teaching and diversifying secondary education to suit groups according to their abilities and motivation are reforms urgently needed to reduce this waste in human resources. Secondary education could be linked to the following:

- A diversity of courses to offer wide opportunities to students, with emphasis on quality
- The alternation of study and professional or social work
- Bridging with other technical, vocational and other educational streams
- Study leaves to acquire specific skills
- Learning through software tutorial packages on the computer in a friendly computer-based environment. These packages are in sequence, systematic and interactive with the learner. It is not the software that determines whether the learner has reached comprehension of the concepts involved in the task, but the quality of the interaction between the learner and the software.

Transformation: From Education to a Knowledge-Based Society

Multi-media software is becoming creative and it is possible for the users to navigate a broad spectrum of topics as well as to explore these topics in depth. The possibilities which computers offer as a tool to help students learn, construct knowledge and comprehend constitute a true revolution of the learning process and an opportunity to transform schools.

Traditional teaching is based on transmission of knowledge, and students are the recipients of this information. The result is a passive student who has little chance of surviving in the knowledge-based society into which we are about to enter. The knowledge society requires creative, critical thinking to learn about learning, working in groups to advance potential, wide vision about economic, social and ecological problems encountered by today's society, and deep knowledge in specific domains. This means that schooling of today must be transformed. This transformation goes much deeper than simply installing a computer as a new educational tool. Computers must be inserted into the learning environment to allow "construction of knowledge," comprehension and development of capabilities that are necessary to function in the knowledge society. Learning becomes the product of a knowledge-constructing process through projects undertaken by the student using the computer network as a source of information. Through the process of solving problems, students can learn how to get and select the right information to incorporate it into the solution – to learn about how to learn – to be critical of results obtained, to develop strategies and to understand that debugging is the engine that drives learning. In this way, students can acquire capabilities and values necessary for the knowledge society instead of them being transmitted by the teachers.

New Teachers for a New Age

Teachers also need to be trained to become facilitators for the knowledge construction rather than the current traditional role of the teacher as a transmitter of information, a role which indeed will very soon become obsolete. Therefore, teachers need to be trained in terms of computer technology and educational software, and in how to integrate knowledge into the classroom. This will stimulate the learning process. Teachers will become experts as they use multi-media packages with their students. Gradually, teachers with their students become "constructors of knowledge" and migrate gradually from their current role of "information providers."

Transforming the School

The knowledge society we are about to enter will require the transformation of the school. More adequate tools for identifying problems and absorbing technologies are needed. Schools should become places of empowerment, learning environments that will improve the student's mental capacity for new actions and ideas and direct the thinking of future generations. It is a challenge to keep the environment stimulating, where conceptualization is achieved. In addition, schools must have ethics at the core of their education. Common core elements to be strengthened are the languages, science and general knowledge, and using up-to-date information technology. Intercultural understanding and science for sustainable human development in terms of quality of education should be provided. Schools for secondary education become so important in adapting and orienting people to their changing world of interdependence, creativity and active citizenship are fully developed here at this stage.

Diversifying Education

Courses should be structured which allow:

- choices to various work needs
- choices to advance student potential, and
- choices to fit individual capabilities.

Curriculum reform is needed with the full participation of policy planners, teachers and civil society in determining what education at the secondary cycle should deliver. Guidance and counselling are essential so that students will make the right choice, according to their motivation and aptitudes, and to avoid waste. Modular education is a suitable formula to respond to challenges of the future and accommodate individual differences. In addition, bridges should be built between modules to allow flexibility and mobility according to emerging trends and market forces. A modular system of secondary education will facilitate encompassing all types of technical, vocational and academic education, whether in preparation for work, or for continuing higher education. Modules could be added in every situation where the knowledge-based economy has new demands for another style of human capital. The responsibility of secondary education is vast in shaping the diversity of education for future generations. Technical and vocational education should be widely diversified at this cycle to prepare quality and relevance to the work-life. Training should be closely linked to the employment sector.

Length of courses should also be diversified. Alternating periods between schooling and working by means of sandwich courses could be introduced. Also short-term and long-term sandwich courses are introduced for continuing education. Recognition of the training and incentives of employers for in-service training should be pursued. Points of credits could be created for all alternating periods of study and professional activity. There should also be learning about science and technology and innovations in introducing industrial technology. Additionally, some central schools can be equipped with staff, information and computer capacity to act as central servicing satellite schools in countries where cost is a problem. Secondary education is the point at which people choose their paths for life.

Reforms in Higher Education: Restructuring

With the challenges of globalization in mind, higher education requires an immediate restructuring in terms of governance, relevance, quality, access, financing, link with cyber-economy and information technology, research development, partnerships with industry, and life-long education and training.

Governance

Higher education has to be independent of both government and institutional beneficiaries. It should be structured on:

- autonomous, efficient decisions taken with less bureaucracy
- flexibility to allow changes
- quality assurance for all academic activities
- decentralization of academic decision and accountability
- evaluation of academic and research profiles, and
- efficient funding mechanism.

It would be structured on four levels as outlined below:

1ST LEVEL (I.E. BOARD OF TRUSTEES)

Level 1 should represent public government and private business, industry, and the banking sector to insure financing the university, thus safeguarding its autonomy and assuring good governance.

2ND LEVEL (I.E. UNIVERSITY COUNCIL)

Level 2 would cover strategy, a plan of action, and assurance of execution of various programs and evaluation.

3RD LEVEL (I.E. FACULTY COUNCIL)

Level 3 would cover curriculum development, courses of disciplinary and interdisciplinary nature, recruitment, promotion, R&D and innovations.

4TH LEVEL (I.E. DEPARTMENT COUNCIL)

Level 4 is the basic unit for supervising teaching and research to ensure quality and excellence. It should be left to departments, schools and faculties, deans, vice-presidents and presidents to execute the program and budget of the university in the most efficient way for the delivery of quality education.

Appointment of faculty and staff should be based only on merit and not subject to any other interference by government, ethnic, race, sex or religious groups. It should be open to all intellectuals, and should allow renewal and changes to suit an ever-changing environment.

Rotation of the president, vice-presidents, deans, directors and department heads is to be encouraged to allow a fresh style of management and also to allow professors not to be absent too long from their research and academic activities.

Relevance for Twenty-First Century

Globalization will lead to greater unity, not the Napoleonic unity envisaged two centuries ago. It is a unity with diversity based on the principle of subsidiarity. Universities will become increasingly interlinked with one another while each will be distinct. The anomaly of "national university" which existed at the first half of this century can only be alluded to in the past tense, when nations were living in isolation.

Networks become increasingly unique in placing the university in a new international setting under one roof of a global village. Any crack in this roof will affect all humanity, and education must respond to the new challenge of interdependence. The university of the next millennium may have campuses across the globe, like international, multi-corporate businesses, evolving all the time.

Common in this international arena is the curiosity which will be the basis of all scholarship, generating knowledge for the advancement of humankind. What is important is to develop the university setting as a dynamic place to incite people and catalyze a process of learning to allow creativity, capacity-building, critical thinking, professionalism and innovative power so that everyone reaches his/her maximum potential in order to produce scientists and entrepreneurs.

The university should always be measured within the time and space of its setting. Even old universities – the *Madrasa* (mosque university), Al Azhar, Zaytona, the Monastic schools, Plato's Akademia and the Alexandria Library – have battled for scholarship and science. The question here is, can the momentum be maintained when we look into the future with a vision that knowledge has no boundaries or limits, or shall we confine ourselves to "limits to growth," the scenario of Dennis Meadow's Club of Rome?

The knowledge-intensive economy is replacing rapidly the work-intensive or capital-intensive economy. It rests on three basic assumptions.

1. More knowledge will be produced, doubling every five years. Universities will manage the floods of knowledge.
2. The shelf-life of knowledge will decline. Effects of patent may slide down to six years.
3. The average level of education will rise. The concept of life-long education will emerge, replacing structured education.

The university library will shift to a knowledge stock exchange to function at the world level with Internet and with e-mail; knowledge will be processed in seconds to function as an interactive partner in the learning process.

The power of technology is no longer imaginary. We are surrounded by super computers which scan and analyze. Artificial intelligence is on the rise, as is virtual reality.

Quality, Efficiency and Competitiveness:
Measures for Performance

Higher education has witnessed an expansion of growth in both industrialized and developing societies. According to UNESCO statistics, the total population grew from 20 million in 1965 to 60 million in 1990. Although a great achievement was made in terms of quality and the "education for all" policy adopted by UNESCO mission, it has not addressed quality as it should, as manifested by over-crowded campuses, out-dated teaching methods, over-burdened professors and, in many cases, good professors shifting to research where teaching is given less priority, and cooperative learning, creative problem-solving and individual tutoring were absent. With mass production of graduates, the need for students with high potential was neglected.

Striving for excellence means striving for quality professors, a richer curriculum, advanced content and methodology, innovative multi-media of learning and access to knowledge through computer networks to realize the student potential to nurture his or her talents. The question of education equity was not addressed.

Education policies must be planned for the long term and should rise above short-term responses. They should be based on accurate diagnosis, forward-looking analysis and awareness of the needs of a knowledge-based society.

Deregulation of the university system based on decentralization, autonomy and effective participation of local stakeholders is required. Increases in student enrollment should always be followed by an increase in physical facilities, qualified teachers and an academic support system. Political decisions and interference exerted on the university should not be tolerated. Where equity and quality of the education system are concerned, education policy requires reliable policy-oriented and user-friendly data to establish reliable indicators for assessing students' performance, teaching techniques, contents and pedagogy. Data management can help in bringing new scenarios around different policy options to diagnose and determine actions to be undertaken.

Learning technologies can provide students with state-of-the-art training for their professional development. The educational process becomes more efficient and cost-effective. It enables professors to stream-line and monitor performance and support the management of complex institutional processes.

Some universities are responding to the challenge of producing quality graduates who can compete easily for jobs in the marketplace through:

- reorientation of the curriculum and learning environment to student potential and needs

- an accelerated investment in interactive multi-media learning technologies and networking
- case studies, project management and R&D for entrepreneurial development
- software development oriented to fit the curriculum
- interdisciplinary and study courses mixed with on-the-job training, and
- continuing education to allow an added professionalism for a new dimension.

Access to Higher Education

Although basic education is a human right issue, higher education is based on merits. Policy on higher education cannot become an open-door policy. It has to be built on scholarship. It should be realized that mobility of students horizontally and vertically should be allowed. This will enhance student potential. Flexibility, often found in the American system of higher education, is instrumental in promoting the capacity of the individual toward a new dimension in the society.

Sustainable Financing of Higher Education Institutions

The root of the problem lies in the continuing growth of student enrollment imposed by a liberal admissions policy of governments unmatched by public expenditure on higher education. Reforms in financing higher education need to be addressed seriously to respond to the requirements of globalization for competitive graduates. But what is the role of the state in terms of financing higher education? Most universities are state-run and heavily subsidized by the public sector. These subsidies cannot be met by many governments. So the university has to find other sources for finance. One option is to charge fees covering the running costs of the students at various specializations. Another option is a combination of annual government contribution and student fees.

These options need the will of the government and the university to address only newcomers of students to the university and should be done gradually. To avoid student unrest, the government contribution could be given to the university by way of scholarships to deserving students who come from low-income families.

Another way to cover the tuition of low-income students would be to create revolving funds to give loans to students to cover their tuition at low interest rates, paid by the students upon employment after graduation. The university should also streamline its operations to reduce its running costs. Other options can be found to cut down the cost per student without affecting quality. Also, adequate salaries for staff could be insured to attract top-quality faculty members to the teaching profession. Another way to help students finance their educations is to offer evening courses at the university (full- or part-time) to allow students to work during the day in order to cover the cost of their education. Another possibility is to allow sandwich courses for those who are fully employed; with time, they will accumulate the credit-units for completion of their degrees. Distance education and the open university system is another formula for mixing work with higher education. The newly developed "virtual university" and interactive learning on computers and networks may offer great opportunities for employed students to obtain higher education and life-long education.

Since many governments are facing difficulties in supporting the costs of higher education, it is imperative that governments relinquish authority over state universities and give them full autonomy to run their own affairs, accountable to an independent board of trustees (governing board), to promote investing ways and means of meeting the cost of teaching at the university. Housing, dormitories and catering at the university should be run separately as self-sustaining operations covering their own costs and should not be dealt with as part as the academic budget of the university.

R&D in the university should not be part of the academic teaching budget and should be covered totally by contractual R&D projects with private and public enterprises. Graduate studies could also be covered by research grants.

Preparing for the Future

The US is reforming its educational system to invest more in science and mathematics in future American generations in order to harness science and high technology as a major force to economic leadership in a global world. US science received an increase in budget equal to inflation in 1997. This federal spending on scientific R&D increased 2 percent to US$75.5 billion. Non-defense R&D was increased by 4 percent.

Integration of Generation and Dissemination of Knowledge: Mixing Teaching and Research

American universities flourished by mixing higher education and research, whereby universities became centers of research excellence. This has strengthened the research graduate work, funding it and producing excellent PhDs and post-doctorate graduates. The strength of the American university system comes from linking the creation of new knowledge with the transfer of that knowledge to students and community through extension, life-long education and contractual R&D with production.

However, with reward systems based on "publish or perish," faculties are buying-out of teaching responsibilities, and tenure and promotions are based entirely on the ability to attract federal research funds. These reports have fueled a backlash against higher education. Some states have gone so far as to institute minimum requirements for classroom and office hours for faculties at public research universities. Surveys show that faculty teaching responsibilities declined from 69 percent in 1973 to 53 percent in 1993.

The integration of teaching and research is at the heart of the American university system. Imbalance between research and teaching is occurring at the expense of teaching. Learning and discovery are inseparable processes, and both lie at the heart of the university mission. University as a place of learning and generating knowledge will have to secure flexibility and meet the challenges of globalization.

Japan, Taiwan, South Korea and Singapore – unlike the United States – have concentrated on raising the educational standards of their entire populations rather than only an elite fraction. As a consequence, failures of students are more often encountered in the US system of education. In an increasingly knowledge-based global economy, unsuccessful students tend to be only marginally employable, and the wages of unskilled workers have been steadily falling. Unless changes are made, the social and financial costs of educational failures are likely to increase.

Start with the Young

During the first seven years of life, children make great leaps in cognition, language acquisition and reasoning which correspond to dramatic neurological changes.[2] Educational attainment could be increased through better skills and enthusiasm of the teacher's formal education. Schools may have the primary responsibility for children's formal education, but their success is influenced by other pre-schooling, religious and community institutions, family, neighbors and friends, and the mass media.

From the ages of three to five, when brain activity is high, parental involvement is important to foster the love of learning and the concrete habit of life-long learning. However, parents who work long hours outside the home in this demanding consumer-driven economy leave very little time for their children. This vacuum has been replaced, to a large extent, by the TV set. A few TV programs are suitably educational; others are simply trash. There are now between 20 and 25 violent acts per hour in children's programs. By the time they reach the age of 18, children in North America, on average, have watched 15,000 hours of TV – which is more time than they have spent in the classroom. This will lead to deterioration not only to the educational system, but also in the long term to the economy and national security.

Broadening the Vision:
Learning with Technology

Some countries seem to educate their children much better than others. No comprehensive answer has emerged yet but plenty of lessons are being learnt from the tests which reveal the educational discrepancies. The tests were set for the largest-ever piece of international education research, the Third International Math and Science Study (TIMSS). Of the 41 nations participating in this first phase, Singapore was at the top; the average scores of its pupils were almost twice those of South Africa, bottom of the class (see Table 1:4).

East Asian countries have overtaken nations such as America and Britain which have had universal schooling for much longer. America came 17th in science and 28th in mathematics. England came 25th in math and Scotland came 29th. The four richest East Asian economies took the first four places in math.

TABLE 1:4
13-Year-Olds' Average Score in the Third International Maths and Science Study
(by Rank)

Rank	Maths		Science	
1	Singapore	643	Singapore	607
2	South Korea	607	Czech Republic	574
3	Japan	605	Japan	571
4	Hong Kong	588	South Korea	565
5	Belgium	565	Bulgaria	565
6	Czech Republic	564	The Netherlands	560
7	Slovakia	547	Slovenia	560
8	Switzerland	545	Austria	558
9	The Netherlands	541	Hungary	554
10	Slovenia	541	England	552
11	Bulgaria	540	Belgium	550
12	Austria	539	Australia	545
13	France	538	Slovakia	544
14	Hungary	537	Russia	538
15	Russia	535	Ireland	538
16	Australia	530	Sweden	535
17	Ireland	527	United States	534
18	Canada	527	Canada	531
19	Belgium	526	Germany	531
20	Thailand	522	Norway	527
21	Israel	522	Thailand	525

Rank	Country	Score		Country	Score
22	Sweden	519		New Zealand	525
23	Germany	509		Israel	524
24	New Zealand	508		Hong Kong	522
25	England	506		Switzerland	522
26	Norway	503		Scotland	517
27	Denmark	502		Spain	517
28	United States	500		France	498
29	Scotland	498		Greece	497
30	Latvia	493		Iceland	494
31	Spain	487		Romania	486
32	Iceland	487		Latvia	485
33	Greece	484		Portugal	480
34	Romania	482		Denmark	478
35	Lithuania	477		Lithuania	476
36	Cyprus	474		Belgium	471
37	Portugal	454		Iran	470
38	Iran	428		Cyprus	463
39	Kuwait	392		Kuwait	430
40	Colombia	385		Colombia	411
41	South Africa	354		South Africa	326

Note: The international average is 500.

Source: Third International Maths and Science Study (TIMSS).

Some former communist countries, notably the Czech Republic, Slovakia, Slovenia and Bulgaria, also did significantly better than their richer Western neighbors, even though they spend much less on education. Six of the top 15 places in both math and science went to the East Europeans. It seems that how much a country can afford to spend has less to do with how well educated its children are. American children have three times as much money spent on their schooling as young South Koreans, who nevertheless beat them hands down in tests.

TIMSS is the largest and most ambitious study taken by the International Association for the Evaluation of Educational Achievement (IEA) to focus on policies and practices in order to enhance mathematics and science learning across systems of education. The study covered half a million students at five grade levels in 15,000 schools and more than 40 countries around the world (4th, 7th, 8th and 12th grades). Thousands of researchers participated in this worldwide study. Reports were released on the 7th and 8th graders.

In most countries and internationally, boys had significantly higher mean science achievements than girls at both the 7th and 8th grades. This is attributable mainly to a significantly higher performance by boys in earth science, physics and chemistry.

International educational comparisons like the TIMSS study have been the subject of growing academic enthusiasm and criticism since the 1960s. Teachers, though, have been almost entirely hostile and most governments have held themselves aloof from the arguments, fearing embarrassment. Now attitudes are changing, at least among politicians. Over the past 10 years, governments' desire to know more about how their schools compare with others, and what lessons can be learned from the comparison, have begun to outweigh fear of embarrassment. More countries took part in TIMSS than in its predecessors, and the attention paid to its findings by the world's politicians, educators and the news media was much greater than for previous studies.

Results of the evaluation have shocked most of the OECD countries (the world's 29 richest countries) particularly the US, Britain, France and Germany. OECD governments spend a total of US$1 trillion on their annual education budgets, but are not benefiting fully.

Knowledge Workers

Leaving aside the results of the tests, two main factors lie behind governments' increasing willingness to take part in international education studies. The first is the growing consensus that education is the key to getting rich – for countries as well as for individuals. It is widely believed that one of the main reasons why tiger economies like Singapore and South Korea have grown so quickly is that their governments have made determined and successful efforts to raise their educational standards.

The other factor is value for money. Governments everywhere have woken up to the full economic significance of education just as they are making desperate attempts to rein in public spending. OECD countries already spend about 6 percent of national income on education; given the pressure to trim budgets, there is no prospect that governments will chuck money at schools without checking to see whether standards are improving. Hence, the enthusiasm for comparisons. If governments could discover what it is about their education systems that helps growth, then perhaps, they hope, they could do better without spending more.

Indicators in Science Development: Disparity between North and South

The main trend revealed by the UNESCO 1996 *World Science Report* is one of continuing asymmetry in the way science is distributed around the world. We see that all the developing countries taken together are responsible for a mere 10 percent of the total gross expenditure on R&D, while the member countries of the OECD can claim 85 percent. The industrialized countries commit between 2 percent and 3 percent of GDP to R&D, whereas the countries of the south only manage a fraction of this. In Latin America and Africa, for example, the investment ratio is 0.4 percent or below. Even countries with important scientific communities in certain disciplines, like India, Brazil or China, are not able to devote more than 0.7 percent.

The pattern is repeated if we take the numbers of active scientists and engineers. Although some 25 percent of scientists are found in the developing countries, the regional figures again show a striking imbalance. While the European Union (EU) supports two scientists per thousand population, the US 3.7 and Japan 4.1, developing countries have much more modest levels. For example, Sub-Saharan Africa has less than 0.1 of the Japanese value.

It is clear from these few examples that for many parts of the world two things are needed. The first is a clearer commitment toward science by governments and politicians, and the second is a broad investment in capacity-building – the strengthening of scientific infrastructure and the development of human resources. The other overriding impression is one of change and adaptation to new circumstances. The richer nations are being obliged to rethink their science and technology (S&T) priorities in the face of severe economic constraints and new political and ethical challenges. The developing countries are striving to build up their individual and collective self-reliance in S&T leading to sustainable development. The countries in socio-economic transition are attempting to replan their science without throwing away valuable assets from the past. By the same token, governments everywhere are seeking ways to tie investment in research more closely to economic and social goals without endangering the fundamental research that is the basis of tomorrow's innovation. This is not easily achieved, and great care needs to be taken to ensure that the balance between pure and applied research is not distorted.

Investment in Science and Higher Education in the Arab Region

Although the Arab region is an homogenous culture with values, religion, language and a common history stemming from Islamic civilization, it is nevertheless heterogenous when we address new indicators of a contemporary system of governance within a well-defined socio-economic context. There are three distinct sub-regions as listed below.

1. The Magreb sub-region
2. The Mashraq sub-region
3. The Gulf sub-region

The first region has been influenced by its proximity to a Francophone culture, while the other two regions have been influenced to a lesser extent by an Anglophone culture and the culture of proximity to neighboring countries.

TABLE 4:4
S&T Students in the Arab Region

	1991	1996
Community Colleges	44%	48%
Bachelors	35%	29%
Masters	46%	49%
Ph.D.	66%	65%

Source: UNESCO *World Science Report, 1998.*

Financing Higher Education

The total expenditure on higher education in the region was US$6.9 billion (1996) which amounts to 1.3 percent of GDP. This has increased over the US$4 billion in 1991 due mainly to the expansion in newly established higher learning institutions. Ninety-three percent is government financed. The average investment per student is US$2,400 per annum. The investment per student in the Gulf states ranges from US$9,000 to US$12,000, while in lowest income countries it is US$600 per student annually.

The new trend in the region is the active role of the private sectors in financing higher education. This will emerge as a strong new phenomenon in the next millennium.

Staff-Student Ratio

The average staff/student ration in S&T higher education was 1:12 in 1996, compared to 1:13 in 1991, while in humanities and social sciences it was 1:47 in 1996, compared to 1:40 in 1991. Table 5:4 shows the distribution of the ratio among Arab states.

Link with Industry

The challenge to Arab universities is to become both centers of excellence for quality higher education and centers of R&D to advance knowledge and its applications to commercial technologies.

TABLE 5:4
S&T Staff-Student Ratio in the Arab Region

Countries	Ratio
Bahrain, Egypt, Oman, Tunisia	1:9
Iraq, Morocco, Qatar, Saudi Arabia	1:12
Kuwait, Lebanon, Somalia, UAE	1:15
Algeria, Jordan, Mauritania, Palestine	1:18
Libya, Syria, Yemen	1:24

Source: UNESCO *World Science Report, 1998.*

Postgraduate links to research and to industry are very weak. Postgraduate students make up less than 6 percent total of tertiary education. To foster links with industry, the university professor should have a matching role in conducting contractual research with industry or the public business sector in addition to that of teaching. R&D should be fused to departmental research and graduate theses, so as to build bridges with the production and service sectors.

Research in universities is mostly, if not totally, funded by governments and it is geared toward academic promotion and publication in accredited journals. So a new approach is needed wherein private funding is lured to create a partnership between the university and industry. The UNESCO University–Science–Industry Partnership (UNISPAR) has been successful in developing linkages for R&D between universities and industry in Africa. This linkage is currently funded by the African Technology Fund created by UNESCO for S&T for African development. It funds the bridging of the transfer of research outcome to production. The program has reinvigorated researchers to advance their research toward application and it has also invited private enterprises to become partners in this venture.

R&D units, where researchers in the university are mobilized for problem-solving, have been modestly created in some Arab universities. Funding instruments by the state are established in some countries (e.g. KFAS in Kuwait, KAAST in Saudi Arabia and HCST in Jordan) to create contractual research on priority projects undertaken at the research facilities in the universities and to promote competitive research among researchers.

Business Parks: S&T Incubators

R&D expenditure in the Arab region is still very low compared to other regions in the world. In 1996, it amounted to US$782 million, which is 0.4 percent of GDP. It also varies among states from 0.4 percent to as little as 0.03 percent in some states; Egypt, Kuwait, Morocco and Saudi Arabia amount to 72 percent of total R&D expenditure for the Arab states.

The number of researchers, full-time equivalent (FTE) in the Arab region was 19,000 (1996) or 0.8 of the labor force as compared to 6–14 per 1,000 in OECD.

In some Arab universities, R&D marketing centers and offices were established. Very few universities created incubation parks to establish links between the researcher and industry. A project budget has been created to allow an important tool in this direction. However, there are still difficulties in matching the Western universities in this domain. Bureaucracy and heavy-load teaching are counter-productive to successful incubation.

The Arab region can learn from the successful educational models that are being developed in this rapidly changing world. In a nutshell, the challenge to educational planners is to devise a system of higher education that will successfully meet the needs of the future by combining the British sense of realism, the American sense of flexibility and the Arab sense of culture and heritage. This lofty ambition to achieve requires concerted efforts by enlightened men and women.

JIT learning is set in contrast to the factory model of knowledge acquisition in traditional models of education. The factory model of information delivery (see Diagram 3:5) matches the traditional factory model (see Diagram 1:5).

DIAGRAM 3:5
Factory Model of Information Delivery in Schools

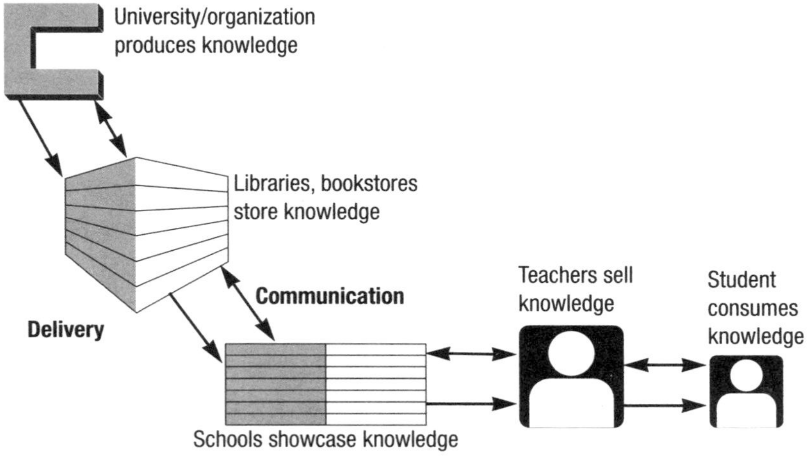

Knowledge is produced in universities and organizations (factories), stored in textbooks and learning materials (warehouses), distributed to schools (stores) and delivered to students (consumers). Teachers, like knowledgeable salespersons, are cast in the role of matching the needs of the students with the information resources. In many cases, they adjust the timing and organization of the delivery of the information but accept the content as determined by others. The lines of delivery are marked by the single direction arrow in Diagram 3:5. The two-directional arrows represent the hierarchical system of information sharing. Students and teachers talk about classroom learning; teachers, school administrators, parents and the community discuss school needs; administrators interact with suppliers; and suppliers talk with producers.

JIT learning conjures up an educational system that responds rapidly and flexibly to changing societal needs. Concepts, ideas, theories and learning tools are "delivered" as they are needed to solve real-world problems. The Internet makes it possible for learners to have contact with knowledge producers and to access information when and where they need it with less dependence on schools or teachers to mediate the access (see Diagram 4:5).

DIAGRAM 4:5
Just-In-Time Information

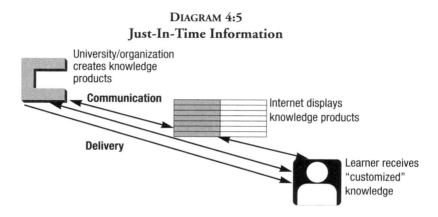

In both industry and education there is a belief that ready access to primary information sources will eliminate the need for knowledgeable mediated guidance. These models assume a transformation of learners and consumers into individuals who understand what they need, where to find it and how to use it. What is missing from these diagrams is the support system that makes this direct communication with primary sources effective.

Characteristics of JIT Learning

JIT learning suggests a highly individualistic model of learning with the following dimensions:

- learner-control
- time-independent and place-independent access
- functional use of information.

The help functions of many machines and computer programs meet these three dimensions of JIT learning. When trying to format a document, run a statistical comparison, create a graphic effect or remove a paper jam, computers often provide help menus or help "knowbots" that show the user how to accomplish his/her task in the moment of need. The presence of this form of JIT learning resource embedded in the machines reduces the need for extensive group training or expensive repair visits. But what happens when we extend this type of learning model beyond training to education? Can we assume that knowledge acquisition is a similar process?

What does it mean to have learner-controlled, time- and place-independent access and functional need drive intellectual development? Examination of these dimensions with respect to school learning points to concerns over the use of the "Just-In-Time" metaphor to characterize changes that are taking place in education.

Learner Control
"Just-In-Time" learning implies that the learner's need is what drives the delivery of information. Educator reformers who use JIT learning are often those who advocate learner-directed, constructivist modes of learning in contrast to information delivery systems or programmed learning tutorials. They are not focused on delivery of information as much as on the skill that the learner must have to find the information that he/she needs. Student learning is described as a process of constructing, elaborating and modifying representations of knowledge.[1] In traditional classrooms (the factory model), decontextualized information delivery is the mode of instruction. In this system, students retrieve the information but are unable to use it to solve problems or understand relationships. These shortcomings of the traditional system are used to argue for an inquiry-based approach to learning. Constructivists argue that integrated learning directed by the students helps them to understand why, how and when to use information and tools.[2] Because students direct the learning, there needs to be access to extensive resources.

Designing a comprehensive curriculum from multi-discipline, project-based activities is the challenge faced by many of the New American Design Schools,[3] as well as many on-line teacher development programs.[4] What is missing in these descriptions is how the learner acquires the skill to be an expert consumer of learning resources.

Opponents of constructivist learning approaches claim that "learning-controlled," "project-centered" or "theme-based" instruction fails to provide strong content knowledge in any discipline. The result is that students do not know even the most basic elements of the different subject areas.[5] Hirsch fears that these progressive ideas create an instructional context that lacks intellectual coherence. Instead, he calls for a more traditional approach to curriculum which emphasizes student mastery of a scope and sequence within a discipline – an ordered, logical sequence of foundational ideas, concepts and tools to be presented to students over a period of years. Basic skill educators are unsympathetic to constructivist notions that suggest learners should control education. They place the teacher and national or state agendas as the central force in directing the course of learning.

This debate between directed and discovered learning, between Locke's and Rousseau's conceptions of the learner, between fixed and flexible characterization of knowledge, delineates educational battles throughout this century.[6] Students need guidance and assessment by skilled teachers. Projects need to be placed in larger contexts. Students need help in understanding how their project work relates to the larger field, and to the community of people who are involved in creating, organizing and preserving knowledge. Building knowledge is a community activity.

Time-Independent and Place-Independent Access
JIT learning is time- and place-independent. The learner can access information when and where it is needed. Computers linked to the Internet provide this flexibility of access because it connects to vast collections of information and tools. Any group or individual can make digital information (in the form of photos, sounds, text and images) available to anyone who wants this information at any time and from any place. This is the feature that leads some to suggest that teachers will no longer be needed to organize the learning experience.[7] The claim is that students will "learn how to learn" and will be able to pursue their interests and projects independently with little need for teachers.

It is this claim that JIT learning will make teachers obsolete that is challenged. Ready access to rich informational resources from many different perspectives *increases* the need for skilled educational direction from teachers. Students need to learn how to evaluate information and information sources, what other resources are available and how their work integrates with that of others to create a comprehensive understanding of a field of study. Creating cross-discipline, project-based learning requires exceptionally talented teachers who understand the scope and sequence of each discipline well enough to make sure that students are receiving a comprehensive education. Those who argue against constructivist learning have some valid concerns. However, the solution is not a return to "basics" – information delivery education. What is needed, instead, is a move forward to basics integrated with rich interconnected projects within knowledge building communities.[8]

Ultimately, a good education is the result of interactions with good teachers. An effective way to accomplish this is by increasing both the number and quality of teachers, and to utilize students as resources for each other. We need to create learning communities that will make it possible for many more people to participate in classroom interactions. Acknowledging the power of flexible, on-demand learning tools and technology, this chapter presents a very different structure for their use from that of many who advocate JIT learning.

Functional Use of Informational Resources

JIT learning suggests that knowledge is a stockpile of *discrete* ideas, concepts or tools that can be delivered as needed. The systemic relationships among skills and concepts are minimized in this way of thinking about knowledge. It also assumes that ideas only have value in terms of their functional use in solving specified problems. But knowledge is about reflection and debate as much as it is about solving practical problems efficiently. Knowledge is not built from the needs of individuals; it is a process of weighing many different perspectives and of thinking beyond what is needed for the current activity. Information resources need to be examined from the multiple perspectives of the community and analyzed in ways that lead to comprehensive integrative learning.

The notion that we will all become self-directed learners working with computer terminals to learn what we need to know undervalues the role of teachers and experts and of conflict and multiple perspectives. Experts open new avenues of inquiry, challenge the learner in new directions, and encourage the process of evaluation and reflection. We can use the wealth of new tools for teaching and learning within communities working together to build knowledge.

The Internet is a stunning collection of global knowledge, with distributed control by experts and communities. This information is available to more people, more quickly and with less effort. At a superficial level, this increases our independence from particular places and people. This is the point that is made by those who argue that JIT learning gives us a new way to think about education. At a deeper level, though, this enormous amount of information ultimately increases our dependence on each other. The Internet contains far more data than any one person can read, evaluate or use. We need to be a part of learning communities to build knowledge in ways that help us understand our world.

Just-In-Time for What?

The organic model of learning in which students take over the role of educating themselves with JIT learning modules is the 1990s' version of the free school movement of the 1960s.[9] It assumes that students know what they need to know, are motivated to learn and can determine their own courses of study. This assumption contrasts sharply with the traditional model of classroom instruction that is found in most US schools.[10] In the traditional model, the teacher sets the course of learning (based on school, district and national frameworks) for a class of students who can all be taught, for the purpose of instruction, the same content and in the same way. Traditional classrooms operate on the implicit assumption that the teacher is dealing with each independent learner but in a group context.

With the knowledge base rapidly expanding, the traditional model of teaching and learning is at a breaking point. There are far too many students for one teacher. There is far too much content for any single teacher to master. The tensions in this model are different at different levels of schooling. In elementary schools, where the focus is on the learners, the tension appears in finding a single teacher who can provide rich, extensive, multi-subject learning experiences. In secondary education, the tension results from having a large number of single subject teachers working with different groups of students hourly. In these schools, class members are grouped by age and ability to be as similar as possible. They are expected to work independently to master the content in the curriculum.

This traditional model no longer serves the needs of a society rich in information and in need of citizens who know how to use diverse talents in concert to solve complex problems. JIT learning suggests that students can work more independently with less need of teachers. Instead, I argue that technology contributes to more *inter*dependency than to *in*dependence and creates a need for more skilled teachers.

From Classrooms to Learning Communities

The claim that JIT learning tools will make it possible for students to pursue independent learning within a computer-delivered personal learning plan is not consistent with changes that are taking place in our society. A team of representatives from industry, unions, government and education studied 15 jobs in 5 employment sectors to find the common skills necessary for success in these occupations.[11] The Secretary's Commission on Achieving Necessary Skills (SCANS) report for America 2000 describes 3 foundational skills (conceptual, problem solving and personal) and a set of 5 competencies that are critical to job performance across diverse occupations. The competencies include learning how to work with people of differing talents in teams using resources, information and technology to create shared understandings of systemic relationships and consequences.

Rather than using new communication and computer technology to further individualize learning, classrooms can be organized into learning communities with students, teachers and community members all playing vital roles in directing the course of education. The premise that JIT learning should or will lead to more individualized learning is not the only possible outcome. The opposite is also possible – that these tools will transform classrooms into learning communities.

How is a "Learning Community" different from a class of students? What would it mean to involve students in learning communities? In this section of the chapter, a traditional classroom is compared to a learning community. This is followed by a description of the new "power tools" and practices that help create this transformation. It is within this larger context of change that JIT learning tools have value.

What is a Class?
A "class" in mathematics or science is a collection of objects that share the same properties or characteristics. The word "class" is used to refer to a group of learners matched on characteristics that effect their learning, their knowledge base, their age and their skill in learning. This grouping of students is an effort to create a homogenous class so that a teacher can talk to each student as if she or he were the only person. Each class member works independently to demonstrate what she or he has learned,

with help between students viewed as cheating. Class rules and "discipline plans" are created to increase uniformity of actions. This effort to create uniformity has resulted in rigid ability tracking.[12] Even before some students are old enough to read the signpost, they will find themselves on paths that will not lead them to the futures they may later desire.[13]

Students do not naturally fit into this rigid structure. They are different. They begin school at different ages, some with very different backgrounds and experiences, and all with unique strengths and weaknesses. They learn at different rates and need to have different experiences.

What is a Learning Community?

Knowledge construction in our society is rarely done in isolation. People in a field work together building on the ideas and practices of the group. Culture and cognition create each other.[14] Learning increasingly takes place in "communities of practice."[15] A community of practice is a group of people who share a common interest in a topic or area, a particular way of talking about their phenomena, tools and sense-making approaches for building their collaborative knowledge and a sense of common collective tasks. These communities of practice may be large, the task general and the form of communication distant, as in a group of mathematicians around the world developing math curriculum and publishing their work in a set of journals. Alternatively, the community can be small, the task specific and the communication close, as when a team of teachers and students plan the charter of their school.

The community of practice in schools can be a number of subject or topic specific "learning communities." Learning communities share a way of knowing, a set of practices and shared value of the knowledge that comes from these procedures. Communities support different ways for novices and experts to work in the same system to accomplish similar goals. Community members are recognized for what they know as well as what they need to learn. Leadership comes from people who can inspire others to accomplish shared goals.

How is education different when students are members of learning communities? Consider these comparisons in Table 1:5.

TABLE 1:5
Differences between the Organization of a Classroom and a Learning Community

Class Structure	Learning Community
Homogeneous groupings	Heterogeneous groupings
Class discipline	Community organization
Competition	Collaboration
Knowledge delivery	Knowledge construction
Teachers centered	Student centered
Independent, individual work	Interdependent, teamwork
Expertise flows from one to many	Expertise flows in many directions

Learning communities recognize that students arrive with different skills, at different ages and with different experiences and interests; this diversity is then built into the learning context. In a learning community, students learn to work in teams and learn how to make teams work. The accomplishment of the team is primary and each member of team contributes in some way to the outcome. This makes students in a learning community *inter*dependent. They build from each other's strengths to develop a sense of competence and empowerment in areas where they are most motivated or skilled, and can pull others who are weaker in these areas up with them. Distributed knowledge is a building block for such learning communities.[16]

Some reform efforts are currently experimenting with transforming graded classrooms to multi-age and ability learning centers. For example, the Los Angeles Learning Center (US) demonstrates effective patterns of student learning in multi-age communities with differing expectations based on the evolving skills and abilities of each of the students.[17]

The most important difference between classrooms and learning centers revolves around the control of new learning opportunities. When students are participants in learning communities that include a network of people who organize around a specific issue, problem or debate, the resources and direction of the learning are less predictable. If the learning community is exploring the origins of human behavior or the shape of an equation, they are not limited to the people who are in the room who are all at the same "level" of understanding. The inclusion of many people with differing areas of expertise does not make the direction of the community either under the complete control of the teacher

[147]

or under the complete control of the learner. Instead, the control of learning is an interactive process that develops as the community works together to create shared understandings. All members of the community, including the teachers, are learners, and teachers model skilled learning.

Internet technology provides a rich format for the larger community to participate in the education of the next generation. Past technologies (print, photography, film and computers) have made it possible for many people to share their ideas with students without actually entering the school, but only in a one-way transmission mode of communication. With communication on the Internet, it is possible for students to interact with many more people and ideas, in some cases through multi-media interaction. Students, teachers, experts and resources around the world can pose challenging questions to each other, point to valuable resources and provide instant responses to the questions posed. Transforming the classroom into a learning community makes it possible for many more people to be a part of the learning process in an open and continuing dialogue. Using the metaphor "learning communities" in place of JIT learning highlights this different approach to education (see Diagram 5:5).

DIAGRAM 5:5
Knowledge Building Communities

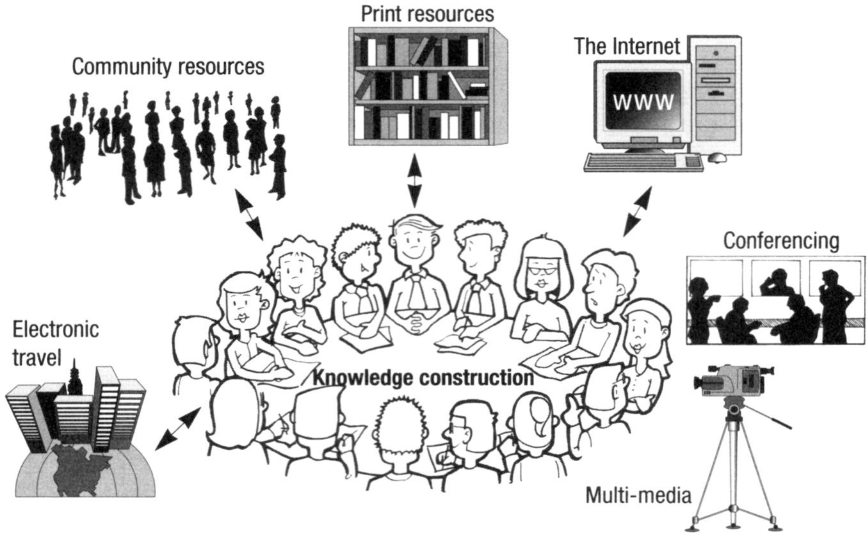

Print resources

Community resources

The Internet

WWW

Conferencing

Electronic travel

Knowledge construction

Multi-media

seconds from any location in the world, and many people can use the same materials at the same time.

Using these resources, students can be asked to adopt the role of different historical figures and reenact discussions and debates from other periods. To understand history, students need to understand the frame of mind of the people who lived in different periods; primary sources make it possible for students to engage history directly. Furthermore, telecommunication projects invite the collaborative investigations and participation of students from around the world. These students, by nature of their various geographic locations and cultures, will have very different perspectives on historic events, and their multiple perspectives offer a richer tableau for testing ideas and theories.

From Linear Text to Hypertext

Linear texts are increasingly being replaced by hypertext with links to extensive information. Students with access to encyclopedias on the computer have tools for finding information that would have been difficult to locate in the past. While traditional text-based indexes helped students find key terms or concepts, students can now search for any or every occurrence of a word in the collection. Internet search tools, though still primitive for educational use, give students access to more information than could ever exist in a single school library.

Students can use hypertext to organize their learning, but they can also use hypertext as a form of expression. Writing in hypertext is a new skill. It is conceptually different then sequential writing. It allows for a different form of interaction between author and reading and larger communities of people. Writing collaboratively with a larger community of people, all of whom care about a topic is a powerful lesson in group problem-solving and thinking.[19]

Students learning how to use and compose in hypertext are participating in new evolving forms of communication.[20] They are learning to write in a format that is integrated with other forms of expression including color, formatting, graphics, photography, audio and video. These skills are increasingly valued as the ability to work with current technological advancements requires specialized communication skills such as graphic design and multi-media hypertext and video production. These are the "basic" skills for the communication age.

From Hands-On Models to Virtual Simulations

There is no doubt that the use of three-dimensional models in schools help students understand concepts, relationships, functions and structures. When students have hands-on experience with objects that they can touch, move and assemble, they gain a better conceptual understanding. Math manipulatives are standard learning tools recommended in most curriculum framework or guides. Students use blocks, dice, triangles and rulers to understand number relationships. Science labs and scaled models help students to visualize, for example, what is hidden beneath skin or rotating far off in space. In social science, students build models of missions, forts, castles and other communities of the past. These multi-sensory constructions serve as concrete representations of ideas that are complex and interlinked.

The computer extends our ability to model. With the ability to create virtual objects with complex properties and relationships, we can begin to simulate functions and processes that are invisible without these tools. Simulations make it possible for students to see and experiment with the way atoms bond, winds flow or planets orbit.

One example is the Virtual Frog Project by Researchers at Stanford University.[21] Over the Internet, students can access the virtual frog, a visual three-dimensional rendering of different systems that constitute a frog. In classroom dissections of "real" frogs, students see only the remains of a dead frog. With a virtual frog, they can make the skin transparent and stain food to watch the digestive process. Virtual creatures model internal processes and interactions with their environment. These relationships are not visible through the process of examining the skin, bones and organs of a dead frog. This technology enables students to experiment with the relationships between the structures and functions in these virtual creatures. For example, students can be challenged to breed or engineer a frog that will jump higher or further than that of their peers. Doing this would require an understanding of how size and length of bones interact with the development of muscle tissue. Hypotheses can be formed, tested and analyzed using these virtual objects.

From Direct to Remote Observation

It is, and will remain, important for students to use their observations of the world as part of their investigations. Dewey, concerned by the *rapid growth of technology* of the last century, feared that direct learning experiences would be replaced by a poor substitute, book learning:

> As societies become more complex in structure and resources, the need for formal teaching and learning increases. As formal teaching and training grows, there is a danger of creating an undesirable split between the experience gained in direct association and what is acquired in school. This danger was never greater than at the present time, on account of the rapid growth in the last few centuries of knowledge and technical modes of skill.[22]

Today these same words are echoed by a new generation of educators. Today, however, the concern is that *computers*, rather than books, will replace direct learning experience.[23] Used appropriately, however, computers, like books and other resources, can be companions in the investigation of reality. Projects designed today, using the computer as a research tool, send students into the physical and social world to collect observations, measurements, surveys and other data using appropriate scientific tools. Telecommunication networks make it possible for them to then exchange, analyze and discuss this information with their peers from around the world. In the Global Learning and Observation to Benefit the Environment (GLOBE) project,[24] students from around the world collect, compare and analyze data on air temperature, air pressure, wind speed, precipitation and other environmental measurements.[25] Visualization tools make it possible for their data to be displayed in the same full color maps that they download from science centers.[26] Students in Learning Circles often create projects that require their peers in other countries to conduct investigations,[27] collect surveys or design interviews with people in their communities.[28] In the Global Lab Project,[29] students locate, measure and mark an open area of land near their school. They share measurements and investigations both above and below the surface of the earth with students from around the world, each working on the same size section of the earth. These examples describe learning environments supported by computers that *increase* rather than *decrease* student direct experiences with their physical and social world.

As computers become smaller and more portable, they become valuable field guides and research tools in the laboratory and in the field. Students can use microcomputer-based measurement and monitoring devices for collecting and analyzing data.[30] Using laptop computers and a set of monitoring devices, students can collect, record and graph their data on temperature, relative humidity, light intensity, pressure and voltage right on the spot. More in-depth analysis and descriptions can occur back at the school site.

Tele-Robotics make it possible for students to direct a telescope to look out in space from their classroom,[31] tend a garden located in Austria or experiment with light and heat in a model house in Australia.[32] Students can also participate in electronic field trips using a range of tele-robotic devices to explore the ocean floor or view out into space.[33] Scientists and researchers are reaching out to schools, inviting students to be part of their learning communities. In this past year, students were able collectively to reserve time on the Hubble telescope,[34] work with scientists exploring the Monterey Bay and follow a team of adventurers as they traversed the rainforests of Mexico, Guatemala and Belize in search of lost Mayan cities and clues for saving the environment.[35]

Scientists using new technology extend their observational range – to look out in space, under the seas and into the microscopic world. Small, inexpensive sensors may make it possible for students to place micro-sensors down a snake hole or up a tree in a bird nest. This would enable them to make observations that are simply not possible when they rely only on their own senses. These observational tools would make it possible for students to share what they find locally with those in other environments in the same way that scientists share their data with distant colleagues, building knowledge in collaborative learning communities.[36]

From Broadcasting Video to Creating New and Virtual Worlds

Photos, filmstrips, slides and video have given students the opportunity to learn about a range of topics that extend and expand textbook learning. While typically motivating, these are passive media. Teachers worry that students may be watching but are not thinking or being actively engaged with the materials they viewing. In contrast, when students create their own films and video reports, either originally or based on their involvement with the content they have viewed, their involvement in the content area and learning process is much greater.

Virtual reality adds additional interactive options to the learning environment, making it possible for students not only to see what exists but also to place themselves in different settings. In these worlds, they can make choices and see the consequences of their actions. For example, students can now watch dynamic videos taken by remote vehicles that explore the deep canyons of the Monterey Bay off the coast of California.

Students are encouraged to use these materials to create their own narrated explorations. In a few years, they may be able to assume the identity of one of the inhabitants of this underwater world and see if they can survive in a simulated bay. This "Virtual Canyon" would not simply be a game. It would be a visual database of current information about this complex ecosystem in which students could manipulate objects, make choices and view consequences of their actions. Virtual environments which model real life may be, in some senses, more real than the videotape representations that we now see as real.

From Student Reports to Students as Teachers

With better access to resources, students can become experts on different topics. They can share this expertise not just by completing assignments given to the teacher but by creating learning resources for other students, using today's technological production tools. Powerful examples of this can be seen in the library of Web sites created by students as part of the ThinkQuest Contest.[37] Since its inception in 1996, students from around the world have been forming partnerships and creating educational environments for their peers. Examples include the following five student-created products.

EduStock – Economics and Investment: A Stock Market Simulation
Students can create their own stock portfolios and experiment with making and losing money in real time with the free real-time stock market simulation on the Web. Once students create their portfolios, they are saved and updated every 20-minute period with the actual values from the exchange. This is a great math activity for students of all ages. It also provides an easy way for anyone to experiment with personal investments.

Design Paradise: A Simulation Game of Land Use
As chief executive officer (CEO) of a major development company, students are challenged to create a balance among the needs of industry, environment and citizens to create a stable and prosperous economy on an island. The island of Kauai in the state of Hawaii serves as the

"laboratory." The game can be played for hours as the island takes shape. The game players are given a numerical score on their success as a developer and they also receive "happy points" based on the satisfaction of the inhabitants of their island paradise.

From The Ground Up: A Guide to C++ and The On-line Point of View-Ray

These tutorials are interactive lessons helping students to learn more about the technical tools that are used to create the Web. Students who master these tools will be able to create new forms of learning and artistic expression in the networld.

Anatomy of a Murder: A Trip through Our Nation's Legal Justice System

The drama begins with the body of an unidentified young woman found in a car on a deserted desert road by a police officer. The officer must secure the scene and wait for a team that will begin the work of collecting evidence from this crime. While you read, optional mood music plays. Each chapter of the story provides the foreground. Fact sheets give the background legal work that explains what is taking place at the scene, in the police station, the lawyer's office or the court system. Every detail of police and lawyer work has been researched to help the readers understand what happen behind the scenes from the time the murder is committed to the end of the trial. While the story is fiction, the education is real.

Welcome to Himalayas – Where Earth Meets Sky

This site explores Himalayan altitudes, lands, geologic past, trekking, flora and fauna and environmental problems, and also provides an atlas, traveler's corner, guided tour and quizzes for users to test their knowledge.

Students and teachers of music, art, chemistry, history, culture, war, math and physical education will find that students have provided high-quality educational experiences that others can share. These contest winning entries show what students can create using computer tools and how they can be creators of information, teachers as well as learners. And, as every teacher knows, teaching is one of the best ways to learn.

When students take part in programs like "Facing History and Ourselves" and the Holocaust/Genocide Project, they learn to look back into history and then look at their own actions in a new light.[38] This provides a resource for teachers and students to study conflict and effective strategies for conflict resolution.

Cyberfair involves students in "service learning" as part of a worldwide contest.[39] Students form partnerships with different segments of their community and help them by designing a Web site for them. Students learn about their community and how to use technology in the service of community goals. As part of the contest, students must evaluate Web sites created by other schools. Participating in this process of peer review helps students to understand the process of evaluating and validating information placed on the Web.

These projects and Web sites, created by students from around the world, represent the best efforts of students working collaboratively to teach each other. But there are many ways students can help teach within their local communities as well. Students who are comfortable with mathematics and understand mathematical concepts quickly can help students who need additional time and assistance to help them see a relationship. Often these exchanges are helpful to both parties. A student who finds it easy to create ideas but harder to edit them can be paired with a student who is a better editor than creator, creating a symbiotic learning relationship. These relationships within the learning community can both increase the human resources for teaching and expand the possibilities for learning.

From One Expert to a World of Experts

Communication tools make it possible for people anywhere in the world to be a part of a classroom lesson. Increased human resources extend the topics that students can explore. Electronic field trip opportunities make it possible for students and teachers to join teams of researchers, scientists and technicians exploring distant places such as Mars, a rainforest or Antarctica. Additionally, teachers can invite distant "team-teachers" from any field, with any expertise, to work in the classroom.[40] For example, subject matter experts are matched with teachers in programs such as the "Electronic Emissaries." Adult mentors are also matched with students to provide support and direction in school learning through the Hewlett-Packard Mentor Program.[41] The Writers-in Electronic-Residence program matches professional authors with classrooms, providing students with feedback on their writing. In Passport to Knowledge projects, scientists schedule regular video conferences to discuss ideas and concepts over live broadcasts and in on-line projects.

Distance education is providing flexible on-line materials that share information in a different format than traditional classroom lectures. Videotaped demonstrations and explanations give learners a high degree of control over the time, location and method of study, and make it possible for teachers to work with students in distance locations. Multiple modes of delivery can augment time spent in class, and communication technology can make it possible for group work to take place from individual terminals. For example, in the Collaborative Visualization Project,[42] students can get help from scientists by clicking on their images. Using video conferencing, they can share their computer display and discuss their data and ideas.

Charting the Course of Learning: A Communal Activity

Many of the properties identified as JIT learning – student-centered projects, ease of access to instructional tools and tutorials of authentic tasks – are important ingredients in the design of new learning environments. However, the premise that the overall effort is to individualize instruction is not the only possible outcome. Increasingly we are coming to understand learning as a social interactive process.

With the emerging Networld and with it more powerful communication tools, the classroom walls no longer need to isolate students from the community. As we have seen from the many examples, students are now being of service to government agencies and community groups. Increasingly, there are opportunities for partnerships with industry. Students are forging new relationships with companies and industries involving students in "service learning" relationships. This development challenges educators to use these new tools and to structure these new relationships so that student learning is primary, with service as an important outcome.

New partnerships are forming between industries that market to children and schools. Some provide opportunities for students to work for companies in tele-apprentice relationships from the classroom. An open question is, can we create an integration of students with the business community without returning to the abuse and exploitation of children that characterized the last century? The media brings stories of how these new tools are leading to new forms of child endangerment, pornography and abuse. We need skilled teachers to help design new learning environments alert to the possibilities of exploitation of students as knowledge workers.

The tools that are now making a difference in the classroom are those that help students to connect and create. The connections are both inside and outside of the classrooms where experts of all ages can be a part of the resources for learning. And the ability to create is what makes it possible for every student to share what they discover with others. Teachers are likely to continue to play a vital role in helping students to shape, evaluate and share ideas.

6

Applications of Total Quality Management in Education and Training

Robert A. Cornesky

Introduction

This chapter will discuss how the principles and approaches of Total Quality Management (TQM) experts have been and are being applied in education and training and the effect it will have on the future education, training and development of human resources.[1] Most of the chapter will address the TQM efforts in the US, although the factors affecting quality in higher education are global in nature. They include such items as rising costs, increase in number and types of student, and a desire to produce an educated, productive and competitive workforce.

TQM is defined as a philosophy that promotes an organization's mission and objectives using continuous quality improvement (CQI) tools and techniques as a means to achieve mutual and simultaneous satisfaction of all stakeholders. This definition of TQM demands the wide deployment of data-driven, empowered cross-functional teams to improve processes to meet the needs of stakeholders. This definition is much more than the forming of either committees or classroom groups in order to make recommendations for process improvement.

Because of the missions and complexity of our modern institutions of higher education, it is almost impossible to apply totally a model from one of the experts to every segment.[2] Attempts to do so will probably result in failure. Each institution can, and should, develop its own model of TQM. However, successful models inevitably incorporate the commonalities in the principles and approaches to TQM. Let us first examine these commonalities and some examples of how they are being applied in higher education. An understanding of these principles is essential if one is to appreciate the power and complexity of TQM and how it differs from traditional committee work found in most educational institutions.

Commonalities in Principles and Approaches

Although the models of the quality experts are different in some respects, they enjoy common elements.[3] The common elements that bind the foundations of TQM are:

- processes and systems
- teams and teamwork
- customers and suppliers
- management by fact
- complexity
- variation.

Let us briefly examine each element or principle and show their inter-relationships.

Processes and Systems

Process is defined as all of the combined tasks or steps necessary to accomplish a given result. Quality leaders champion the processes ("P") approach over the more commonly used results ("R") approach. The basic difference in the approaches is that the "R" approach focuses almost entirely on the results regardless on how they were achieved, whereas the "P" approach employs teams to focus on the processes used to generate the results. The differences are further analyzed in Figures 1:6 through 4:6. Quality leaders stress the importance of improving the processes and systems in which people work in order constantly to increase the quality of products and services.[4]

Understanding the "processes and systems" principle is central to successfully implementing TQM in not only managing a college or university more efficiently, but also in improving learning in classrooms.[5]

Every work activity is a part of a process and system (see Table 1:6). It follows that quality can improve if the processes and systems in which the people work improve. If we improve the processes and systems, we will receive better quality results and achieve higher levels of productivity. This is true not only for administration, but also for teaching and learning.

TABLE 1:6
Interactions between Processes and Systems and Quality

- Process is a group of tasks.
- System is a group of related processes
- "Result" (including learning) is the end product of a system.
- Work (including learning) is part of a system and countless processes exist in most systems.
- Improving processes improves the system that delivers superior quality and excellent results (including learning).

By definition, a "system" is an arrangement of persons, places, things and/ or circumstances that makes, facilitates or permits things to happen. The very nature of the system will determine what will happen and how it will happen. In Figure 1:6, for example, an input (a "product-in-process," e.g. a student, an invoice etc.) is introduced into the system of Unit A and undergoes a series of tasks in three processes. Before exiting, the "product-in-process" (PIP) must undergo further modification in a system of Unit B, then in the system of Unit C and then finally back to Unit B where the PIP undergoes further transformation in the processes of System 2.

FIGURE 1:6
Conceptual Model Showing a "Product-In-Process" Through Three Units and Four Systems: 1

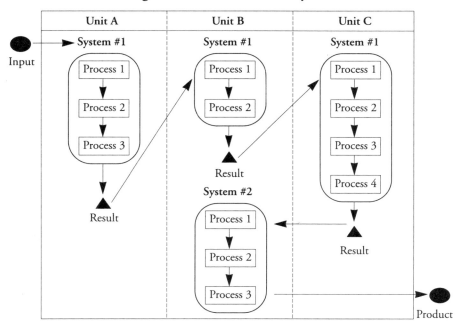

Most managers – including thought-leaders (my term for professors) – inherit people that come from systems where only results were emphasized. The results or "R" approach yields a predictable attitude that generates predictable behaviors. This "R" cycle of predictability is not only difficult to alter, it is also an inhibitor to developing a quality culture. It is precisely at this juncture where many of the problems in higher education are focused. This is illustrated in Figure 2:6 where a predictable end result of the PIP from the system of Unit "A" generates predictable attitudes and behavior. The PIP from the system may or may not end up conforming to requirements.

FIGURE 2:6
Conceptual Model Showing a "Product-In-Process"
Through Three Units and Four Systems: 2

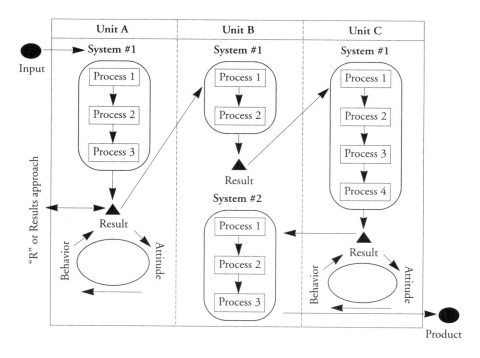

Note: In this example, the results of "R" approach concentrates on the result (output of a system) which usually generates predictable attitudes and behavior.

Since managers, and thought-leaders as managers of the classroom, significantly influence the processes and systems under their leadership, it is management's role to commit the academy to quality PIP.[6] Faculty, staff and students will work energetically if convinced that quality will be the end result. Quality is contagious. Research has shown that if managers and thought-leaders support people under their tutelage to work as a team towards improving the processes and systems for quality results, most people will develop an attitude of pride-in-workmanship.[7] The resulting behavior becomes focused on teaming and the use of data. As shown in Figure 3:6, the consequence is a workplace (classroom) culture directed toward achieving quality.

Teaming

As shown in Figures 3:6 and 4:6, teaming is extremely important in improving processes and systems and producing quality services and products. In classrooms promoting group learning activities and teaming, deep learning increases.[8] In their books, Robert Waterman[9] and Robert Levering[10] stress the importance of teamwork in effecting change and in keeping morale high in American businesses. I have found the same to be true in the management of colleges, universities and classrooms.

Effective teams are necessary for institutional and collaborative classroom learning to occur. Teams must understand the Plan-Do-Check-Act (PDCA) cycle and the need to concentrate on improving processes in the systems where people work. Team members also have to understand the customer/supplier concept, another commonality to quality. Effective teams, like effective organizations, must learn from their experiences.[11] To learn, teams need data to manage by fact, another commonality to TQM.

As shown in Figure 4:6, when the "P" approach is used to analyze and improve the processes in System 1 of Unit A, the data generated from the results ("product-in-process") are supplied to the team. The team is to use these data to plan and implement additional modifications to the processes within the system to further increase the quality of the results.

FIGURE 3:6

Conceptual Model Showing a "Product-In-Process"
Through Three Units and Four Systems: 3

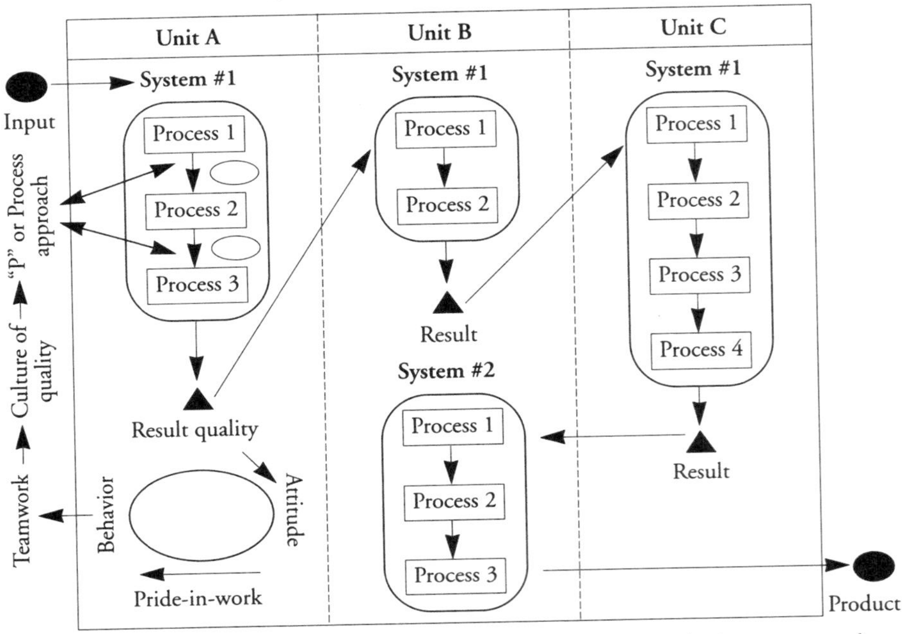

Note: In this example, the process or "P" approach concentrates on having teams work on improving the processes within the system to generate quality results. The predictable pride-in-workmanship attitudes reinforce a teaming behavior and a culture of quality.

Customers and Suppliers

Generally, the concept of customers within educational institutions differs from the private sector's definition because, in education, repeat customers are usually undesirable. It can be argued, however, that if parents, alumni and current students are well satisfied with their school experience, they will recommend the institution to others. This is true of the classroom setting as well; it is well known that great teachers almost always have a waiting list for their classes. Likewise, colleges and universities that are very satisfied with the graduates of a particular high school may admit additional graduates from that school. Thus, students, alumni and employers do share some of the characteristics of traditional customers.

A further parallel to the customer concept lies in the relationships among various employees within the same institution. Virtually every

FIGURE 6:6
Deployment Flow Chart:
Course Scheduling Procedure after Process Revisions
from a PDCA were Incorporated

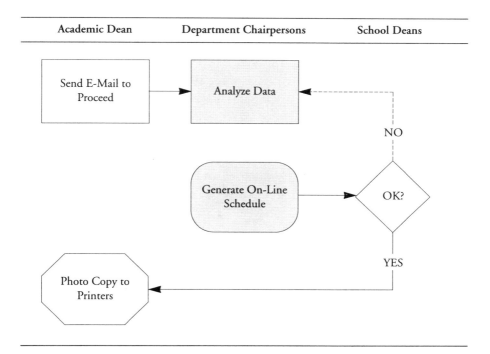

Here is another problem that TQM helped solve. You all have jobs. So, you went through a hiring procedure. Figure 7:6 shows how we were hiring new faculty members. The process involved department faculty, the School Dean, Associate Vice-President, Academic Vice-President, Council of Deans, Council of Vice-Presidents and the President. It took an average of 210 working days from the moment an opening was identified to the moment a contract was offered. Of course, the faculty hiring procedure was instantly improved when a management team began to focus on eliminating non-value-added work and redundant processes. The 210-day procedure was cut to 60 days, a far more reasonable time in which to hire anyone.

FIGURE 7:6
Deployment Flow Chart of a Faculty Hiring Procedure

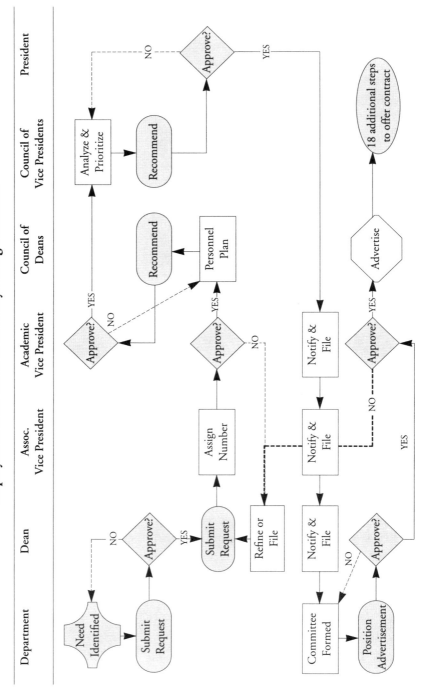

There are literally thousands of examples in higher education where quality improvement teams using the PDCA cycle improved systems. Some of these are listed below:

- transcript processing time reduced
- reduction in invoice reviews
- implementation of improved computerized data base
- redesigning curricula
- reorganizing the budgeting procedure
- reduction in application review time
- streamlining purchasing procedures
- expediting registration procedures
- establishing employee recognition programs
- reducing photocopying costs
- tie budgeting procedure to institutional mission
- establishing a comprehensive student assessment program, and
- improving teaching and learning.

Major TQM Successes of Other US Colleges and Universities

There are approximately 3,600 colleges and universities in the US. Probably one-third of these institutions are involved in what we would consider TQM improvement efforts. I am aware of significant TQM improvement efforts in several hundred institutions and of these, less than a dozen have incorporated TQM principles throughout their entire institution.

Babson College

Babson College is based in Massachusetts. It is a private business-oriented institution that is ranked as the top business school in the US for entrepreneurship.

Babson began its quality journey with the writing of the Malcolm Baldrige National Quality Award (MBNQA) Education Pilot application as a TQM class project in 1994. The draft of the application with a scoring estimate was presented to the President's Cabinet, which then decided to participate in the pilot program.

They quickly discovered a lack of data, weak communications and inconsistent management for continuous improvement. They even realized they occasionally lost sight of their students in uncoordinated "stovepipe" administrative processes. The College had a good quality approach, but spotty deployment achieved limited results.

The MBNQA application process improved awareness of the College, gave direction for improvement, suggested ways to collect data and created a budgetary process for generating institutional research. In addition, the results forced the institution to concentrate on assessment. One of the "best" discovered that it could improve significantly.

Belmont University

This private institution in Tennessee began following MBNQA Criteria in 1993. It is the only educational institution in Tennessee that has achieved Level 3 (of 4) in the Tennessee State Quality Award.

Fear and uncertainty in decision-making have been replaced by teams busily generating innovations. In fact, there are so many quality improvement teams busily examining the university's processes that it is difficult to keep track of everything that is going on. Belmont plans to work on improving areas that show deficiencies. They have established a quality culture that has an attitude of "the better we become, the more we want to improve."

Belmont University is also a leader in applying TQM to the classrooms. Students are taught to function as collaborative teams to improve classroom processes so that active learning can take place. Faculty are mentors and coaches; students are workers responsible for a large part of their own learning.

Defense Systems Management College

The Defense Systems Management College (DSMC) in Virginia was established in 1971 to increase the capability and effectiveness of acquisition managers in the Department of Defense. DSMC started the Quality Journey to increase customer focus through process management. It also participated in the MBNQA Education Pilot to get objective feedback on its Quality Journey. The DSMC learned that it did not have a systematic way to collect, analyze and use data, and benchmarking against other institutions was not a common practice.

The college realized that it will take years to establish certain quality changes. This includes developing thinking and behavior patterns that focus on customer requirements and getting everyone involved in continual improvement.

The college was one of two institutions of higher education to receive a site visit by Baldrige quality examiners.

Northwest Missouri State University

A pioneer in quality, Northwest Missouri State University (NMSU) began its journey in 1986, two years after the arrival of Dr. Dean Hubbard as President. In 1991, NMSU upgraded its "Culture of Quality" with a study of the original MBNQA document. In 1994, the University made an application for the Missouri Quality Award, which is based on the Baldrige criteria. (NMSU won the Missouri Quality Award in 1997.) Incorporating the recommendations from the Missouri Quality Award feedback report, NMSU made an application for the 1995 MBNQA Education Pilot that culminated with a site visit.

After adopting the Baldrige criteria as a planning model, NMSU restructured its governance system, introduced a seven-step planning process and revised its "Culture of Quality" plan. As a result of writing the application, administrators were able to see many gaps, including what they had to measure and benchmark. Additional changes in the institutional culture included breaking down the department silos causing people to focus on processes and systems, and developing empowered focus teams.

When NMSU adopted a culture of quality, a list of over 200 ideas was generated by faculty, students and staff about possible changes on campus. From the list, 42 items were chosen to be implemented over seven years. At the end of that time, NMSU has successfully:

- consolidated seven colleges into four
- eliminated 34 programs that were undersubscribed or of poor quality
- reallocated 6 percent of the budget from administration and academic support areas to instruction
- increased faculty salaries from 15 percent below those at peer institutions to a point of above average
- eliminated a 6- to 18-month backlog of maintenance projects

- identified core competencies to be mastered by every student and courses for delivering the instruction
- converted a US$1 million deficit to a US$3 million reserve
- increased enrollment by 26 percent to capacity
- established the first comprehensive electronic campus in the nation, and
- established a comprehensive senior exit exam in almost all academic departments.

This list is only representative of TQM successes at Northwest Missouri State University. From a TQM perspective, NMSU is probably the finest institution of higher education.

TQM in College Classrooms

In a recent article by David Johnson et al., indisputable evidence is presented on the effectiveness of cooperative learning in college classrooms. They state:

> The research on cooperative learning has a validity and generalizability rarely found in the educational literature. This research has been conducted over eight decades by numerous researches with markedly different orientations working in a variety of different colleges and countries. Research participants have varied with respect to economic class, age, sex, nationality and cultural background. The researchers have employed a wide variety of tasks, subject areas, ways of structuring cooperative learning and ways of measuring dependent variables. Vastly different methodologies have been used. This combination of research volume and diversity is almost unparalleled.[14]

By examining the theoretical roots of cooperative learning through the lens of TQM, you can see that both students and faculty members must understand and utilize the basic quality principles. Actually, many of the principles of TQM have been used in the educational classrooms for over eight decades – long before TQM was even considered and named by businesses and industry. One of the differences between what we were doing in higher education and what businesses were doing was in the descriptors – e.g. students versus workers, terminal competencies versus operational definitions. Another difference is that businesses have developed and refined their processes and systems to better meet the needs of their stakeholders. Let us examine several commonalities between TQM in businesses and in classrooms.

Thought-leaders who successfully incorporate group learning in their classroom do the same thing that businesses do to successfully incorporate TQM into their corporate culture. For example, businesses work through a managerial prospective to utilize the personnel in order to incorporate a learning organization paradigm into their culture. This permits the organization to survive and thrive in a highly competitive environment. They perform as the CEO of their classroom and treat their students as workers who are responsible for the quality of the product – i.e. their learning. They incorporate an active learning paradigm in the classroom where both the CEO (teacher) and workers (students) contrive to improve processes and teamwork. As a result, they reduce complexity and variation, and deeper learning occurs as the students master the terminal competencies. There are great similarities between successfully incorporating TQM into an institutional culture and successfully incorporating cooperative learning into a classroom.

How We Teach and What Industry Wants

As can be seen in Table 2:6, there are considerable differences between the instructor-based paradigm and the active-learner-based paradigm. In the former, knowledge is transferred from the instructor to a passive recipient, the student. In the TQM-based active-learning paradigm, the instructor becomes a leader, coach or mentor and helps the student not only to learn how to learn, but also how to work in teams.

In 1993, a US national report finally revealed what most of us in higher education probably already knew. The Wingspread Report, "An American Imperative: Higher Expectations for Higher Education," identified a disturbing and dangerous mismatch between what American society needs from institutions of higher education and what it is receiving.[15]

Despite the passage of time and the application of a variety of "solutions," the problem still exists. We do not need another report to discover, if anything, the situation has gotten worse. Many of the issues that face higher education today are the result of poorly designed, outdated or irrelevant curricula that fail to meet the needs of the real world, especially in an economic environment filled with dynamic change.

TABLE 2:6
Instructor-Based Paradigm vs. Active-Learner-Based Paradigm

Characteristic	Instructor-Based Paradigm (Traditional)	Active Learner Paradigm (TQM Based)
Knowledge	Transferred from instructor to student	Co-created
Student purpose	Passive recipient	Worker, responsible for obtaining knowledge and skills
Faculty purpose	Provide opportunity for learning and to sort students	Develop students' competencies and skills
Student-Faculty relationship	Do for/Do to	Active learner/Provide support
Classroom environment	Competitive, individualistic	Cooperative, group learning
Assumptions	Expert can teach	Teaching is difficult and requires considerable training

The Wingspread Report, however, was not a death knell. It heralded an opportunity for improvement, as C. Peter Magrath, Executive Director of the National Association of State Universities and Land Grant Colleges, realized:

> If we focus on the clear national need to give and be seen as giving more attention to the undergraduate student, as well as the other issues raised in the Wingspread Report, we will have a better opportunity to demonstrate the existing and enormous strengths of American higher education . . . thereby assure our competitiveness in the future before us.[16]

What can institutions of higher education focus on? What are the real answers to the questions raised by the Wingspread Report? Here are some suggestions.

• Listen to the voice of the customer – translate customer requirements into appropriate course competencies.

- Measure the results – evaluate the systems and processes for learning, as well as teaching, academic program and institutional effectiveness through criteria such as the Malcolm Baldrige National Quality Award Education Pilot Criteria.

Table 3:6 shows what is expected of the students in a typical instructor-based paradigm versus what employers expect from their employees. As you can see, there are considerable differences between them.

TABLE 3:6
Comparison of Skills of Students Graduating from a Traditional Education System Based on the Instructor-Based Paradigm and the Skills Required of Employees in a Modern Organization

Instructor-Based Paradigm (Students)	Workplace Requirements (Employees)
Memorize facts	Critical thinking and problem solving
Individual effort	Teams and teaming skills
Pass a test (surface learning)	Learning how to learn
Individual courses	Interdisciplinary knowledge
Receive information	Receive and process information critically
Technology aids learning	Technology is integral to learning

Discussion

There are many factors that affect quality in colleges and universities. At the ninth International Conference on Assessing Quality in Higher Education, held July 21–23, 1997 in the US, 24 countries were represented. Keynote speakers came from the United Kingdom (UK), the EU and the US. All had similar concerns such as rising costs with decreased funding, increase in the number of students wanting an education and the desire to meet the expectations of their customers. Speakers addressed significant improvements in their various quality assurance efforts. Although I have not elaborated on all of these findings, one can be assured that there are significant TQM efforts in virtually every country in the world. TQM efforts are being applied to the accreditation, management and learning efforts of educational institutions as they train and develop our human resources.

In the US, there have been other institutions of higher education that have successfully implemented TQM.[17] For example, Samford University in Alabama, Delaware County Community College in Pennsylvania, and Fox Valley Technical Institute in Wisconsin are worth benchmarking. Others have made significant progress. Still, many other institutions have moved away from implementing what is known as a "TQM program" towards establishing a culture of Continuous Quality Improvement by implementing efforts to Assess Value-Added Learning (AVAL). TQM is not dead, it is simply transformed into other verbiage more readily acceptable to those in education. By the same token, the genetic material of TQM has always been incorporated into the gnome of the educational nucleus. It simply responds differently to various societal stimuli. Regardless of what we call the continuous improvement efforts in educational institutions, we must remember that quality is much more than a degree of excellence as measured by stakeholder satisfaction, including the wants and needs of employers. With this in mind, I must close with a warning: if the voice of the professoriate, the true thought-leaders of society, is removed from the top of the list of stakeholder concerns about the quality of our graduates, we will have extinguished the single most important flame that guides civilization.

This, in turn, means that the school's decision-making is closely allied to students' needs.

Grant Maintained Schools

In the UK, the new wave in education can be seen in the Grant Maintained Schools. An important driver of the Grant Maintained Schools was the demand by parents for greater accountability by schools and for greater parental involvement in their children's education. Grant Maintained Schools are government funded, but they share many of the features of the Charter Schools in the US. They:

- enjoy a high level of administrative and financial autonomy
- are directly accountable to their communities, and
- are controlled locally.

They must also have a parent representative on the governing board, follow a nationally determined curriculum (the National Curriculum) and be open to all students.

The Australian Context

Here are some pertinent experiences encountered by the Australian State of Victoria over the past five years while grappling with this challenge. For the best part of a hundred years since the founding of the Australian federation in 1901, Australia has been an isolated place, a long way from the main markets of the world, inheritors of a European culture in an Asian-Pacific setting, protected from international competition by high tariff barriers and a highly regulated financial system which buttressed its currency against the pressures of the international markets. Behind these protective mechanisms there developed a peaceful, prosperous and stable nation in which governments, organizations and individuals were, by and large, not especially required to exhibit innovation, take risks or strive for efficiency. (Although some did!)

Because of global changes which have affected us all, in the space of a single decade from 1983 to 1993, this protective cover was all swept away. Tariffs were dramatically reduced, the financial system deregulated and Australia was exposed to the forces of globalization, accelerated by the revolution in information and communications technologies. It was in this climate that, in October 1992, a newly elected government in Victoria set out to reinvent its education system and equip it to prepare young people for this new demanding and uncertain world.

Future Schools: The Victorian Experience
Toward Self-Management

In Victoria, a reform program under the titles of *Schools of the Future 1992–1998* and *Schools of the Third Millennium* (1998) was carried out.

Self-Management

A fundamental feature of Australian reforms – and common to those in a number of countries including the US and the UK – was the delegating of powers, previously held by the central education and regional authorities, to individual schools. These included powers to:

- determine their curriculum program and priorities against a state-wide common standards framework
- decide how to spend the school's budget
- raise money from external sources, and
- hire and deploy staff, including the acquisition of specialist staff from outside the traditional teaching service.

A fundamental feature was the introduction of greater accountability in return for giving schools greater freedom and authority. The accountability framework contained the following initiatives.

- A state-wide curriculum framework from years P through 12 within which each individual school is free to design its own curriculum program and to specialize if it so chooses.
- The setting of state-wide performance standards for students in each year-level of school, with periodic state-wide tests to assess student performance. These tests are given in years 3 and 5 (primary schooling), and are being introduced in years 7 and 9 (junior secondary schooling).
- Mandatory face-to-face reporting of student progress, and above-noted test results reported to individual parents.

- Creation of School Councils as corporations with a limited but real range of powers set in constitutions approved by the state government.
- A School Charter in which the School Council sets its own goals and priorities within the parameters of the state-wide policy framework after consultation with all parents. The school's performance is audited in detail by the central education authority against the goals and priorities laid down in the charter.
- Each School Council reports annually on the school's performance to each parent and to the central authority.
- Each School Charter is renewed every three years following a comprehensive internal and external review.

In Victoria, these changes were carried out under *Schools of the Future Program*. One of the most delicate policy issues to arise was whether *Schools of the Future* meant the end of a systemic basis for government schools; whether each individual school would now compete in an open market against every other school for pupils and for government money; whether the diversity in schooling that would inevitably follow would disturb the equilibrium of the education system.

However, there were two prior questions to be answered:

- Do education systems support or stifle individual schools?
- Can education systems be sufficiently responsive to the needs of individual students?

It is probably important to spell out the private-public split in Victorian education, the competition and pressures this engenders and the important ongoing role of the government education system. Within the government (and indeed any Catholic) system, there is the unavoidable tension between "center" versus school. Many current reports indicate that the pendulum is swinging toward greater independence within centrally determined boundaries for government systems.

The Victorian answer to these questions was to retain some of the essential and valuable characteristics of a system while giving individual schools scope to tailor their services to the needs of their own students. The School Charter process was deliberately developed as a dynamic process to secure the commitment of each school community to both the central and locally developed goals and priorities. To retain the essential characteristics of a system, we introduced a policy platform centered on a budgetary process which ensured an equitable distribution of funds to schools, taking into account such factors as the socioeconomic composition of the school's catchment, special needs such as those arising from a large proportion of non-English-speaking students and geographic isolation.

Also introduced were a state-wide curriculum and standards framework which laid down as detailed learning outcome statements, the skills and knowledge that all students were expected to acquire at different stages of their schooling. Alongside that were introduced the state-wide testing at two fixed points in their primary schooling and, in the near future, at two fixed points in junior secondary schooling. In addition, the quality and standard of the year 12 or matriculation level examination were extensively upgraded.

Below is a summary of what happens under the *Schools of the Future* program.

- Schools may decide their own curriculum priorities and program – including for example, whether they choose to specialize in a particular area of study – but must do so within a strong overall curriculum and standard framework expressed as educational outcome statements, which is laid down by the central authority.
- Schools may decide their own spending priorities, but must do so within a "one-line" global budget provided by the central authority, which takes into account overarching issues of equity. At the same time, schools may raise additional funds on their own on a voluntary basis.
- Schools are required to conduct their own student assessments at all levels and report annually on outcomes, but must also offer all their students in primary and lower secondary school the opportunity of sitting the state-wide tests in literacy, numeracy and science. The results of these tests, which 97 percent of students now take, must be given in writing to each student's parents, in a face-to-face interview situation in addition to comprehensive reports in all subjects twice a year. If a student is achieving below the expected level, the teacher must negotiate a plan with the parents, to assist the student to reach the required level.

Decisions on the implementation of these issues are made by a school council, which consists of parents, community members and the teaching staff. The council's central task is to produce a School Charter which sets out curriculum, budgetary and assessment policies. The school's performance against this Charter is monitored by the central authority, as indicated in the discussion of the Accountability Framework above.

Access to the *Schools of the Future* program was voluntary. Each community had to make a conscious choice to join, with all joining over a two-year period. Annual surveys over the last five years have indicated that not one school wants to go back!

It can be seen, then, that *Schools of the Future* contains five elements that have been found internationally to be critical to successful school education.

1. An active focus on the individual school as the unit which has the capacity for improved performance by delegation of greater freedom, authority and responsibility to principals and school councils.
2. Flexibility to respond to the needs of the school's own students.
3. Commitment of the community to the schooling system.
4. High but realistic standards to which all students can aspire.
5. Accountability to the community and to parents for what goes on in the classroom.

In the recent World Bank study as part of the Education Reform and Management series, it was noted that: "[t]he reform to school education in Victoria is marked by comprehensiveness, coherence and a focus on clear outcomes – all aspects of system reform."[3]

Having given schools greater autonomy at the managerial and operational levels, we are now moving to the next phase – greater autonomy at the level of school governance. This is being carried out under *The Schools of the Third Millennium* program. It will empower a school to make more far-reaching decisions about employment of staff, about its curriculum specializations, about financing and about asset management. Each school will be exemplary in its use of sophisticated educational technologies for teaching administration, accountability and reporting. In these ways, it continues the trends established by *Schools of the Future* and by similar policy developments in other countries. Access to the program is voluntary but not automatic. Schools will have to demonstrate readiness for self-management. Accountability will be further strengthened by a resource service agreement aligned to performance.

These changes have positioned our schools to better face an uncertain future. They will equip our schools to harness fully the technologies of the future, which is the next big challenge. Professor Larry Cuban of

Stanford University, California says: "[n]ew technologies do not change schools: schools have to change before they can make effective use of the new technologies."[4]

That is what Victoria is trying to do. In parallel with the reform program, Victoria is trying to ensure that its schools are ready in every way for the new technologies so that they have the best position on the so-called information superhighway of the digital age.

What Future Schools Must Do

The objectives of our *Schools of the Future* and *Schools of the Third Millennium* programs are consistent with the requirements identified by educationalists in many countries as being necessary if schools are to provide a quality education for today's and tomorrow's students. A review of current thinking among educationalists shows some strong patterns emerging. These patterns point the way to successful future schools being developed in terms of nine linked strategies of which Self-Management described earlier is the first (see Figure 1:7).

FIGURE 1:7
Nine Linked Strategies to Develop Future Schools

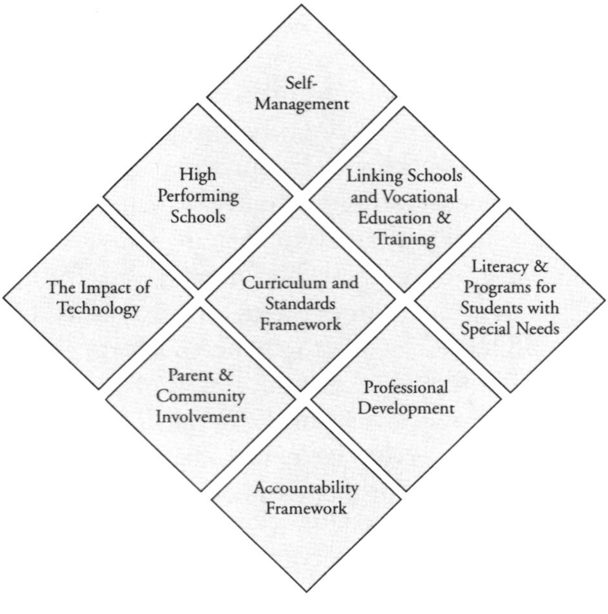

Self-Management

High Performing Schools

Linking Schools and Vocational Education & Training

The Impact of Technology

Curriculum and Standards Framework

Literacy & Programs for Students with Special Needs

Parent & Community Involvement

Professional Development

Accountability Framework

9

The Singapore Education System: A Quality Model?

Daphne Pan

Introduction

In the keynote address at the 7th International Thinking Conference,[1] Goh Chok Tong, Prime Minister of Singapore, emphasized that the future scenario would be one where success depends on knowledge and speed in responding to changes which will impinge on every aspect of life.[2] In this dynamic information age of exponential knowledge increase, knowledge and expertise determine to a great extent national development and viability. Key challenges of globalization and rapid technological advances have introduced the shift from cost competitiveness to capability competitiveness so that competition is based not so much on the lowest cost of doing business as on the highest level of competence. As the *Asian Wall Street Journal* has pointed out in its *Asian Economic Survey 1997–1998*, "[f]or the long-term . . . the struggle for economic success will be fought more in the classroom than in the currency market . . ."[3]

This, then, is the age of "survival of the smartest," and for many countries, education is or is becoming a top priority.[4] An OECD survey across 17 OECD countries presented a rise in average population of those aged 18–21 in higher education from 14.4 percent in 1985 to 22.4 percent in 1995. Graduation rates in the US topped the list at nearly 45 percent of the population at theoretical graduation age, while those of Canada, UK, Norway and New Zealand range around the 30 percent mark. Education featured importantly in the UK general election of May 1997, and was identified as a key issue in the last US elections.

People see no hope and no opportunity for their children unless they have access to a good public education.[5]

President Clinton had announced in his State of the Union address of February 1997 that as education will be the primary tool to keep America ahead, a budget of US$51 billion will be deployed to improve national education standards, teacher training, school discipline and character education for good citizenship. At a recent East Asia Economic Summit organized by World Economic Forum, the Hong Kong government was urged to make education a priority since "education policy is arguably the most important economic policy at this stage of the territory's development . . ."[6]

These are but some examples of the attention being paid to education. Particularly for a small country such as Singapore whose chief asset is its human resources, education is pivotal. It must gear up to compete in the international marketplace, and well-trained and highly skilled manpower is needed to support its drive to regionalize, globalize, seek new economic opportunities and consolidate an external economy. Hence, education has been identified as a key strategic thrust that will launch Singapore into the twenty-first century. Concomitant with this decision is the awareness that the education must have quality.

Defining Quality

Definitions of quality vary, shaped as they are by expectations and ideologies about the nature and function of education. Smith and Smith point out that: "[t]he word (quality) is commonly used with two quite different meanings. Sometimes 'quality' implies the Ball concept of 'fitness for purpose,' whereas on other occasions it is used to mean the Pirsig concept of 'high standard' or 'excellence.'"[7]

Quality is also often equated with value-for-money. Clearly, all these aspects are important; maintaining standards needs no defense, but the "product" must not only be excellent in the abstract but also be practically useful and have high added value. Ideally, quality education should be estimable, effective and efficient.

Measuring Quality

A range of performance indicators has been devised for measuring quality.[8] As numerical values, such indicators help to systematize what is complex and difficult to measure, but there is little doubt that as a tool they are liable to be simplistic. At best they tend to address a systemic and predominantly extrinsic set of values; at worst, they encourage number-crunching without due regard to the central issue of the objectives of education. Excessive reliance on quantification is suspect, as is strict adherence to a rigid set of parameters. Vigilance is vital as it is only too easy for the concept of quality to become corrupted by politically correct representations. There is also the danger of assuming a purely instrumental approach which would be reductive, and concerned only with accountability and bottom lines.

Barnett states that:

> [i]mproving the quality of higher education cannot be accomplished simply as a set of tasks in a technical mode of operation . . . We cannot sensibly employ the term "quality" in a value-free way . . . the identification, the assessment and the improvement of quality cannot be conducted purely as a technical exercise.[9]

Nor is any monolithic set of indicators likely to be good for all time. In this fast-paced era, responsiveness and adaptability to changing circumstances are critical. For operative purposes, it is perhaps more useful to keep some fundamental questions constantly in mind. What are the desired learning outcomes? What core skills and competencies need to be transferred? What values and attitudes should be inculcated? And what would be the best means of effecting and assuring such transfers? Again, answers necessarily vary because meaningful measures of quality are context-dependent and must be correlated with context-specific goals and consumer needs.

This chapter offers the Singapore experience. Hopefully, however, it will have some implications and applications for other countries and systems. For instance, there appear to be some common denominators in the Emirati and Singaporean environments. Both are rapidly developing countries with a relatively small population; human resource management and development are therefore crucial success and survival factors. Both have fairly centralized control so that top-down initiatives can be very efficient and effective. There is also some similarity in the learning milieu: Singapore's is one that is structured, prescriptive, nationally coordinated and well-funded. Within the UAE, where religious schools play an important part and reinforce a culture tending towards the didactic, learning likewise is largely mimetic and relatively passive. There is great respect for authority and learning, and students are consequently more disciplined and trainable. With such and other commonalities, exchanges of ideas and experiences should be of mutual value.

Singapore: A Case Study

1946–1959: Post-War Reconstruction
The education system in the post-war years until the attainment of independence in 1959 was rather lackluster. Apart from financial constraints (expenditure on education was only 5 percent of the national budget), there was insufficient leadership and political will.

1959–1978: Expansion and Consolidation
From 1959 onwards, however, there was rapid expansion in response to economic, social and national objectives. With its separation from Malaya in 1965, efforts at qualitative consolidation were intensified. Major reforms of the preceding period gained momentum in the implementation and, among other things, the next 20 years saw:

- implementation of free, compulsory primary education, more secondary schools and greater attention to tertiary education
- more emphasis on teacher-training
- increased attention to educational research and curriculum development
- introduction of the policy of bilingualism (English and a mother-tongue) to increase productivity, social harmony and national cohesion, and
- emphasis on mathematics, science and technical subjects and the creation of schools for training in vocational, technical and commercial streams to provide the manpower base for industrialization.

1979–1990: Fine Tuning and New Direction
The Goh Keng Swee Report in 1979 initiated a period of review and revision. Low teacher morale, the unsatisfactory outcomes of policies (e.g.

Generic and Thinking Skills

This involves training in process skills (e.g. logical, analytical, critical, creative and reflective thinking skills) as well as mind-set changes. A desire for learning, or at least the recognition of the desirability of continuous learning, will engender independent, self-motivated learning. Some strategies suggested for effecting this include the use of active learning, project-based learning and assessment through open-book examinations.

Values and Social Responsibility

Educating for good citizenship goes beyond political socialization to an integrative role. It creates a sense of identity, both national and individual, and shared values which make for harmonious and productive coexistence. Hence, among other things, Singapore has introduced moral education into the school curriculum. Efforts have also been made to educate the public at large to become a more gracious and caring society. Education is likewise perceived as a powerful tool for socializing the young into a survivalist "can do" culture. Prime Minister Goh Chok Tong states:

> We want to bring about a mind-set change among Singaporeans . . . we want to bring about a spirit of innovation, of learning by doing, of everyone each at his own level all the time asking how he can do his job better.[43]

Three Priorities for the Singapore Education System

In response to the times and in projecting for the future, the three priorities identified as part of the strategic planning for the next millennium are developing/enhancing thinking skills, exploiting information technology (IT) for teaching and learning, and national education.

Developing thinking skills

Goh Chok Tong states:

> We must get away from the idea that it is only the people at the top who should be thinking, and the job of everyone else is to do as told . . . We do not even know what these problems will be, let alone be able to provide the answers and solutions to them . . . But

we must ensure that our young can think for themselves, so that the next generation can find their own solutions to whatever new problems they may face.[44]

For a country that has been considered autocratic, such a statement by its Prime Minister is all the more significant evidence of the imperative of equipping students with the higher-order thinking skills.

Interest in intelligence development has intensified since the 7th International Conference on Thinking of June 1997. While not entirely novel to Singaporean audiences, such views as Howard Gardner's on multiple intelligences,[45] De Bono's on lateral thinking,[46] Daniel Goleman's on EQ[47] and Robert Sternberg's triarachic theory of human intelligence[48] received reinforcement and a good deal of high-level follow-up. Several proposals are being implemented, including:

- introduction of innovative teaching methods (e.g. role-play, simulation), and
- revision of curriculum to ensure relevance and eliminate the superfluous, with the caveat, however, that: "whichever way we cut back and redefine the curriculum, we will ensure our students retain mastery over the core knowledge and concepts that give them the basis for further learning."[49]

The Vice-Chancellor of the NUS has announced that the curriculum will be progressive, trimmed by up to 30 percent within the next few years. The intention is to create graduates who, being less encumbered by fact accumulation, will have more time for acquiring other skills, such as the ability to think and to function competently as working adults. There is growing recognition that education is not an activity restricted to the classroom. It is also to educate for life, for the development of individual potential, continued self-actualization and, more immediately, for the workplace. Both the fitness-for-use and value-for-money definitions of quality are predicated on the usefulness of education for gainful employment and asset-creation. To better enable this, the school–industry articulation should be soundly established through such means as ensuring a relevant and up-to-date curriculum, developing the practical skills (e.g. computer skills and modern finance) and interpersonal skills (e.g. teamwork, communication and organization) so necessary for efficient operation in the marketplace. Singapore students are good at studying, but critics have remarked that they are not sufficiently "street-savvy." It has been suggested, therefore, that they should be taught, for instance, how to commercialize ideas and start up companies, and have nurtured in them the enterprising and entrepreneurial spirit underpinned by a broad global outlook. This would ensure that they are "marketable" and possess a reasonable shelf life.

To support this, formal education should be extended by informal (self-directed inquiry) and non-formal continuing professional education. The Prime Minister states:

> We will make Singapore a Learning Nation that goes beyond schools and educational institutions . . . Our collective tolerance for change and willingness to invest in learning as a continuous activity will determine how we cope with an uncertain future. We must make learning a national culture. Learning Nation begins by recognising that education is a continuum, starting with the early pre-school years and continuing throughout life . . . We must set up comprehensive mechanisms to continually retrain our workforce, and encourage every individual to engage in learning as a matter of necessity. Even the most well educated worker will stagnate if he does not keep upgrading his skills and knowledge.[50]

Exploiting IT For Teaching/Learning

Recognizing that IT is a potentially powerful educational tool, a Master Plan for schools was announced in April 1997, with S$2 billion (US$1.16) allocated to create "smart" schools by year 2001. This involves:

- installation of physical and technological infrastructure: equipping schools with start-up hardware[51] and whole-school networking, so that pupils will have access to multi-media computer resources; materials from CD-ROMs and the Internet
- the use of IT for up to 30 percent of curriculum time
- developing software, content and learning resources,[52] and
- providing training and human resource development.

The IT Summit in December 1997 reported impressive progress but more needs to be done, and harder questions need to be more thoroughly addressed, such as the ones that follow.

- How do institutions decide about investments in technology – how much and what kinds?

- How can we plan when technologies are changing so rapidly?
- How much technological skill do institutes require of faculty and students?
- Should we see technology as an instructional tool, academic content or both?

Evaluating our academic and administrative structures in the light of the increased use of information and instructional technologies, what changes do we need to make? And how would these changes impinge on teachers, learners and the learning process? "Smart" technology and "smart" schools do not automatically produce "smart" students. Much depends on "smart" teaching and learning. The following are but some of the "fine print" meriting careful attention.

TEACHING
- How is the role of the teacher changing through the use of technology?
- How do we promote use of IT in teaching and learning?
- How much and what kind of training do we need to provide?
- How can teachers be prepared to best fulfill this new role and meet these demands?
- Can technology enhance pedagogy without sacrificing the benefits of face-to-face interaction?
- How is technology influencing the teacher/learner, learner/content transactions?

LEARNING
- In what ways can technology facilitate cognition, information processing and real mastery?
- What learning outcomes are demonstrably derived from the use of technology?
- Are we accurately measuring these outcomes?
- What forms of technology-aided learning are proving most effective, and why?
- How may the rapid increases in information resources be best incorporated into curricula?
- Are students acquiring the skills of self-managed learners through technology-assisted learning?
- Do students learn differently in different formats? If so, how?

Current educational responses to the changing nature of work emphasize first, staying longer in school; second, closer links between schooling and work; third, stress on work-relevant skills; and finally, closer collaboration among governments, education systems and the world of business and industry. Many of these initiatives are of recent origin and there is very little systematic information and research on their effectiveness in improving the transition process or ensuring better access to stable and rewarding employment.[29] Nor is there universal agreement that the closer links between education and business are necessarily benign.[30]

We must remember that a job is one kind of work, work is one part of life, and that education has many important individual and social goals beyond work preparation. Yet a crucial question remains: Where is work going in the coming decades, and what can and should education do to prepare young people for the future?

The Future of Work

It is impossible to predict with any certainty the future of work in society. Too little is known about the supply and demand of human resources at the present time, the factors which will shape this supply and demand in the future, how these factors will interact, the kinds of work that will be available or the requirements of that work. How these patterns develop will determine how the education and training systems of a nation can meet these needs and the social and political impact of different work contexts.[31]

The major forces that will shape the demand for work in the future are already in evidence.

- Knowledge and innovation, especially in scientific and technological fields.
- Communication and information technologies, and their impact on productivity and other forms of input (especially labor).
- The nature and extent of economic growth, its cycles and its sustainability.
- Global and regional competition.
- Consumer patterns and expectations.
- Demographic patterns affecting the age of the workforce.
- Political decisions about social and economic support systems, and the role of government intervention.

- Cultural values related to the hierarchy of prestige of different forms of work and the access of minorities, women, immigrants and the young to different careers.
- Political stability and infrastructure.
- Vision, creativity, initiative and leadership.

Some of these factors are cyclical (notably economic growth), others are structural (especially competition and technology) and others still are idiosyncratic (vision, for instance). Together they will shape the extent of the demand for work and workers, and the nature of the work demands. This should be in some kind of balance with the supply side, the education and training system both for the young and for adults, though this balance is by no means easy to anticipate or attain.[32]

It may be helpful to explore some of the options open to us by considering seven scenarios of the future of work.

Scenario 1: Work Continues to Change and Evolve
In many developed and developing societies, work has been changing over time. Some kinds of work decrease in importance, some new forms of work arise and are given special importance. These patterns continue. Unemployment continues to be high but is moderated as young people are kept out of the labor market by extended schooling and older workers are given incentives to retire. Jobs continue to shift from resource and manufacturing sectors to the service sector. The polarization of work between good and bad jobs eases as more middle-level jobs are created, partly as a response to public backlash against impersonal technologies (such as voice mail) and partly because of the need to bridge low-skill temporary personnel with high-skill professionals.

Education systems continue to stress the importance of school retention and post-secondary credentials; current initiatives like work-study and transition programs continue to be priorities. Social inequalities remain a problem, mitigated to some extent by social redistribution programs and incentives for high-productivity industries to provide job experiences and other forms of social assistance.

Scenario 2: Work Becomes Scarce
In most developed countries, increasing productivity and competitiveness become less dependent on labor and more on technology, inventiveness

and management. Good jobs are restricted to those with advanced education in scientific and technical fields, and those with unusual talents or experience, social skills or proper connections. And there is an ample supply of such people. There is little work for everyone else.[33]

Education becomes a funnel through which large numbers of students are led, with smaller and small numbers coming out the other end with good job prospects. The remainder are left to become perpetual students or enjoy lives as entertainment consumers, supported by general government redistribution of wealth. Social, gender-related and class violence increases as large numbers of poorly educated and frustrated men have few outlets and opportunities. A new version of the Roman "bread and circuses" evolves as fast food and television sports occupy the leisure of the masses.

Scenario 3: Work Increases

In many societies, and in many regions in all societies, the advance of technology falters – its social and environmental effects outweighing its benefits. Anti-technology movements become more powerful, technology is increasingly vulnerable to terrorism and fraud, and there is a movement toward self-reliance and "medium technology" to enhance labor, not replace it. As a result, people work longer hours to attain financial independence and there are shortages in many economic areas which depend on skill and experience.

Schools stress "survival skills" and practical arts, including cooking, machine repair, inventiveness, agriculture and a work ethic that sees rewards as commensurate with work. Independence is a virtue, dependence on public funds condemned. Sustainable economies are the goal, human labor the means. Many societies introduce public service corps comparable to military service to handle the floods and weather devastation that are increasingly frequent.

Scenario 4: Work Becomes Polarized

The trend towards the polarization of jobs increases. Most companies and professions follow the "core and cloud" metaphor, with a small number of elite full-time, highly paid and competitive people and a large amorphous group of JIT workers, part-time and temporary workers with low-level skills, or specialized skills of personal relations or data inputting. More and more, the core is composed of men and women who have acquired advanced degrees and the cloud is composed of men and women who do not have the education or opportunity to qualify for the core or improve their skills.

Education systems become more clearly sorting devices for an elite, stressing "high-stakes" subjects such as mathematics and science, and high-stakes tests to determine placement in elite post-secondary institutions and programs. Other students are given culturally-oriented learning experience and basic social and career skills. There is a high degree of violence, drug abuse and frustration as a moderately educated population finds no work opportunities appropriate to their training and becomes marginalized.

Scenario 5: Work is Artificially Created

Society and individuals continue to value the significance of work for individual meaning and for social coherence. A distinction is made between productive work (the activity of a minority) and therapeutic work (the activity of most of the population). Productive work subsidizes therapeutic work, and many kinds of work continue in resource, manufacturing and service sectors because they are socially necessary, even if they are not economically viable. In this system, work is an outcome, not an input, of the economy.

Schools continue to sort students and prepare everyone for work activities of different sorts. Many industries are subsidized for job creation and special programs are established for those with little education, the handicapped and the elderly. Society benefits from the more or less meaningful occupation of large numbers of citizens and individuals acquire an alternative to the passive consumption of entertainment media.

Scenario 6: Work Declines in Importance

As work opportunities and the need for workers decline, and as governments make adjustments to re-allocate the profits derived from greater productivity (the "robot tax"), people begin work later in life, retire from work earlier, work fewer hours, are given longer vacations, and begin to see work, job and career as less important for their personal identity, less a source of fulfillment and less a personal challenge.

Education moves away from career education and vocational programs, and shifts emphasis from employability skills to life skills

– citizenship, media studies, culture, fitness, sports, arts and crafts, tourism and avocational activities. Entertainment, voluntary service and recreation become major life activities; for some, these activities are mainly as spectators, but others participate in fitness, health, crafts, creative writing, video production, outdoor activities and sports. Play becomes the replacement of work as the driving ambition; indulgence or fulfillment replaces discipline or deferred gratification as the driving ethic.

Scenario 7: Work is Redefined

As societies and historical eras have periodically redefined what constitutes work and established the priorities among different kinds of work – hunting, farming, manufacturing, building, fighting, thinking and serving – post-modern society begins to blend the concepts of work (as job or gainful employment), play (as leisure and enjoyment) and learning (as the acquisition of new skills, knowledge and attitudes). To the public and private sectors is added the third sector of voluntary, charitable, artistic, community and civic activity. The major work of most people is lifelong learning.

Academic, cultural and vocational education merge, each leading to the others. Community involvement is a major emphasis of many schools and post-secondary institutions; adult and lifelong education becomes a normal pattern of pathways for both young and old as they make contributions in a variety of activities that satisfy them and contribute to social well-being. Public service, professions and private corporations "lend" members to community activities as part of their responsibilities.

Each of these scenarios is inspired by a different vision of work, society and education, but they are not mutually exclusive. They do not unfold in any inevitable way but are the result of pressures, responses to these pressures, and social and individual choices. A scenario is a text to be written, not a script to be followed.

Learning for the Future

At the present time, it is important to ensure that education maintains its roots in tradition and provides a sense of continuity and identity. It is also important for education to adjust to the present issues of society and the present needs of learners. But it is education's vision of the future and how it can contribute to the future of work to which we need to turn our attention.

We must remember that modern education systems have their roots in industrial society as it evolved in Western Europe and the US. Schools arose to protect the young from child labor, to instill virtues like honesty, religious conformity and civic responsibility that were deemed necessary for social order, to identify promising candidates for social promotion, and to teach basic skills of literacy and numeracy. As school systems expanded, they adopted the structure of the civil service, the military, the church, and especially the emerging organizational patterns of business and industry.

Schools were organized into grades and classes for group instruction; learning was the consumption of teaching; authority flowed down from ministries of education to local authorities, to school principals and teachers in a hierarchical structure; learning programs were divided into subjects, generally based on the structure of post-secondary disciplines, and subjects were cut into weekly and daily timetables; learning was measured in terms of duration (academic credits); attendance at class was considered a necessary condition for learning and compulsory attendance laws were enacted because schooling was seen as necessary for learning (not to be schooled was not to be educated); students progressed through the curriculum and received certification if successful.

Underlying the formal curriculum of languages, science, mathematics and other subjects were the underlying lessons of authority (the teacher), conformity (school discipline, punctuality), persistence (school retention) and effort (promotion, marks). These were the qualities for which schools socialized the young, and the criteria by which students were sorted for further studies and for careers. Graduates were trained to join the professions and related occupations (civil service, teaching, health care), the assembly lines of large manufacturing industries or the clerical pools of large business enterprises.

Schools promoted learning in three ways: through the content of the programs (reading, mathematics, vocational courses, science, current events), through the way teaching was delivered (full-class instruction, memorization, repetition, testing) and through the underlying medium or implicit substructure of the school (grouping of students, expectations, rules, school culture).

As we approach the year 2000, we must ask if the new world of work requires a new world of education.[34]

Eight of the principles of an education for the post-modern knowledge society are listed below.

1. The attitudes and skills of *lifelong learning* are essential elements of preparation for life and work. This involves the will and desire to see learning as continuous throughout life, as embedded in a variety of structures (work, community, institutions, media) and as a personal responsibility of everyone. Governments and other agencies provide a variety of transitions and pathways between learning and working throughout all phases of life. New conceptions of youth learning (especially at the elementary and secondary levels) stress that childhood and adolescence are only the first stages of lifelong learning. And lifelong learning identifies and imparts the skills of "learning how to learn," including: first, the ability of the learner to plan and organize learning experiences; second, the skills and attitudes of self-appraisal; third, the skills of accessing information through computers and technology; and finally, the critical and creative competence to select and organize information in dynamic and innovative ways.

2. The structure of *learning programs* reflects not only a disciplinary organization of subjects but also other approaches, especially problem-based learning and key cross-curricular outcomes such as thinking skills, communication in a variety of media, various forms of literacy (including technological and ethical), and a familiarity with the value and limits of technologies.

3. Links between *academic learning* and *career preparation* are strengthened through approaches such as applied academics that stress the practical applications of science, mathematics, language and other fields, and the theoretical basis of practical skills such as management, engineering, policy-making, gardening and design. In the knowledge economy, the traditional distinction between vocational training and academic education becomes blurred; generic vocational skills are largely academic skills.

4. The focus is on *outcomes* more than on the means of attaining them. Schools, courses, lessons, assignments, computers, tests and

learning activities are means to the end, not ends in themselves. What is important are the skills developed, the knowledge acquired and the values adopted, as well as the ability of learners to transfer and apply these skills, knowledge and values to a variety of situations in the real world. Outcomes provide the coherence for a curriculum and the standard against which the learning of individuals and the quality of institutions are measured. The varieties of learners and learning styles demand a dynamic mix of strategies and experiences, within the school and outside.

5. *Information and communication technologies* form an essential element of education: as a subject of learning (both skills and deeper significance); as a set of tools to acquire, process and communicate information; and as a system to expand access to learning resources, expertise and services. Technology provides an alternative to the tradition of full-time school attendance and classroom instruction; it expands access to resources far beyond what is available in the individual school; through distance education facilities it offers access to those who cannot attend school. We are evolving rapidly from the school as the only means of learning to the mixed mode of school-tutor-technology-resource, to distance education programs and "virtual schools" that are "intentional communities" of teachers and learners relying on face-to-face and/or electronic interaction. People with the basic skills, the technological resources – and the motivation – can be truly independent learners, drawing elements of their program from different schools in different parts of the world.

6. There is an *integration* of learning, working, playing and living in society. One of the criticisms of schooling has been its isolation and separation from the real world of living in community and working. Courses mainly prepared people for other courses. Yet for many people in our society, their work is to learn; many people approach their work as play, a challenge and often a joy; and we all learn through play, through games, puzzles, challenges and pleasurable activities. In an environment of lifelong learning, learners of different ages mix, especially the young and the old who have not been easily fitted into the mainstream. The knowledge society provides equal opportunities for both women and men, as well as for the young

(who know how to ask questions) and the old (who know what questions to ask).

7. New kinds of *teachers* are needed – some to be models of artistic skill or maturity, some to be coaches and mentors, some to be designers of learning programs, some to be communicators, some to be managers of learning systems, some to be experts in different areas. Here the metaphor of the core and the cloud is also relevant: a core of full-time professionally-trained educators and a cloud of part-time or temporary experts who come and go to perform specific services. Child care functions are performed by non-professionals who are responsible and who have the special – and important – social skills needed.

8. *Educational funding* is more dispersed than in the past, divided among schooling for the young and lifelong learning for adults and older citizens. It is allocated to schools but also to media, communities and innovative learning enterprises that provide resources, programs and services for learners of different ages. In learning, as in health care and security, the less the dependence on the system, the more reasonable the cost, and often the more effective the achievement.

Conclusion

The late British economist E. F. Schumacher wrote: "[i]t has been recognized in all authentic teachings of mankind that every human being born into this world has to work not merely to keep himself alive but to strive toward perfection."[35]

Among the various sectors of society – political institutions, health care, entertainment, communications, manufacturing, services – public education systems have been least affected by the transformations taking place in work and technology, and in society at large. Until now.

It is clear that as work changes and as societies change, education must also change if it is to discharge its mandate of preparing people for tomorrow as well as for today. The changes are more than special programs of school-work transition, or career education courses or better career information and guidance systems. The credibility of school systems, in the eyes of the public and in the eyes of the clients, parents and students, depends on their ability to provide leadership in the very areas in which they are supposed to have expertise – knowledge, skill, communication, foresight, culture, learning. This is a responsibility of educators not only to prepare tomorrow's workers but also tomorrow's leaders, tomorrow's thinkers and tomorrow's humane, caring and cultured women and men. People who strive toward perfection.

SECTION 3

EDUCATION IN THE GCC

11

Education and Training in GCC Countries: Some Issues of Concern

Hamad Al-Sulayti

Introduction

The business of education and training is flourishing. Countries, East and West, have embarked on reconstructing their educational systems. In the 1970s, the US started a "back to basics" movement, and the UK went for a more structured competency-based educational system. In 1988, the UK introduced a National Curriculum and reorganized school management almost on a market basis.[1] The West went back to mastery learning, while the East (particularly Southeast Asian countries) is heading for greater child-centered education.

Globalization is driving governments to treat education and training not as a consumer good, but as a productive asset. Governments are shifting their emphasis from education to training. Technical colleges and training institutes, not the universities, are increasingly the main targets of reform.[2] Technological innovations and international competition to capture international markets are pushing countries to improve the vocational qualifications of their workforce.

The governments and people of Gulf Co-operation Council countries are feeling the wind of globalization. To some, globalization is a great threat and a violent hurricane. To others, it is a great opportunity to eliminate bureaucracy, subsequently improving efficiency and restructuring the economy.

Education and training reform has become a hot issue on the business agenda of GCC cabinets and concerned ministries. At present, GCC countries are witnessing a lot of discussions, meetings and conferences on privatization, development of human resources and restructuring the economy. The wind of change is pushing toward viewing education and training as an investment enterprise.

The wave of reform reflects a shift in the political fortunes of education and training. In 1996, the Bahraini Cabinet approved a work plan for restructuring education with an emphasis on development of technical and vocational education. Training also got a big boost in 1996 when the cabinet approved a national strategy for preparing a well-trained workforce with emphasis on re-skilling of school leavers to curtail unemployment.

In Oman, there is a move toward improving the quality of education and developing training standards to meet the increasing labor market requirements of a qualified Omani labor force. Saudi Arabia has embarked on a plan to improve school efficiency and to enhance the role of the private sector in education. It has launched a vocational training strategy to prepare the Saudi labor force for economic development. The United Arab Emirates (UAE) is also working on the development of an educational and training strategy aimed at restructuring its educational system to make it more responsive to labor market needs and to train nationals to replace the expatriate labor force. Kuwait and Qatar, as well, have embarked on upgrading their educational and training systems.

Educational reform is not an easy process. Education deals with tradition, attitudes, social values and societal norms. To reform education, one has to take all these factors into consideration. On the quantitative side, GCC countries have witnessed, in a relatively short time, a dramatic expansion in access to basic education for almost all school-age children. Generally speaking, GCC countries have taken a lead in privatizing primary as well as secondary education for all children. Net enrollment rates are averaging well above the level of 80 percent of school-age children.[3] All GCC countries provide free elementary and secondary public education. Schools are usually well maintained and supplied with good educational facilities such as libraries, laboratories and other equipment.

However, there are increasing pressures on GCC education and training systems to improve their quality. Some of the criticisms have been directed at the role of education as a supplier of relevant skills to the economy in countries which still rely heavily on an expatriate labor force. Education in GCC countries is also criticized for its emphasis on routine learning and memorization, for its high attrition and for repeaters' rates which have reached 31 percent in some secondary schools.[4] Schools are accused of graduating more and more low achievers who are functionally illiterate and lack the minimum threshold of competence.

The process of qualitative improvement of education cannot be as simple as the quantitative expansion of existing educational arrangements. The process of change is likely to be neither simple nor straightforward. The surrounding environment must be taken into consideration. Social, political and economic changes have direct impacts on education and training policies and management.

Despite the common political, economic and social pressures on the educational systems of GCC countries, there is no consensus on how to improve the quality of education. This is true not only in GCC countries, but also among educational reformers worldwide. In the West, for example, improving the quality of education began by departing from child-centered education and concentrating on teaching the basics and improving the academic achievements of students. Meanwhile, in the East, notably in Japan and South Korea, the move is toward more child-centered education and creative learning.

Taking into consideration the present challenges facing education and training in GCC countries (e.g. disparity between education and economy, low achievement standards, bureaucracy, high percentage of drop-outs and failures), reforms and restructuring of education and training in the GCC countries should give priority to the privatization of schools, the relevance of the curriculum, and correlating education and training with labor market needs.

Privatizing Schools

GCC countries have recently taken steps toward privatizing its industry, transportation and communications sectors. The education sector is still outside the privatization process and there is no indication of when it will be included. It is for the benefit of education that the private sector should be encouraged to increase investment in education and training. Private schools work because they are outside the reach of government bureaucracy and because they have more competent leadership and parent involvement. In addition, their teachers are more independent and empowered. Good and productive teachers want respect and the freedom to practice their vocation. Teachers want to have their opinions heard and respected. Good teachers know that teaching is hard and demanding. They are willing to make the effort. They seek dignity, autonomy and support.

Privatizing education and training does not mean allowing private schools to convey whatever sort of education and learning they like or to shift the financial burden of children's education from the government to the parents. In their educational practices, schools should adhere to rigorous educational quality standards set by the central educational authorities. GCC governments should encourage private schools and subsidize their services in order to make their tuition fees less expensive and within the financial reach of more parents. This type of arrangement will encourage the private sector to invest more in education as well as encourage more parents to send their children to private schools and, thus, invest more of their savings in education.

Making the School Curriculum More Relevant

Improving the school curriculum is one of the main imperatives in improving the quality of education. This is the age of information explosion. More information has been produced in the last 30 years than in the previous 5,000 years combined.[5] With this high and ever-increasing minimum threshold of knowledge and competencies required by modern economies, there is clearly a need for profound scrutiny of the present school curriculum.

The literature shows that there is wide agreement among educational reformers in GCC countries that the content and organization of the traditional school curriculum should be reformed. There is a clear need to train students to locate, evaluate and effectively use information. Educational materials should be flexible and relevant enough to stimulate students to take an active role in the learning process. Routine learning and memorization are no longer adequate teaching strategies in the age of globalization. The current literature endorses cooperative learning and the teaching of higher order thinking skills. It goes without saying that many of these approaches require better qualified teachers and almost unlimited access to a variety of information resources. Our schools need support in improving their capabilities to emphasize information literacy and numerical skills in the twenty-first century.

TABLE 1:12
UAE Indicators Compared with other Countries

Ranking by HDI	Life expectancy at birth (Years) 1994	Adult literacy rate (percent) 1994	Percentage registration in elementary, secondary and higher education	Real per capita income (US$)	Life expectancy index	Education index	GDP index	Value of HDI	Classification depending on: (real per capita – value of HDI)
1. Canada	79.0	99.0	100	21,459	0.90	0.99	0.99	0.960	7
4. US	76.2	99.0	96	26,397	0.85	0.98	0.99	0.924	1
22. Hong Kong	79.0	92.3	72	22,310	0.90	0.86	0.99	0.914	17
26. Singapore	77.1	91.0	72	20,987	0.87	0.85	0.99	0.900	15
43. Bahrain	72.0	84.4	85	15,321	0.87	0.85	0.98	0.870	14
44. UAE	74.2	78.6	82	16,000	0.82	0.80	0.98	0.866	17
53. Kuwait	75.2	77.8	57	21,875	0.84	0.71	0.99	0.844	47
55. Qatar	70.9	78.9	73	18,403	0.76	0.77	0.99	0.840	33
70. Iran	68.2	68.6	68	5,766	0.72	0.68	0.94	0.780	9
73. Saudi Arabia	70.3	61.8	65	9,338	0.76	0.60	0.97	0.774	32
88. Oman	70.0	35.0	60	10,078	0.75	0.43	0.97	0.718	49

Source: *UNDP Human Development Report, 1997*, 146–7.

A remarkable improvement was in the percentage of enrollment of students between 6 and 23 years in different stages of education, which increased from 44 percent in 1980 to 82 percent in 1994 – an increase which exceeded that of Hong Kong, Singapore, Iran and other GCC countries (now approximately 84 percent).[5] In addition, enrollment rates for all UAE children up to year 5 level (1990–1995) is almost 99 percent, considered the best among the GCC countries along with Kuwait and Bahrain, with the percentage being higher than in other countries like Iran (90 percent) and Saudi Arabia (94 percent).[6]

With respect to per capita income, there has been a noticeable decline in real per capita income since 1980 in the UAE. This is primarily due to the large increase in the migrant population by almost 85 percent between 1985–1995 and the decline in oil revenues. However, it remained higher than many GCC countries, Hong Kong and Singapore. In comparison, the industrialized countries have experienced a steady growth as shown in Table 2:12. The ranking of the UAE on the HDI scale (-17) was lower than its rating according to GDP per capita share (-52 in 1992). All Gulf countries showed negative values on the GDP per capita scale in 1994. The real GDP per capita rank is higher than the HDI rank.

Development achievements are most noticeable in the areas of female literacy and enrollment rates. According to Table 3:12, the UAE female enrollment in secondary education as a percentage of males (1993–1995) is the highest among GCC countries, and UAE female illiteracy rate and maternal mortality are the lowest.

When taking into account these and other indicators, there is little doubt that the UAE has made significant progress in human development, with all the relevant indicators showing improvement exceeding many other GCC countries who had commenced development programs long before the formation of the UAE Federation in 1971. However, these figures do not give the true picture as they also cover expatriates in the UAE. Accordingly, a more detailed analysis of the UAE education system would be useful.

TABLE 4:12
Education Development in Government Schools
(1985/86 to 1996/97)

Scholastic Year	Students	Teachers and Administrative Staff	Classes	Schools
1985/86	179,276	13,320	6,619	395
1986/87	194,433	14,996	7,241	415
1987/88	209,180	15,867	7,745	431
1988/89	225,391	17,076	8,403	457
1989/90	242,538	18,717	8,973	475
1990/91	257,773	20,074	9,441	499
1991/92	261,692	21,337	9,861	512
1992/93	270,560	22,514	10,255	534
1993/94	278,836	23,421	10,542	560
1994/95	289,066	24,335	10,909	582
1995/96	295,322	25,287	11,260	615
1996/97	300,338	25,984	11,567	639

Source: UAE Ministry of Education, Education Statistical Bulletin – Summary 1996–1997.

Non-national students represent about one-third of the total student population in government schools. However, the slow growth of the number of national students in government schools indicates that the system has either absorbed all students eligible for schooling or a growing number of them are joining private schools (see Table 5:12).

TABLE 5:12
Students in Government Schools by Nationality

Scholastic Year	Nationals	%	Non-Nationals	%	Total
1991/92	17,3118	66.20	88,574	33.80	261,692
1992/93	180,403	66.70	90,157	33.30	270,560
1993/94	187,046	67.10	91,790	32.90	278,836
1994/95	19,3034	66.80	96,032	33.20	289,066
1995/96	197,893	67.00	97,440	33.00	295,333
1996/97	20,1979	67.25	98,358	32.75	300,337

Source: UAE Ministry of Education, Summary of Educational Statistics, 1996–1997

Similarly, the private school system has experienced significant growth in the past 10 years. Private schools almost doubled between 1987/1988 and 1996/1997, thus increasing from 198 schools to almost 388 schools (96 percent) during the period. They now represent about 33 percent of the total schools in the UAE and accommodate 41 percent of the total number of students enrolled in UAE schools. However, national students in private schools increased slightly from 10.2 percent in 1993/1994 to 11 percent of total private school students in 1997/1998 (see Table 6:12). (Asians represent 61 percent, and other Arabs 23 percent.) Over 62 percent of private schools are in the Emirates of Abu Dhabi and Dubai.

TABLE 6:12
Education Development in Private Schools, 1987/88 to 1996/97

Scholastic Year	Students	Schools
1987/88	87,964	198
1988/89	102,619	231
1989/90	115,670	240
1990/91	126,137	270
1991/92	137,057	289
1992/93	149,477	321
1993/94	173,544	359
1994/95	189,773	365
1995/96	192,882	376
1996/97	195,586	388

Source: UAE Ministry of Education, Educational Statistical Bulletin, Summary 1996–1997.

The rapid development of private schools heralds the development of a quasi-market within the education system (Article 9 of the 1972 Federal law), thereby increasing competition, providing wider choices to parents and catering to the needs of different groups in society. However, the quality of services provided by a large number of these schools remains less than satisfactory, operating with little or no direct supervision from the Ministry of Education.

Another area of remarkable achievement is adult and literacy education. Within a quarter of a century, the number of adult education centers rose from 54 in 1971/1972 to 139 in 1996/1997, with the number of students increasing from 4,192 to 18,255 for the period.[15]

Taking into consideration the number of students, schools and organized classes, both government and private, the overall figures in the UAE become impressively high, as shown in Table 7:12.

TABLE 7:12

Education Aggregates in the UAE
(1995/96 to 1996/97)

Scholastic Year	Students	Teachers and Administrative Staff	Classes	Schools
1995/96	530,256	42,817	22,226	1,132
1996/97	514,746	43,578	22,014	1,170

Source: UAE Ministry of Education, Education Statistical Bulletin, Summary, 1996–1997.

The development of education in the UAE can be seen more clearly when considering the budget allocation of the Ministry of Education (see Table 8:12). The increase in education funds relative to the overall budget of the UAE, particularly after 1992, places the UAE at the forefront of GCC countries and Iran in terms of educational expenditure.

TABLE 8:12

Comparison between Education and Government Budgets (1993–1997)

Financial Year	Government Budget (Million Dirhams)	Ministry of Education Budget (Million Dirhams)	Education Budget as percent of Government Budget
1993	17615.4	2657.3	15.1
1994	16047.3	2771.9	17.3
1995	17949.0	2927.4	16.3
1996	18254.2	3044.6	16.7
1997	19863.0	3461.0	17.4

Note: Dirhams 1 million = US$275,00.
Source: Ministry of Education, Statistic and Documentation Branch, Bulletin no. 15, 1996–1997, 2.

According to a 1997 UNDP's Human Development Report, education expenditure as percentage of government budget in the UAE for the years 1992–1995 was 17.1 percent, much higher than that of Bahrain

(12 percent), Kuwait (10.9 percent), Oman (12.5 percent) and Iran (15.9 percent). The proportion was increased again in 1997 to 17.4 percent. While this is considered high by international standards, the proportion of education expenditure as a percentage of GDP is about 2 percent, a low percentage even when compared to other GCC countries.

When assessing education budget components, it appears that the bulk of the allocation goes toward salaries and construction, with very little going to research and development (R&D). For example, in Singapore, educational allocations reached 19.2 percent in 1980 and increased to 24.8 percent in 1995.[16] While a large portion of Singapore's funds (7–8 percent) goes to education R&D, the larger part of UAE's education budget goes to salaries, leaving only 1 percent for educational R&D.

Higher education, like general education, has also experienced significant growth in the past 20 years. The first UAE university was established in 1977 at Al-Ain. It has now grown in terms of number of faculties and student population (approximately 14,459 students by 1997/1998), and has produced about 17,100 graduates since its establishment, the majority of them females. Furthermore, the university has established relationships with overseas universities for the training of medical and agriculture science students, as well as for UAE students seeking further higher education qualifications.

FIGURE 1:12

UAE University Student Enrollment (Selected Years)

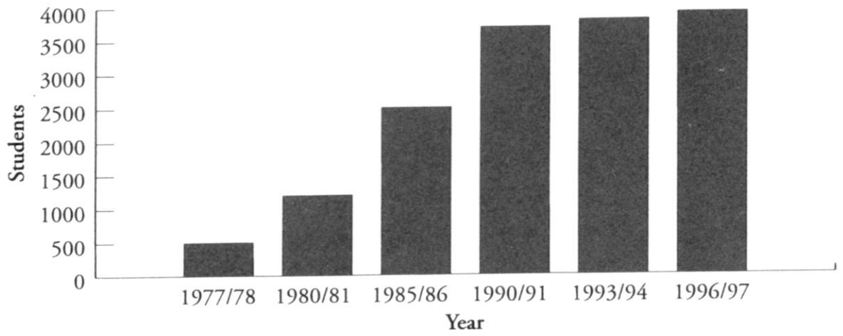

Source: UAE University Annual Report (Several issues).

The 10-college network of Higher Colleges of Technology (HCT) provides training for UAE nationals through a program of two- to four-year

obtained scholarships to study abroad in 1995/96 were in science-oriented programs.[20]

A closer analysis of the link between the vocational education system and the labor market would reveal that the connection is very weak. The labor market has 35,000 jobs in technical, service and administrative areas every year, but the technical education schools and the higher education system turn out a very small number of nationals in relation to market needs. If the current labor force and education graduates rates continue to grow at their present rates, it is expected that the education institutions would fulfill only 7 or 8 percent of the demand for labor by the year 2005. According to a report prepared by the Department of Technical Education/Ministry of Education, the vocational education system meets less than 10 percent of the demand for middle management jobs. The report argued that the number of graduates in five occupational groupings (mechanics, commerce, agriculture, electrical and electronics) ought to be increased five-fold in the next fifteen years in order to meet half of the demand.[21] This means the labor market will continue to tap into its pool of expatriate labor to meet its immediate needs. Such reliance on expatriate labor will have a depressive effect on wage levels in certain sectors and occupations, thus driving away nationals further from productive employment in technical fields.

It is expected that technical education is likely to develop further in the coming years when the necessary academic and administrative infrastructure is completed. However, if certain areas of specialization do not equally develop, it will not be possible to meet existing and emerging needs of the labor market.

In this context, a reassessment of the effectiveness of vocational and science education is required to enable the UAE to meet future challenges.

Training

Post-school training complements the educational process and addresses the gaps in the individual's educational profile. Training also helps adapt the labor force to new job methods. Given the giant leaps in modern technology and the speed by which information becomes outdated, training has become necessary to keep up with the new needs of the labor market, to raise productivity and to maintain the desired standards of proficiency.

There are generally three kind of post-school training.

1.   Pre-service training, which provides the newly-employed with the skills necessary for the work environment.
2.   In-service training, which upgrades old employees' skills and helps introduce new work methods.
3.   Out-service training, which reflects specific individual interests and helps develop personal skills and hobbies.

Most firms do not favor pre-service training as it is costly, particularly when they can easily draw on labor from a pool of qualified, cheap expatriate labor. This attitude has adversely hampered efforts to integrate the national labor force into the labor market. On the other hand, in-service training is more common and is widely used in both public and large private sector organizations.

Training is delivered by many providers, grouped into three major categories. The first category includes centers established by government departments and semi-government organizations. The aim of agency-specific training centers is to upgrade the skills of national employees in order to facilitate their job mobility within the organization, replace expatriates, keep up with the rapid technological changes, and adapt to the needs, objectives and plans of respective organizations. Examples of these centers include those of Abu Dhabi National Oil Company's Career Development Center (ADNOC), Etisalat Corporation, Abu Dhabi's Electricity and Water Department, Ministry of Defense and the Police Department.

Second, training can be provided by National Centers which are supported by government subsidies and are income-generating as well. These centers are more specialized and cater to public and private sector employees. Examples include the Institute for Management Development or the Emirates Institute for Banking and Financial Studies.

Finally, pre- and in-service training are provided at private sector education and training centers. Today there are over 50 institutions of this kind. Some of these institutions represent overseas universities and colleges, and thus provide degree or diploma programs. Most of the training offered is largely centered around English language teaching, computer training and specific management courses.

All of these education and training institutions operate independently and are not officially recognized by the Ministry of Higher Education and Scientific Research. Only five training institutions are recognized by the Ministry of Higher Education and Scientific Research (see Table 12:12). The remaining colleges/institutes operate without the direct supervision of the Ministry. Approximately 48 percent of students in the (accredited) private education and training institutes in 1996/1997 were UAE nationals, compared to 52 percent in 1995/1996 and 60 percent in 1994/1995.

Detailed data on the number of trainees, areas of training and training expenditure of the non-credited institutions are either not available at all or inaccurate and unreliable.

Such centers served the needs of the population well in the early stages of development. They have, however, many deficiencies as outlined below.

- They do not apply to a range of important occupational areas or skill levels.
- They have failed to gain industry and government recognition. Many qualifications, courses and individual subjects were not recognized beyond the institutions within which they were obtained.
- Training has been based on a time-served approach and lacked emphasis on meeting the needs of modern workplaces. Course graduates are "qualified" but not necessarily "competent."
- The centers suffered from a limited ability to articulate from one level of qualification to the rest. Those who obtained vocational qualifications often found them to be of limited value when entering other levels of education.
- The private sector training providers are driven by the profit margin and cost-cutting rather than by the quality or appropriateness of training, and thus may not be in harmony with national goals and objectives.

Reforms of the private training sector have not been seen as essential by the government. As the majority of training providers are not accredited, they are therefore not monitored or even evaluated. In view of the limited capacity of the public training sector to cope with the increasing demand, the number of private training providers has mushroomed. More students are opting now for private education, particularly expatriate students as well as students from other GCC countries.

TABLE 12:12

Students in Accredited Private Universities and Colleges in the UAE by Nationality (1994/1995 to 1997/1998)

	1994/95			1995/96			1996/97			1997/98		
	Nationals	Non-Nationals	Total	Nationals	Non-Nationals	Total	Nationals	Non-Nationals	Total	Nationals	Non-Nationals	Total
Al Ain Scientific College	61	173	234	186	316	502	173	320	503	338	458	796
Ajman's University of Science and Technology	86	488	574	537	1,785	2,322	895	2,779	3,674	666	2,098	2,764
Islamic and Arabic Studies College	687	103	790	1,334	287	621	1,597	471	2,068	1,606	528	2,135
Dubai Medical College	50	90	240	11	24	35	22	35	57	78	152	230
Dubai Police College	221	-	221	682	201	883	658	208	866	-	-	-
Etisalat Engineering College	105	-	105	119	-	119	143	-	143	-	-	-

Source: UAE Ministry of Higher Education and Scientific Research, 1998.

In short, in order for the training sector to be effective and relevant, a better mechanism is required to monitor its operation. Changes of the private training sector are needed to take place in tandem with changes in the broader education system and with other microeconomic reforms.

Policy Change in Education

Due to the dramatic changes that are taking place in the world, particularly in the UAE, the role of the education system has become the focus of critical analysis. This has resulted in a series of rather severe criticisms of the education system in the UAE. Some of these criticisms include:

- unclear and conflicting missions and goals, which may be seen in close relations to problems and discrepancies in study programs and curricula
- inappropriate methods of teaching and learning (inadequate use of technology)
- inflexible curricula and programs which lead to high drop-out rates and long duration of studies
- inadequate resources for higher education and scientific research
- problems in the structures of administration and management, and
- growing gap between quality of graduates and labor market needs.

Probably as a consequence of a certain combination of those important shortcomings, student outcomes, particularly in higher education, are often viewed as unsatisfactory, either in terms of measured achievement or in more qualitative respects.

Quantitative expansion of education in the UAE has perhaps served its purpose well over the past two decades, but is obviously not sufficient to ensure the qualitative shift required by changing technology and the labor market. Accordingly, the Ministry of Education set up a committee on educational development which embarked on a set of important objectives including:[22]

- expanding and redefining the concept of education in different stages to incorporate basic education skills, Islamic teachings as well as science, culture and vocational matters
- re-orienting the educational system in light of society's needs, while balancing collective and individual needs

- reinforcing the principles of justice, participation and creativity in the different stages of education
- stressing the importance of educational planning, implementation and evaluation, and boosting research, evaluation and follow-up techniques
- diversifying the types of education and sensitizing it to the needs of society by providing appropriate educational opportunities to talented, average and disadvantaged learners, and
- stressing traditional and modern values in the educational process and developing the tools of learning, criticism, initiative and dialogue.

The Ministry has adopted a number of programs which aim to overhaul the education system. Some of these programs are underway and include adult literacy, teacher training and school administration, educational policy and research, special education, educational information systems, education research and military education. These programs remain of particular importance to the educational process as a whole in the sense that they develop the potential abilities and skills of students and citizens.[23]

More recently, the Ministry of Education announced the preparation of a comprehensive strategic plan to develop the education system in the UAE. The plan and its programs are based on the realization that a qualitative change in the objectives, structure, curricula and techniques of education are needed, as well as a balance between national interests and the dictates of the modern age. However, it is too early to judge the success or failure of these changes, but observers believe such change may not achieve the desired outcome because the objectives remain vague, "top–down" and are likely to be imposed from above. This may result in measures being ignored, resisted or contested by educators who have been increasingly perceived as implementers of policies constructed elsewhere and by other people. At the same time, it leaves out a major area of the education system – for example, private schools which are operating under no direct supervision of the Ministry of Education with completely different philosophies, objectives and delivery mechanisms, some of which may not be educationally or culturally appropriate.

However, the policy change is important for a number of reasons.

- It acknowledges the vital part that education plays in the structural change of the UAE economy.

- It marks a significant change in government thinking regarding the role of general education vis-à-vis vocational and science-oriented education, and its relationship to national goals.
- It reveals the government's determination to harness the education system to respond to major UAE economic problems and challenges. Not only did the government suggest that there was a need for greater reforms in education, but also that the balance and emphasis of the system needed to change so that it could better meet the long-term needs of the economy and the labor market.

The thinking behind the suggested changes to the education system in general has been paralleled by specific initiatives in higher education. The government has made no objections to the establishment of private universities (and even private training institutions), and has sought to develop a balance between the traditional independence of the education system and the perceived need to link it more closely with the skill needs of the economy. The argument is now for a convergence of general and vocational education, more flexibility and a better articulation between previously segmented sectors, and encouragement of young people to stay much longer in the education and training system. Proponents of change argue in favor of an "outcome" approach to higher education whereby graduates emerge from the system with certain attributes which would equip them for the world of work. If this notion of quality is accepted, then not only will the largely meaningless distinction between vocational or technical and general education be further eroded, but the traditional gulf between higher and vocational education will have been narrowed. The outcome is perceived to serve national interests in the form of value-added human capital and improved employment options for sectors of the population, thus helping neutralize the negative effects of "pre-market" imbalances.

These changes may not enjoy wide acceptance in some sections of the education sector. They argue that the function of the education system is not to prepare generations for economic consequences and microeconomic reforms but rather their main function is to train people to think. Many others argue that the marketization of education, while appearing to offer efficiency and flexibility, may contribute to social stratification and national disharmony.[24] Without the direct and targeted intervention of government in the labor market, skill shortages may result, and the nationalization effort of the labor force will be undermined. This is very much true in the case of the UAE where the labor market is fairly open and unregulated, and where the issues of skill formation and the means by which skills are developed can be obscured. Michael Piore, for example, has argued that where labor market regulation is weak, there is no incentive for employers to invest and use new technologies in a way which raises the value added and the quality of work.[25] Rather, weak labor market regulations lead to a vicious circle whereby profit is extracted through "sweatshop" wages and low productivity. In effect, what regulated labor markets do is to create incentives for entrepreneurs to invest in capital-intensive forms of production in order to generate the high value added to pay the wage levels set by the regulated labor markets.

In any case, the changes marked the beginning of a policy shift in UAE education. For the first time, education is being openly considered in utilitarian terms and being judged by the extent to which it is succeeding in advancing "national goals." This direction is perceived to add quality and flexibility to the national labor force on which UAE's economic future depends.

Education for the Future

There is no doubt that the current education system is unable to sustain future development, cope with change and realize desired national goals. The inability of the present curricula and structure to keep up with rapid technological developments, new demands of the labor market, modern communications and the information age poses a serious threat to the future of UAE society and economy.

The evolving information technology society will mean further fundamental changes with consequences that cannot yet be clearly visualized. The volume of scientific knowledge doubles once every seven years. As new information is generated every day, highly sophisticated networks are being built and continuous efforts are being made to master the techniques of information retrieval and analysis. A fair knowledge of the computer, the Internet, modern means of communication and the English language is now a must. The growing speed of obsolescence is bound to create changes. In an extreme situation, if a graduate's knowledge becomes obsolete within ten years or so and if all graduate education is provided by higher education institutions, these institutions must change in order to keep up with innovation and developments.

Early in the next century, we will expect a significant trend in education reflected in loosening the once-tight coupling between kinds of higher education and career paths. Educational programs would have to prepare students for a much wider range of professions, and serve as starting points for on-the-job (OTJ) training and continuing education rather than as a finishing school. People will need a broader and better knowledge base to be able to equip themselves for working in tomorrow's market.

In this context, should government simply expand the existing system of education or is it necessary to introduce a more differentiated system of education and research with several tasks and ambitions? Should the system involve other actors beside the state? In addition, should the present pattern of delivery be the same or be modified to cope with specific labor market characteristics and new job arrangements which have changed the way one's lifetime is organized?

The transitions between education and work and between work and education or retirement are becoming fluid and reversible. Many people return to school to improve their education after their first employment. The greater involvement of women in employment forces a greater flexibility in the organization of life and working time for men. In such a situation, the education system would come under increasing pressure to adjust. However, for many educators, the existing education system is complex enough as it is now. Trying to cope with all the possible changes and their ramifications on a system-wide planning basis is next to impossible. In this context, it is important to recognize the evolving nature of educational change and labor market development to facilitate change, and attempt to develop broad guidelines or framework within which the system can continually modify its approach or strategies and where cur- riculum and administration can be reconciled to facilitate effective change.

Having reviewed present UAE educational policy and its philosophy as well as international changes and reforms, a number of characteristics of effective learning are considered appropriate for future education which need to be incorporated in future strategies. These include:

- promoting rational and critical methods of thinking
- enhancing creativity and innovation

- satisfying labor demands
- a flexible and responsive curriculum
- core competencies
- continued learning, and
- reinforcing citizenry.

Promoting Rational and Critical Methods of Thinking

The rapid flux of information carries with it foreign – particularly Western – cultural values, which are difficult to screen or eliminate by any traditional sorting mechanism. As local cultures and values are likely to be influenced or compromised by this contact, it is necessary for the student to be able to manage, monitor, judge and critically assess in a rational way what is useful and what is not. That is, regulating one's learning and keeping oneself concentrated and motivated are important roles of the education system.

Enhancing Creativity and Innovation

Creative thinking depends partly on personal endowment and partly on methodological training. Education should inspire self-confidence in learners and stress the patterns of consciousness, thinking and behavior which make them more capable of participating effectively and creatively in social, political and technological fields.

Satisfying the Labor Demands of New Technology and Work Organization

The education system should highlight the skills required for continuous adaptability to new developments in technology and economy which are transforming the means of production, generally creating new services and products. This requires better training links between industry and technical education providers in order to provide appropriate, high quality education and training that keep up-to-date with change.

Flexible and Responsive Curriculum

In the next century, teaching methods and curricula will need to be goal oriented as well as structurally different, emphasizing the skills of critical and scientific thinking and self-learning. New curricula needs to incorporate new educational ideas, scientific research methods, problem-solving and, at the same time, continue to contribute to the cultural enrichment of society.

Core Competencies

Structural changes in work organizations have meant changes in the skills required of members of the labor force. The range of skills required will vary considerably across firms and among groups. Some specialization of skill is likely to continue but each worker will require a wider range of technical skills (multi-skilling). Various skills and educational disciplines require competence in certain key subjects such as mathematics, computing, language and other sciences. The new system of education should stress such interdisciplinary aspects and their extended applications and problem-solving uses.

Continued Learning

Education and learning are not limited to specific time or age but rather are ongoing. Learners do not get the kind of certificate awarded to students of regular educational institutions. Continued learning should be developed to provide students with the opportunity to seek personal advancement and fulfillment and give another chance to those who have failed in the formal system, those who were not successful in the transition from school to work, and those who wish to change direction at a more advanced stage of their life and learn new skills.

Reinforcing Citizenry

In the face of growing internationalism, it is important for developing nations to strengthen the sense of citizenship, and the ability of citizens to participate in different walks of life. Education should reinforce loyalty to the homeland. It should also teach the youth the significance of identifying with national objectives and priorities and the means for effective participation in civic life.

These characteristics of effective learning imply a major alteration in the position and role of students in that not only must they engage in demanding learning activities but they must also become agents in their own acquisition processes. It also requires drastic changes in the role of teachers. The new century requires education facilitators rather than merely information providers. They are expected to create an intellectually stimulating climate with models of learning and problem-solving activities. They must broaden their roles, and increase their involvement in needs analysis, program development, accreditation and evaluation.

Further Reforms

The process of structural change is a phenomenon common to most advanced countries, and the need to develop human resources and improve skill levels is recognized in even the most highly successful economies. Thus the US, Canada, the UK, Germany or Sweden have all recently introduced reforms in their education and training systems as a major strategy for increasing their competitiveness[26] as well as assisting disadvantaged groups to maximize benefit of their stock of human capital.

The UAE education and training system should continue with its efforts to reassess its educational philosophy and approach, and reform its structures and delivery mechanisms – particularly those responsible for developing student personality, capabilities and readiness to the world of work.

Considering the strategic significance of these reforms and what is being developed in this area and throughout the world, a number of other initiatives are suggested as outlined below.

- Establishing the Higher Council for Education and Training Board to oversee the education and training sectors, and plan future direction in line with national goals.
- Developing a comprehensive strategy on the privatization of education and growth of private education.
- Developing appropriate labor market regulations which encourage investment in human capital and the use of capital-intensive production.
- Integrating education and training by such methods as assessment of prior learning, articulation arrangements between provisions, setting competency standards for general education and developing

new models for upper years of schooling which link industry and education.

- Breaking down the dichotomy between technical/vocational and general education, and thereby developing an integrated set of options for all youth up to age 18 and 19.
- Encouraging life-long learning and training programs in industry.
- Developing research into vocational education and training.
- Improving training opportunities for adults.
- Improving training for educators.
- Facilitating the transition from school to work.
- Encouraging partnership between industry and through the development of apprenticeship systems.

Conclusion

There is no doubt that the UAE has made significant strides in developing its human resources. These achievements are a reflection of the government's commitment to the process of balanced national development and trained labor force to sustain growth and progress. However, the process is by no means flawless. The necessary changes of the UAE economy and labor market depend on education and the training system and have, in turn, presented educators with a series of challenges.

The inability of the higher and technical education system to cater to a changing and evolving labor market raises serious concerns for policy makers who are trying to reduce reliance on foreign labor. However, there is potential for the system to improve, requiring a clearer vision and an integrated strategy.

The education system needs to take a different course in a short period of time, moving away from the traditional approach to a more flexible and responsive system that promotes critical thinking, citizenry and creativity, and produces a well-qualified multi-skilled workforce capable of dealing effectively with the challenges of modern age.

Education is the engine of change and is changed by it. The challenge is for education itself as it becomes a more active participant in setting the agenda for change.

13

Developing the United Arab Emirates Workforce for 2015

Roger Benjamin

As we look to the twenty-first century, new workforce challenges for all countries are emerging. All countries may be seen as local economies that are increasingly faced with the problem of responding to the same globalization challenges. Although all states must respond to similar challenges of a worldwide integrated market economy that rewards highly trained, productive workforces, irrespective of their geographic position, each country faces different internal challenges regarding the nature of their workforces and anticipated future trends. This chapter examines the workforce challenges facing the United Arab Emirates (UAE) and proposes a strategic plan as a response – a strategic plan modeled after a similar plan being developed for managing workforce development in the United States.[1]

The basic outline of the argument is as follows. Although all countries face similar global economic challenges, they start from different positions based on the nature and skill level of their workforce. In projections of male, female or family earnings to the year 2015, significant gaps and undesirable trends will appear. It is important to understand where these gaps occur. In the case of the UAE, a diverse, multinational workforce with differing levels of human capital (education levels) exists along with the workforce of UAE nationals. The focus of this chapter is on the UAE component only. How do the projections of the UAE workforce compare with similar projections for either neighboring countries or countries elsewhere at similar or different stages of economic growth? The assessment is that the UAE workforce has certain points of comparative advantages and comparative weaknesses as they face the future. Since education and training are the main remedy to any perceived workforce deficiencies, the next step is to suggest an audit of all UAE education and training assets, particularly the post-secondary education and training assets that are the critical UAE infrastructure public policy tools for improving workforce skill and training levels. Education and training assets refer to all institutions from workforce training centers, technical institutes, colleges, universities and employers. The audit will uncover misalignments and gaps in the education and training structure compared to the UAE's projected human capital needs. Out of this exercise should come a clear set of education and training priorities for the UAE to develop. In the emerging global economy, the quality of a state's workforce (human capital) is the only asset that will count. The stakes are therefore very high. The UAE economy, like all other local economies, will be at one or another economic development stage. UAE governmental and economic leaders will prefer to be at a continuously improving, rather than declining or stagnating, level compared to other countries that will be increasingly focusing on their human capital enhancement.

The Key Questions

The following is a list of key questions that need to be considered. Suggested answers are largely covered throughout the remainder of this chapter.

- What is the shape of the UAE economy today?
- What will the economy look like in 2015?
- What should the economy look like in 2015?
- What is the shape of the UAE workforce today?
- What will it look like in 2015?
- What should the workforce look like in 2015?
- What is the structure of the education system, particularly the post-secondary education and training system today?
- What should the post-secondary education and training system look like in 2015?

What is the Shape of the UAE Economy Today?

Based on the UAE Central Bank Annual Report for 1992, the salient characteristics of the economy broken down into terms of major sectoral origin of gross domestic product are roughly as follows: crude oil accounts for 43 percent; agriculture and fishing 2 percent; manufacturing 8 percent; transport, storage and communications 5 percent; construction 11 percent; commerce and hotels 11.5 percent; finance and insurance 7 percent; real estate 5.5 percent; and government services 13 percent. UAE nationals make up approximately 10 percent of the total workforce and slightly over 1 percent of the private sector. The bulk of the workforce, therefore, is expatriate in nature.

What Will the Economy Look Like in 2015?

Unless steps are taken to alter current trends, the shape of the UAE economy in 2015 will be similar to the current economy's mix. This would mean that crude oil would still account for over 40 percent of the gross domestic product. The remainder of the economy would be similar in mix to the current situation and there would be heavy reliance on expatriates in the workforce.

What Should the Economy Look Like in 2015?

While it is presumptuous for an ill-informed outsider to make recommendations about which questions should be most salient for policy makers in the UAE, there are two obvious issues to consider in addition to looking at emerging worldwide trends that may be of interest to colleagues in the UAE.

First, in looking to the future, policy makers will no doubt attempt to lower UAE's heavy reliance on crude oil exports to support the economy. Over-reliance on a single economic sector is a problem with which UAE leaders must deal. What, for example, are the oil and gas reserves in the UAE? How long are they projected to last? There is a growing international concern about environmental issues which may well translate into a serious effort to develop alternative energy sources.

The second problem is how to increase the participation of UAE nationals in the workforce. Heavy reliance on expatriates may be feasible today, but will it be so in 15 to 20 years? As the economies of South and Southeast Asia develop, their citizens may prefer to remain at home. In any event, it would appear to be an important social – as well as economic – goal to increase substantially the participation of UAE nationals in the workforce.

In thinking about future workforce issues in the UAE, it may be of use to consider the workforce trends and issues facing other countries – such as the US – which would provide a set of benchmarks concerning problems confronted by policy makers elsewhere. The American case is not presented as the end goal to which UAE policy makers should aspire. However, the American economy is a relatively open market. Thus the global economic trends impacting on the US may predict what UAE leaders may expect to confront over the next few decades.

FIGURE 1:13
Increasing Importance of Skills in the Global Economy

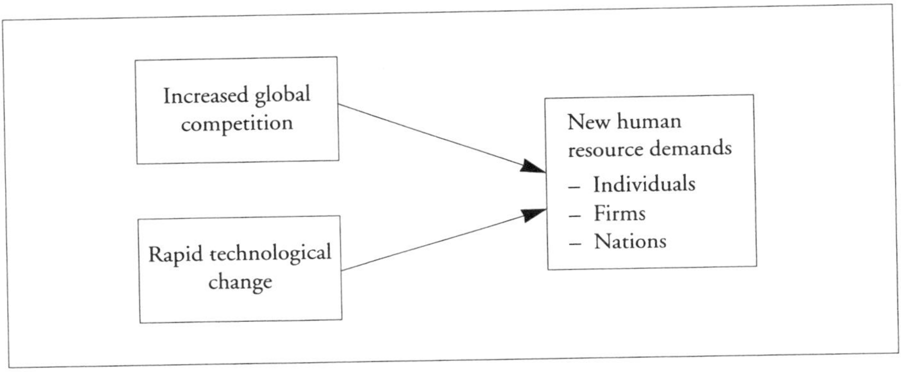

Worldwide Trends and the American Case

The combination of increasingly rapid technological change and global competition places a greater premium on skill or higher educational attainment (see Figure 1:13). Companies can shift production offshore to take advantage of lower wages in other countries. Via the Internet, multinational companies can operate on a 24-hour basis. This places an increasing strain on individuals, firms and nations.

Figure 2:13 shows the distribution of hourly wages among all male workers in real terms, adjusted for inflation and indexed to 1976. (In other words, 1976 is shown as a base, and wages estimated for subsequent years are shown as a percentage of what they were in 1976.) The figure shows only male wages, but disparities in female wages are growing at about the same rate. The top line shows changes in earning levels for workers at the 90th percentile of all male wage earners. It shows slow growth over the 20 years extrapolated out to the future. The message here is that the highest paid workers will hold their own to 2015. Those in the 50th percentile – workers right in the middle of the distribution – have lost about 14 percent in real wages over the 20 years; by 2015, they will be earning about 25 percent less than they earned in 1976. But the most striking consequence of current trends shows up in the figures for workers in the bottom 10 percent. If current trends continue, these workers will be earning little more than half of what they earned in 1976.

FIGURE 2:13
Long-Term Trends in Hourly Wages of Male Workers

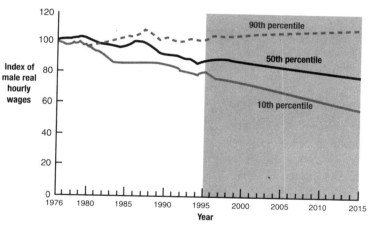

Source: US Department of Commerce, *Census of Population: Social and Economic Characteristics,* Washington, DC, 1990.

The question is: what is the most important factor in determining the level of income? The answer is the level of education. Figure 3:13 shows the distribution of real hourly wages of male workers in the United States by education level. Men with a college education have kept pace with inflation over the 20-year period, men with some college education have seen a decline in real income of 14 percent, and men with only a high school diploma have lost 18 percent. Meanwhile, real wages of high school drop-outs have declined by 25 percent.

FIGURE 3:13
Education and Income: The Intimate Link

By 2015 only college graduates will hold their own

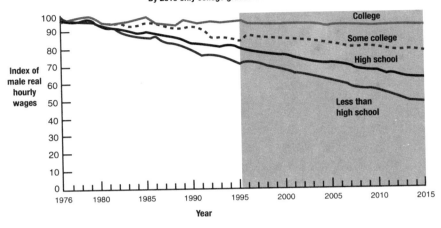

Source: Economic Policy Institute, "Hourly Wage for Men by Education," http://www.epinet.org/fids20.html (January 22, 1998).

If these lines are drawn out another 20 years using the same rates, the result is devastating for the US. By 2015, male workers with only a high school education will have lost 38 percent of what comparable male workers earned in 1976. And those without a high school diploma will have lost 52 percent in real earnings over the same period. If the US economy continues to place a high value on a college-educated workforce, which I believe it will, then only college graduates will be able to hold their own economically out to 2015. Those who attend some college will not do badly, but those who stop pursuing an education before or after graduating from high school will lose ground over their working lives.

I present two additional illustrations that suggest what future trends in global workforce trends will be. First, again from the American case, consider the changes of occupations as a percent of the labor force, as shown in Figure 4:13.

In the US, the growth in professional and technical occupations, in the white collar sector, has been extraordinary – almost 350 percent just in the past 40 years alone. The question for policy makers in the UAE is: what do these American comparisons suggest for the UAE workforce goals over the next 15 to 20 years?

FIGURE 4:13
Occupational Sectors as a Percentage of the Labor Force
(1900–1991)

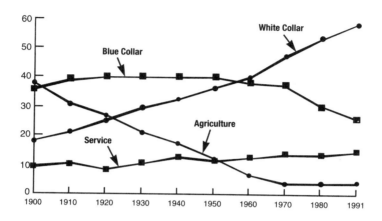

Source: US Department of Commerce, *Census of Population: Social and Economic Characteristics,* Washington, DC, 1995.

Finally, I end this section by presenting Figure 5:13 which charts Moore's Law, the doubling of computing power every 18 months.

FIGURE 5:13
Rapid Technological Change: Explosive Growth in Computer Power

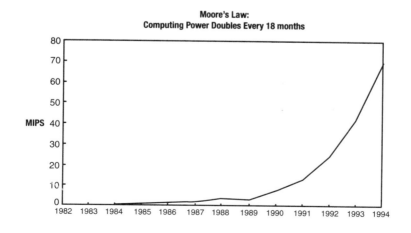

I do so to suggest that as we end the twentieth century, we are beginning another economic transformation based on the microchip, which is the heart of the information revolution. Web-based Internet services will take the place of much of our commercial activities of today. This revolution offers great promise for societies such as the UAE because the transformation may allow the country to leapfrog over existing technologies into this emerging information-based economic world. Of course, this revolution, like all revolutions, also presents dangers to all those who take part in it. Cultural identity issues loom large. Can any nation-state withstand the technological transformation taking place? What does this mean, in particular, for the UAE?

The Arab States Education System in International Context

The next four figures – 6:13, 7:13, 8:13 and 9:13 – are presented to indicate where the Arab states, including the UAE, stand in relation to other regions of the globe. The positive news is that the trends in enrollment in primary, secondary and tertiary education are all increasing. However, there is much distance to go in order to close the gap between the Arab states and Europe and the US.

FIGURE 6:13
Primary Education: Gross Enrollment Ratios (GER) by Gender and by Region, 1980 and 1995 (in Decreasing Order of Female GER in 1995)

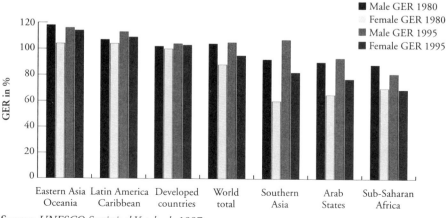

Source: *UNESCO Statistical Yearbook*, 1997.

FIGURE 7:13
Primary Education: Percentage of 1994 Cohort Reaching Grade 5 for Selected Developing Countries

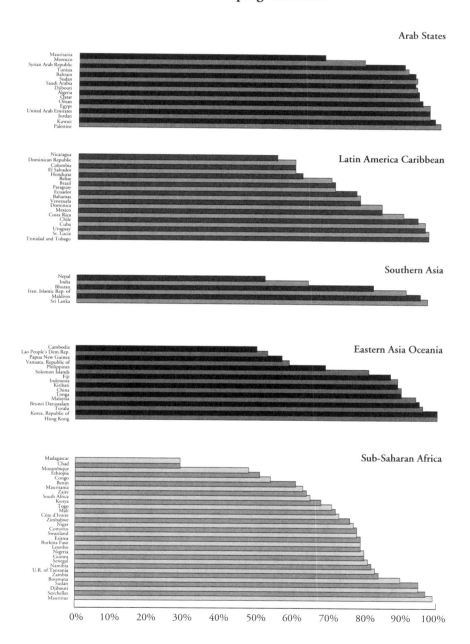

FIGURE 8:13

Secondary Education: Gross Enrollment Ratios (GER) by Gender and by Region, 1980 and 1995 (in Decreasing Order of Female GER in 1995)

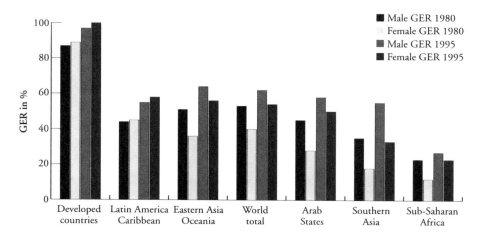

Source: *UNESCO Statistical Yearbook*, 1997.

FIGURE 9:13

Tertiary Education: Gross Enrollment Ratios (GER) by Gender and by Region, 1980 and 1995 (in Decreasing Order of Female GER in 1995)

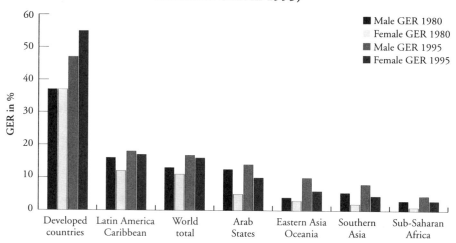

Source: *UNESCO Statistical Yearbook*, 1997.

The UAE Education System

Next, I turn to describe the UAE education system against the backdrop of these summary statistics that place the Arab states in international context. (See the tables that follow.)

TABLE 1:13
Number of Pre-Primary Schools

Year	Number of Schools	Teachers	No of Students
1980/81	20	359	17,263
1985/86	32	590	35,360
1993/94	65	2,886	56,428

Source: *UNESCO Statistical Yearbook,* 1997.

TABLE 2:13
Number of Primary Schools, Teachers and Pupils

Year	Number of Schools	Teachers	Pupils
1980/81	200	5,424	88,617
1990/91	200	12,526	228,980
1994/95	200	15,449	262,628

Source: *UNESCO Statistical Yearbook,* 1997.

TABLE 3:13
Secondary Level

Year	Teaching Staff	Number of Pupils
1985/86	4,237	62,082
1990/91	8,565	107,881
1994/95	12,577	159,840

Source: *UNESCO Statistical Yearbook,* 1997.

Although the UAE, like other Arab states, lags behind Europe and North America in educational infrastructure, the trends are largely positive. The number of students and teachers in pre-primary schools has increased substantially (see Table 1:13), more than doubling since 1980/81. In post-secondary education, there have also been large increases in the absolute number of teachers and students since 1980.

TABLE 4:13
Post-Secondary Education by Field

Year	Law/Social Science	Maths/Natural Science/Computers	Engineering	Agriculture
1991/92	838	266	281	185

Source: *UNESCO Statistical Yearbook,* 1997.

TABLE 5:13
Post-Secondary Education – Universities and Equivalent Institutions

Year	Number of Teaching Staff	Number of Students Enrolled	Percent Female
1980/81	50	2,646	46
1991/92	354	8,668	N/A

Source: *UNESCO Statistical Yearbook,* 1997.

TABLE 6:13
Post-Secondary Education – Other Training Institutions

Year	Number of Teaching Staff	Number of Students Enrolled
1980/81	50	215
1991/92	354	1,737

Source: *UNESCO Statistical Yearbook,* 1997.

Table 7:13 also lists the graduates of universities by field in 1992. This list indicates the relatively small number of graduates in the natural sciences, engineering, and math and computers as compared to fields such as education, business, law and the social sciences and humanities.

TABLE 7:13
Graduates by Field

Year	Total	Business/ Law/Social Science/ Education Humanities	Agriculture	Natural Science	Engineering	Maths/ Computers
1981	783					
1992	1,371	1,100	29	90	57	43

Source: *UNESCO Statistical Yearbook,* 1997.

TABLE 8:13
Public Expenditures on Education

Year	Total in billions of US$	As percent of GNP	As percent of government expenditure
1980/81	1,460	1.3	10.4
1990	2,280	1.8	14.6
1995	2,927	1.8	16.3

Source: *UNESCO Statistical Yearbook,* 1997.

Conclusion

The percentage of government expenditures to education has increased in the UAE from 10.4 percent in 1980 to 16.3 percent in 1995. This is a strong indicator of increasing awareness on the part of UAE policy makers of education's critical importance to UAE's future. And yet, recall the first section of this chapter which noted economic trends for the future. The gap between the UAE and other regions of the world in educational attainment goals is a serious problem. The trends, from the American case, that suggest the increasing importance of college attendance will also increasingly affect the UAE. This suggests the urgent need to increase the investment in education in the UAE and to increase dramatically the proportion of UAE citizens going on to some form of post-secondary education. If the UAE is not successful in bridging the gap by increasing its number of college graduates, they may be doomed to the bottom of the economic ladder – particularly when oil and gas reserves expire. I end this chapter by posing questions for UAE policy makers.

- What economic points of comparative advantage does the UAE possibly have over the next two decades? Tourism? As a conference center for Arab states? In financial services?
- Can the next generation of students be made computer literate to allow the UAE to leapfrog over other regions of the world in fully entering the information age? For example, can all schools at all levels of education be given sufficient hardware and software? What about the teacher training needed to insure students can use the software properly?

The Internet will give UAE an opportunity to shrink distance to and from other nations all over the world. This could mean a considerable positive shift in UAE's trading relationships and other economic and social transactions.

14

Zayed University: A New Model for Higher Education in the United Arab Emirates

William F. Halloran

In June 1996, His Excellency Sheikh Nahyan Bin Mubarak Al Nahyan, Minister of Higher Education of the United Arab Emirates (UAE), instituted an Advisory Planning Committee (APC) for the Future of Higher Education in the UAE. Composed of individuals who had worked with the UAE University in Al Ain, this committee was asked to examine all aspects of higher education in the country, assess its current status, identify problems, propose solutions, and recommend policies and actions to assure that high quality, federally supported, post-secondary education would be available for citizens of the UAE well into the next century. The committee submitted its report to the Minister in November 1996.[1]

The report recognized the great progress the country had made in a brief period of time in providing education for its young citizens. It also recognized the achievements of the UAE University since its establishment in Al Ain in 1977 and those of the Higher Colleges of Technology (HCT) since their establishment in 1988. It praised the national policy of providing higher education opportunities for all citizens of the country who earn a secondary diploma or its equivalent.

Projected growth of enrollments in institutions of federally supported higher education based on the rapid growth of enrollments in tertiary institutions in the past stands out as an imminent problem. For the past decade, the number of students enrolled in the UAE University and in the HCT has been increasing at an annual rate of between 7 percent and 10 percent. A count of children who have already been born, taken from national census data, indicated that if the country maintains its policy of providing access to higher education for all qualified students seeking it, enrollments will continue to grow at an average annual rate of about 7 percent for the next 10 years. In autumn 1996, total enrollments in federally supported higher education institutions were about 21,000; at that growth rate, they will more than double to about 44,000 by autumn 2006.

APC also noted that a high proportion, 68 percent, of students attending the UAE University and the HCT for the 1996/1997 academic year were females. If other higher education opportunities continue to be available for young men in the government and the private sector, the proportion of female enrollments in federally supported institutions of higher education will rise to about 80 percent of the total in the next few years and then begin to drop. That means places must be found by 2006 for an additional 13,000 female students. With a current enrollment of 13,000 female students, the University in Al Ain is stretched beyond its capacity. Classes are oversubscribed and dormitories are crowded. It makes little sense, APC concluded, economically or practically, to continue building classrooms and dormitories for female students in Al Ain, more than doubling their number by 2006. To the cost of building additional dormitories and classrooms for women students in Al Ain must be added the high cost of maintaining the students in dormitories during the week and transporting them to and from their homes at weekends.

Given these considerations, APC recommended the creation of a new university in the UAE that would initially have two non-residential campuses for female students who live in Abu Dhabi and Dubai, the two major population centers of the country. This recommendation resulted in a decision by the federal Cabinet earlier this year to create a new university named in honor of the founder and President of the UAE, His Highness Sheikh Zayed Bin Sultan Al Nahyan. Zayed University admitted for the 1998/1999 academic year approximately 400 first-year female students to a campus prepared for it in Abu Dhabi and about 1,100 female students to another campus in Dubai. I was invited by the Minister of Higher Education to come to Abu Dhabi for an eight-month period – January through August, 1998 – to assist in the establishment of Zayed University. I would like to set our efforts in their national and international context, and describe briefly the kind of institution we created.

Zayed University

Planning and building post-secondary education institutions to accommodate the large projected enrollment increases is both a challenge and an opportunity. Identifying the necessary resources at the federal level in the UAE will be a major undertaking. Facilities and personnel – faculty and staff – will have to double in the next decade. The percentage of GNP allocated to higher education in the UAE is only 0.6 percent. This is despite the rapid growth over the past two decades of higher education expenditures in the UAE. Per student allocations, moreover, have been dropping in recent years as increasing expenditures have failed to keep up with enrollment increases. If current access policies are maintained, expenditures by the federal government must increase substantially in the decade ahead in order to accommodate the growth in student numbers. Furthermore, the country will need to develop a funding formula that provides a stable base of income for current institutions and those that must be created. That is the challenge.

There is another side of the coin. The UAE now has the opportunity to create new kinds of colleges and universities that are particularly appropriate for its young citizens and capable of moving the country successfully into the next century. The opportunity is similar to that enjoyed by western countries in the 1960s and 1970s when they expanded existing institutions into state systems and created new institutions to accommodate the huge numbers of students who were born in the post-World War Two years – the so-called baby boomers.

The expansion of colleges and universities in the West at that time changed both the structure of higher education and its methods of delivery. New state-supported, non-residential institutions were created in all the major cities of the US, institutions that came to be called Urban Universities. In the UK, new colleges and universities with special missions were produced, along with an expansion and shift in focus of the polytechnics that have now become universities. There were also new publicly supported experimental colleges in the US and elsewhere that were student-centered and designed as alternatives to the established state universities which were becoming larger and more impersonal in their delivery of instruction and other services.

The face of higher education in the West changed dramatically in those decades and, on the whole, the changes were positive. For all the problems of inadequate funding – of sustaining support for the vastly expanded enterprise – that now plague state-supported colleges and universities in the US, those institutions have become a permanent feature of the landscape and continue to attract large numbers of native students and growing numbers of students from other countries. Post-secondary education in the US is frequently said to be one of the country's most popular products. Because of its diversity, open access and ultimately its quality, it rivals even Nike and McDonald's in its attractiveness for people from other countries. The economic prosperity the US has enjoyed in recent years owes a great deal to its huge investment in its higher education infrastructure during the 1960s and 1970s. That investment opened the system to accommodate increased numbers of students resulting from demographics. More importantly, it enabled an unprecedented expansion of the percentage of citizens who were able to benefit from post-secondary education. Fourteen and sixteen years of education ceased to be a privilege for the relatively well-off; it became an expectation for young men and women of all social classes and economic strata. The same can be said for other countries in Western Europe, Australia and Japan where post-secondary education is no longer a luxury, but a right for a large percentage of the population.

On a smaller scale, but with similar consequences for their future, the countries of the Gulf region, including the UAE, can now change existing colleges and universities and build new ones in accordance with new models. As the countries seek to provide places for increasing numbers of college-age people, they have a one-time chance to change the face of higher education in the region. They can, if they choose, equip their young people with the attitudes, knowledge and technical skills that will enable them to flourish as members of the family of nations in the twenty-first century. While the challenges are great, the opportunities are greater. How these countries meet the challenges will affect their ability to prosper and provide satisfying lives for their citizens through the next century.

It is in that spirit, recognizing the long-term importance of the opportunity at hand, that we are engaged in planning, under the far-sighted leadership of Sheikh Nahyan, the new Zayed University. While other campuses of Zayed University may develop in other locations in future years, the first two campuses are being designed for female students in the country's two major population centers. From the start we have been in contact with women educators abroad and with prominent women, including educators, in the UAE, and we have been guided by what they said. Indeed, many women are directly involved in our planning, and women will constitute a significant portion of the campuses' faculty and staff. Leaders of the UAE with whom we have spoken recognize that the country cannot depend for its future prosperity on only half of its population. Women must be prepared to enter the workforce and contribute directly to the business of the country. One of our most important challenges and responsibilities is to undertake the preparation of women nationals for productive roles in society in a way that respects and preserves their traditional roles in that society. Within the country, the UAE University in Al Ain and the Higher Colleges of Technology have been undertaking this task for the past 10 years. A visitor to the UAE in 1989 who returned nine years later would see immediately the difference those two institutions have made in enabling women to participate in the work of the country. Zayed University will join those two institutions in this enterprise and contribute positively to it.

In planning Zayed University, we have adopted as our first principle "student-centeredness." Student learning and student development will form the heart of the institution. Students will spend nine hours a day, five days a week on their campuses. The design of the campuses will foster interaction among students and teachers. Faculty members will work closely with individual students both in class and outside class. Instruction will be interactive; it will encourage students to take responsibility for their own learning and to become lifelong learners. Classes will be relatively small, and instructors will come to know their students as human beings. A unique feature of the curriculum will be the requirement that each student take during the first and second semesters of their first year a University Seminar which will be limited to 15 students. Each semester the seminars will focus on broad topics that interest students and increase their understanding of themselves, their culture and the world. They will prepare reports, deliver those reports both orally and in written form, and engage in discussion of assigned topics during the three hours each week that the seminars take place. We are making a special effort to recruit those who have the ability to make these seminars lively and interesting. The unifying theme of the first semester seminar in 1998/99 will be "The Contemporary City," and the theme of the second semester seminar will be "The City in History."

A second unique feature of the first two campuses of Zayed University will be the emphasis on the most current technology for teaching and student learning. We are acquiring hardware and software that will provide every classroom with computer access for every student. All students will learn the basics of computing using desktop computers during their first semester. They will then acquire a notebook computer to use in all their subsequent classes and for homework assignments. They will take their notebooks to class and plug them in; they will then take them home in the evening for further work. Requiring every student to have a notebook computer is increasingly common at colleges in the US; it will be unique in this part of the world. Our goal is to have every graduate of Zayed University not only computer literate, but also computer dependent. As they go out into the world of work and return to their homes, they will carry their computers with them. Their computers will be their principal link to the information they need for full and productive lives.

The first emphases are on student-centeredness and technological expertise, but what will be the content of Zayed University's curriculum? How will it differ from other universities in the region? Most non-European universities still follow the traditional European model. Students who have been streamed as either arts or science track in their secondary schools are required to choose a specialty – or a faculty – when they enter university. This model assumes entering students have received a broad education at a very high level in their schools and that they are informed enough to choose the direction of their lives at the age of 18 or 19. This model came into being in the nineteenth century when only a small minority of people pursued formal education beyond the secondary level. It remains an appropriate model for some students. Distinguished private secondary schools in some Western countries continue to educate students broadly at a sufficiently high level for them to specialize immediately at university. The model is not appropriate for most young people in the world. Most universities in Western countries have either discarded it or modified it beyond recognition.

For Zayed University, a different model has been chosen. Students will spend their first two years (or equivalent) in classes designed to improve their language and computational skills, and to increase their understanding of their own culture and other cultures of the world. They will study the world's "civilizations" as Samuel Huntington uses the term.[2] In the second year of study, students will be required to take two courses, one each semester, which introduce them to two of the specialties, or majors, offered by the university. Only toward the end of their fourth semester, when their second specialty course is nearly over, will they be allowed to select their field of specialization. This restriction will enable them to make more informed choices.

In selecting the first specialties or majors for Zayed University, we have taken account of the needs of the society and the fact that the first two campuses are for female students. Initially, there will be seven specialties that will, over time, become colleges headed by Deans. These are listed below.

- Education, which will produce excellent teachers for the nation's schools.
- Business, which will produce graduates who compete successfully for top entry-level jobs in local businesses and the local offices of international corporations.
- Information Technology, which will produce graduates who know the latest methods for obtaining, processing and retrieving information.
- Communication Sciences, which will produce graduates who are excellent journalists, able to work successfully in both the print and electronic media.
- Family Sciences, which will produce graduates who are knowledge-able about human development, nutrition and food science, family resource management, consumer science, community development and social organizations, and who are able to train others in these subjects.
- Fine Arts, which will produce graduates who are painters, sculptors, musicians, dramatists and film makers who have a solid understanding of the arts and the important role they play in human societies.
- Arts and Sciences, which will grow out of the courses in the lower division program and in which students will be able to construct broad field specialties that draw on all the resources of the University.

All specialties at Zayed University will include internships that enable undergraduates to experience the interrelationships between their theoretical study and their society. The curriculum of Zayed University is being designed to reflect the typical design of colleges and universities in the US so it will qualify for accreditation – or its equivalent – by regional and professional accrediting associations in the US. That, in turn, will facilitate transfers to US institutions and entrance to US graduate programs for students with those aspirations.

The principal goal of Zayed University is to produce graduates who are prepared to take their place in the workforce of the country and to become leaders of the nation in the twenty-first century. Those of us who are privileged to be involved in planning the university are determined to take advantage of the opportunity to create a new kind of university that combines skill-building with solid learning in the arts and sciences. The carefully sequenced core or general curriculum will generate half the credits required for the bachelor's degree. The remaining credits will be earned in a specialty that includes a continuing emphasis on improving and perfecting language skills, both Arabic and English. Basic to the curriculum of Zayed University is the belief that the ability to communicate effectively in Arabic and English, and the ability to use numbers and evolving technologies, are the skills that will enable citizens of the Emirates to participate fully in the global economy in the twenty-first century.

Those involved in moving Zayed University from the drawing board to reality are deeply aware of their responsibility. They know that other institutions, indeed other campuses of Zayed University, will come into being in the UAE with different goals and objectives and different curricular designs. Those will be welcome and healthy developments. In the meantime, we are designing two campuses that will provide a relevant, useful and humane education for women who enroll in Zayed University. Our success, and their success, will be vital for the continued well-being and prosperity of the country and for the quality of life their children will experience as they grow to maturity in the decades ahead.

Conclusion

Jamal S. Al-Suwaidi

Education and Human Resources Development in the Gulf: Challenges of the Twenty-First Century

Education and learning are key components in the development of society which have changed greatly with the tremendous scientific achievements of the twentieth century. The current pace of innovation promises new achievements that may surpass the imagination and transcend the limits of reality as we know it, with far-reaching implications for the social, political and economic systems of the future.

The new communications revolution and emerging social needs and aspirations make it necessary to direct more attention to education, particularly in the developing countries. Furthermore, the persistence of conflict in many parts of the world and the widening gap between developed and developing countries create additional responsibilities in the process of defining the objectives and methodology of education. However, efforts in the developing countries tend to emphasize quantity in education at the expense of quality due to pressures arising from high population growth rates and the inadequacy of funds allocated to education, training and continued learning.

In this context, it is important to examine the domestic challenges that lie ahead in the field of education and study the successful experiences of other countries in order to formulate an appropriate education policy that addresses the future needs of Gulf societies.

In today's highly competitive global environment, many countries must contend with major structural changes while maintaining their political stability and the integrity of their social systems. Educational reforms are needed to deal with this new situation, to contribute to economic growth and to lead to better management of resources in both developing and developed countries.

[331]

New approaches to education, training and human resources development must be implemented. Education planners should always keep an eye on new developments in this dynamic field and be ready to respond by modifying their approaches accordingly. Fruitful educational planning also requires the commitment of greater financial resources to boost the effectiveness and relevance of the system and to develop new educational tools to enhance the productivity of future generations.

Consequently, the role of teachers, students and schools will be very different in the learning environment of the twenty-first century. Educators will have to master new personal and professional skills to replace traditional approaches. The information menu available to students will not be limited to textbooks, as students will train to access a new range of experiences. Parental guidance will be crucial in preparing the younger generation to deal properly with these new learning conditions.

The new curricula must emphasize basic skills, initiative, dialogue and rational and critical thinking. They should be designed to reflect national culture and values, and to promote creativity, innovation and the capacity for continued learning, the ultimate aim being to meet the demands of the work environment in the new high-tech age.

Now more than ever before, coordinating the role of schools, universities, training centers, industry and the community is crucial as reform of education and training systems is becoming a collective rather than an individual responsibility. One recommendation I have is the establishment of a National Council for Education and Training to undertake the overall planning of education in the UAE. Another recommendation is to create a Ministry of Information and Technology to coordinate the efforts of government bodies in the areas of information management, technology transfer, training, labor and human resources development.

Moreover, it is important to bring higher education closer to career paths, to remove barriers to the entry of nationals into the Gulf labor market and to enhance the productivity and efficiency of the workforce. Greater integration of education and vocational training will make it necessary to introduce English and information technology courses throughout the different stages of education, and to design new models to assess prior learning and link education in the upper schooling years with industry.

Furthermore, extracurricular activities should be emphasized to allow for more social interaction and cultural communication. Faculty members should be offered rewarding compensations, and teachers' colleges should insist on the highest academic and professional standards. I recommend that a center be established to design curricula and to develop teaching methods and school management techniques. Private education institutions must not be ignored in the process. Their role and the extent to which they serve national interests should be carefully assessed and supported.

The projected increases in Gulf populations, the need for long-term economic diversification projects and the demands of the constantly changing international environment make it necessary to set more aggressive policies to develop national labor assets in the Gulf. Indeed, these imperatives place the issue of human resources development high on national and regional security agendas for the next millennium.

Contributors

Hamad Ali Al-Sulayti is the Assistant Secretary General for Political Affairs in the GCC General Secretariat. He has held several posts, including Director of Educational Planning and Cultural Affairs, Ministry of Education from 1972 to 1975 and Assistant Deputy Minister for Planning, Curricula and Cultural Affairs, Ministry of Education, Bahrain from 1975 to 1982. He has been Acting Secretary General of the Bahrain Center for Studies and Research since 1981.

Dr. Al-Sulayti has a PhD in Methodology and Librarianship from Indiana University (US). He earned his MA in Management and Educational Planning from the American University in Beirut, Lebanon. He has authored several studies and books, including *Political Decision in Educational Development: Implications for Natural Planning Requirements of Scientific and Technological Development in the Gulf Region, The Strategy of Education Curricular Development in Bahrain* and *A Global View of Education in GCC States and Its Role in Human Development.*

Jamal S. Al-Suwaidi is Director of the Emirates Center for Strategic Studies and Research in Abu Dhabi, United Arab Emirates (UAE) and Professor at the UAE University in Al Ain. He has taught courses in political methodology, political culture, comparative governments and international relations at the UAE University and the University of Wisconsin.

Dr. Al-Suwaidi earned his MA and PhD degrees in Political Science at the University of Wisconsin-Milwaukee and his BS degree in Political Science at Kuwait University. He is the author of numerous articles on a variety of topics including perceptions of democracy in Arab and Western societies, women and development, and UAE public opinion on the Gulf crisis. Dr. Al-Suwaidi is author of "Gulf Security and the Iranian Challenge," *Security Dialogue* vol. 27, no. 3 (1996); a contributing author to *Democracy, War and Peace in the Middle East*; editor of *The Yemeni War: Causes and Consequences*, the award-winning

Iran and the Gulf: A Search for Stability, and *The Gulf Co-operation Council: Prospects for the Twenty-first Century.*

Adnan Badran joined UNESCO as the Assistant Director-General for Science in 1990, in charge of all science activities. He was nominated as Deputy Director-General and Secretary General of the Third World Academy of Sciences in 1993. Prior to his work with UNESCO, Dr. Badran was the Minister of Agriculture and then Minister of Education in Jordan. He also created the Higher Council for Science and Technology of Jordan.

He has written numerous articles on higher education, science and technology policy, and published 60 scientific papers and books in biosciences. He is co-author of the book *Strategy of the Development of Science and Technology in the Arab World*, and author of *At the Crossroads: Education in the Middle East.*

William E. Becker is Professor of Economics at Indiana University, Bloomington (US). He is editor of the *Journal of Economic Education* and also serves on the editorial board of the *Economics of Education Review*. He is the author of *Statistics for Business and Economics*, co-author of *Business and Economic Statistics*, and co-editor of *Academic Rewards in Higher Education*, *Econometric Modeling in Economic Education Research* and *Higher Education and National Growth*. His most recent volume on the economics of education is co-edited with William Baumol, *Assessing Educational Practices: The Contribution of Economics.*

Dr. Becker earned a BA degree in Mathematics from the College of St. Thomas, an MA degree in Economics from the University of Wisconsin, and a PhD in Economics from the University of Pittsburgh (US). In 1987, he received the Henry H. Villard Research Award for his work in education.

Roger Benjamin is the Director of RAND's Education Program and President of the New York-based Council for Aid to Education. He is leading the national effort to restructure post-secondary education and training in the US. Prior to his appointment in 1990 to RAND, he was Professor of Political Science, Dean and Provost at the University of Minnesota, and Provost and Senior Vice-Chancellor at the University of Pittsburgh (US) from 1966 to 1989.

Dr. Benjamin is the author and co-author of 11 books and monographs and numerous articles including *The Limits of Politics: Collective Goods and Political Change in Postindustrial Societies, The Democratic State, Fairness; The Scylla and Charbydis of US-Japan Relations, The Redesign of Governance in Higher Education, Balancing State Intervention: The Limits of Transatlantic Markets,* and *Breaking the Social Contract: The Fiscal Crisis in Higher Education.*

Robert A. Cornesky was the first to apply what is known as Total Quality Management (TQM) to the administration of colleges and universities, including the classroom. He was the first to publish a book on applying TQM to academic settings. Since 1991, Dr. Cornesky has served as President of his own consulting and publishing firm, which specializes in providing TQM services to educational institutions. He recently served as Provost and Vice-President of Institutional Excellence of Southwest Colleges of Naturopathic Medicine and Health Sciences.

His recent books include *Six Steps to Quality: How to Plan and Implement a Continuous Quality Improvement Program for Colleges and Universities, Quality Indices: Self-Assessment Rating Instrument for Educational Institutions, Turning Continuous Quality Improvement into Institutional Practice: The Tools and Techniques* and *Quality Fusion: Turning Total Quality Management into Classroom Practice.*

Don Davies is Founder of the Institute for Responsive Education (IRE), a non-profit public interest organization working to encourage family–community–school partnerships. As an outgrowth of his work with IRE, Dr. Davies established the League of Schools Reaching Out, a 90-member international association of schools working toward education reform through parental and community involvement. From 1974 to 1996, he was Professor of Education at Boston University (US). He served as Associate and then as Deputy Commissioner of the US Office of Education during the late 1960s and early 1970s.

He received his BA and MA degrees from Stanford University (US) and his PhD from Teachers College, Columbia University (US). He is the author of many policy reports and several books, including *Portrait of Schools Reaching Out, Communities and Their Schools* and *Where Parents Make a Difference.*

William F. Halloran is currently a Professor at the University of Wisconsin-Milwaukee (US). In 1989, he helped review the academic programs of the Department of English of the UAE University. In 1990, he assisted in developing a new curriculum for all first-year students in that university, and has since continued to provide advice to the Minister of Higher Education regarding many aspects of the UAE University and higher education in the UAE. He served on a task force that prepared a report on the future of higher education in the Emirates in the fall of 1996; from the fall of 1997, he assisted with the establishment of a second national university, Zayed University, which admitted its first class of students in September 1998 on two campuses – one in Abu Dhabi, the other in Dubai.

Dr. Halloran received his undergraduate degree from Princeton University (US) and his PhD in English from Duke University (US). He served as Dean of the College of Letters and Science at the University of Wisconsin-Milwaukee from 1972 to 1995. In 1989, he received an honorary doctorate from the Justus Leibig University in Giessen, Germany, in recognition of the contribution he made to the exchange of students and faculty between that university and UWM.

Masanori Hashimoto is currently a Professor and Chairman of Economics at Ohio State University, where he has been since 1987. Previously, he taught at Wayne State University, the University of Washington (US), and Indiana University (US). During 1983–84, he was a National Fellow at the Hoover Institute at Stanford University. Professor Hashimoto's research specialties are labor economics and applied microeconomics.

He received his BA degree from Columbia University (US) and his PhD in Economics from Columbia University. He has published many articles on the theory of specific human capital and its applications, specifically comparative studies of Japanese and American labor markets. Professor Hashimoto has testified twice before US Senate subcommittees on the effects of minimum wage laws. He currently serves as an associate editor for the *Journal of the Japanese and International Economics* and on the board of editors for the *Journal of Economic Development*.

Norman Henchey is a Professor Emeritus of Education at McGill University in Montreal (Canada). He is also a consultant for the Government of Canada's Department of Human Resources Development, has been Chair of a national working group to establish an Internet-based Canadian Education Research and Information System and has been studying school–work transition as part of a Canadian report for an OECD project on the transition from school to working life.

He holds a PhD in education from McGill University, Canada. His teaching and research interests include curriculum theory and development, the future of education and education policy in Canada. He has a number of publications and has given over 400 presentations and workshops in Canada, the US, Europe, the Caribbean and Africa.

Abdullah Mograby is a Senior Researcher at ECSSR. He has vast academic and professional experience as an economist, a management consultant and a policy advisor in Australia. He has held senior government and research positions, and played an important role in developing and implementing labor market policies and services in the State of New South Wales (NSW).

He obtained his BA and MA degrees in Economics from Macquarie and Sydney Universities (Australia), respectively. He received his PhD degree in Economics from Macquarie University. Dr. Mograby is a former member of the NSW Advisory Council on Multicultural Affairs and the State Advisory Committee on Immigration Research and former Director of the Middle East Research and Information Association.

Daphne Pan is Director of the Centre for Development of Teaching and Learning, and Senior Lecturer at the Department of English Literature at the National University of Singapore. Her current responsibilities include conducting workshops on learning and committee work. While in the Department of English Language, she teaches Shakespeare and Local Literature.

She obtained her BA degree from the University of Singapore, and MA degree from York University, Toronto (Canada). Some of her research on education includes *Teaching of Literature in Singapore Schools, Teaching Methods and Educational Objectives: A Multi-disciplinary Study at the National University of Singapore, Ensuring Quality in Higher Education* and *Teaching Creative Thinking: Some Answers, but Mostly Questions.*

Margaret Riel is the Associate Director of the Center for Collaborative Research in Education in the Department of Education, University of

California (US). She also teaches courses on school reform with technology in the graduate program at the University of California, Irving. She has been involved in developing and researching models of "Network Learning," especially cross-classroom collaboration designs.

Dr. Riel's early research at the University of California, San Diego, involved experimentation with models for educational networking and the use of interactive learning technology, particularly in the area of writing and social science. She designs and moderates Learning Circles on the International Education and Resource Network. She published the Learning Circle Curriculum Guide on-line. She writes extensively on issues related to the implementation and evaluation of on-line learning environments.

Monther Sharè is Dean of the Faculty of Economics and Administrative Sciences at the Hashemite University, Jordan and Vice-President for Administrative Affairs since 1996. Previously, he was Chairman of the Economics Department as well as Assistant Dean and Deputy Dean of the Faculty of Economics and Administrative Sciences at Yarmouk University, Jordan. He has also worked as a consultant and economic expert in Saudi Arabia and Yemen.

He obtained his BA degree in economics and political science from Beirut Arab University, his MA degree in Economics from the University of Wales (Swansea, UK) and a PhD in Economics from Wales. His publications include books and articles in the field of economics of education, labor economics, international trade and development.

Geoff Spring is Secretary of the Department of Education and is responsible to the Minister of Education and the Minister of Tertiary Education and Training for the overall management of the Department of Victoria, Australia. He is currently Chair of Language Australia, the Open Learning Technology Corporation and the Ministerial Council on Education, Employment, Training and Youth Affairs, and Working Party on the Australian Vocational Training System. Prior to moving to Victoria, he was Secretary of the Northern Territory Department of Education for nine years and former Chair of the Australian Curriculum Corporation.

Mr. Spring's work as an education reformer is highly regarded across Asia Pacific. Since 1980, he has been associated with the Southeast Asia and Pacific Region Educational Administrators and Managers Symposium, serving as Chair for 10 years. He is committed to the globalization of education and has overseen the development of several Memoranda of Cooperation in Education and joint educational programs between the Government of Victoria and many Asia Pacific countries.

Notes on the Text

INTRODUCTION

1 See Jeremy Rifkin, *The End of Work: The Decline of the Global Labor Force and the Dawn of the Post-Modern Era* (New York: G.P. Putnam's Sons, 1996).

1
THE ROLE OF EDUCATION AND TRAINING
IN ECONOMIC DEVELOPMENT

1 For example, in 1759 Adam Smith wrote that "no acquirement which can possibly be derived from what is called a public education can make any sort of compensation for what is almost certainly and necessarily lost by it." Adam Smith, *The Theory of Moral Sentiments* (Indianapolis, IN: Liberty Classics [1759] 1976), 363–4. John Maynard Keynes added, "Education is the inculcation of the incomprehensible into the indifferent by the incompetent." Jon Winokur, *The Portable Curmudgeon* (New York: Nal Books, 1987), 89. In the US, Frank Knight viewed teaching as "a form of original sin." Frank H. Knight, *Freedom and Reform: Essays in Economics and Social Philosophy* (New York: Harper & Brothers, [1947] 1982), 386. Nobel Laureate George Stigler considered teaching to be preaching.
2 Donald McCloskey, "Writing as a Responsibility of Science: A Reply," *Economic Inquiry* vol. 30, no. 4 (October 1992): 689–96.
3 Paul H. Douglas, "Are There Laws of Production?" *American Economic Review* vol. 38, no. 1 (1948): 1–41; Theodore W. Schultz, "Education and Economic Growth," in N.B. Henry (ed.) *Social Forces Influencing American Education* (Chicago, IL: National Society for the Study of Education, 1961).
4 John W. Kendrick, *Productivity Trends in the United States* (Princeton, NJ: Princeton University Press, 1961); Edward Denison, *The Sources of Economic Growth in the United States and the Alternatives Before Us*, Supplementary Paper no. 13 (New York, NY: Committee for Economic Development, 1962); Angus Maddison, "Growth and Slowdown in Advanced Capitalist Economies: Techniques of Quantitative Assessment," *Journal of Economic Literature* vol. 25, no. 2 (June 1987): 649–98; John Pencavel, "Higher Education, Productivity, and Earnings: A Review," *Journal of Economic Education* vol. 22, no. 4 (Fall 1991): 331–59.
5 Robert Lucas, "On the Mechanics of Economic Development," *Journal of Monetary Economics* vol. 22, no. 1 (July 1988): 3–42; Paul Romer, "Endogenous Technological Change," *Journal of Political Economy* vol. 99, no. 5 (1990):

S71–S102; Robert Solow, "A Contribution to the Theory of Economic Growth," *Quarterly Journal of Economics* vol. 70 (February 1956): 65–94; and "Growth Theory and After," *American Economic Review* vol. 78, no. 3 (June 1988): 307–17.

6   Theo Eicher, "Interaction Between Endogenous Human Capital and Technological Change," *Review of Economic Studies* vol. 63 (1996): 127–44.

7   William J. Baumol, "Multivariate Growth Processes: Contagion as Possible Source of Convergence," Mimeograph (November 7, 1991).

8   Robert J. Barro and Xavier Sala-i-Martin, *Economic Growth* (New York: McGraw-Hill, Inc., 1995); Lant Prichett, *Where Has All the Education Gone?* Policy Research Working Paper 1581, The World Bank Policy Research Department, March 1996: 1–48.

9   Gary S. Becker, "A Note on This Issue," *Educational Researcher* vol. 18 (1989): 4.

10 Kevin Murphy and Finis Welch, "Wages of College Graduates," in William E. Becker and Darrell Lewis (eds) *The Economics of American Higher Education* (Boston, MA: Kluwer Academic Press, 1992), 121–40.

11 John H. Bishop, "Incentives to Study and the Organization of Secondary Instruction," in William E. Becker and William Baumol (eds) *Educational Practices: The Contribution of Economics* (Cambridge, MA: The MIT Press, 1996), 161–82.

12 The "value added" by education is often measured by the difference between an after-program test score (post-test) and a before-program test score (pre-test). The change in test scores may have administrative value to school administrators, but they may have little relationship to the economic concept of value. Just as water has a high "value in use" but a low "value in exchange," some basic skills, such as an ability to reconcile a checkbook, may have high value in use but low value in exchange. Other skills may have a high value at one point in time and little value at another – for example, the ability to manipulate a slide rule has fallen in value with the availability of the cheap hand calculator. Although some skills may be viewed as essential for education, their market value is determined by demand and supply. The normative beliefs of a school administrator, faculty, business leader or politician about the importance of intellectual skills are elusive without reference to what employers are paying for the bundle of skills embodied in the graduate, and what skills they desire from the graduate. William E. Becker, William Greene and Sherwin Rosen, "Research on High School Economic Education," *American Economic Review* vol. 80, no. 2 (May 1990): 14–22, and an expanded version in *Journal of Economic Education* vol. 21, no. 3 (Summer 1990): 251–3.

13 Eric Hanushek, "The Economics of Schooling: Production and Efficiency in the Public Schools," *Journal of Economic Literature* vol. 24, no. 3 (1986): 1141–77. Larry Hedges, Richard Lane and Rob Greenwald (1994a, 1994b) use a meta-analysis involving an aggregation of p-values to cast doubt on Hanushek's assertion regarding the relevance of expenditure on instructional methods in generating test scores: "Does Money Matter? A Meta-Analysis of Studies of the Effects of Differential School Inputs on Student Outcomes," *Educational Researcher* vol. 23, no. 3 (April 1994): 5–14 and "Does Money Matter? A Reply to Hanushek," *Educational Researcher* vol. 23, no. 4 (May 1994): 9–10. Contrary to their interpretation, however, a case-by-case review of their presentation of Hanushek's data suggests that the focal point of much discussion in education,

the teacher/pupil ratio (or class size), is irrelevant in explaining student performance when measured by test scores. As Hanushek (1994) concluded, their method of aggregation may be producing their results.

In concluding that certain instructional variables are insignificant in explaining student test scores, however, researchers like Hanushek are accepting the null hypothesis of no average effect in the populations. Statisticians cringe at the idea of "accepting the null hypothesis." The null hypothesis of no learning effect can never be accepted for there is always another hypothesized value, in the direction of the alternative hypothesis, that cannot be rejected with the same sample data. The Type II error inherent in accepting the null hypothesis is well known but largely ignored by researchers in education and economics alike.

The power of the test (ability to reject the null hypothesis) can always be raised by increasing the sample size. Thus, if statistical significance is the criterion for a successful instructional method, then ever larger sample sizes will "deliver the goods." Statistical significance of an instructional method might be demonstrated with a sufficiently large sample, but the difference in change scores will likely be trivial on multiple-choice tests of 25 to 40 items (the number of questions typically required to demonstrate a valid and reliable test that able students can complete in a 50- to 75-minute period). Differences of only a few correct answers in pre-test and post-test comparisons of control and experimental group results are the rule, not the exception, even after adjusting for sample selection.

14   David Card and Alan Krueger report a consistency across studies showing the importance of school quality on a student's subsequent earnings. They recognize that tests can be administered easily at any time in the education process and thus provide a cheap tool for monitoring programs. In recognition of time lag for measuring earnings effects, they recommend the use of drop-out rates as an alternative to test scores for immediate and ongoing program assessment. After all, unless students finish their programs, they cannot enjoy the potential economic benefits. David Card and Alan Krueger, "The Economic Return to School Quality," in William E. Becker and William Baumol (eds) *Assessing Educational Practices: The Contribution of Economics* (Cambridge, MA: The MIT Press, 1996), 161–82.

15   Russell E. Rumberger defines surplus schooling as the number of years of schooling completed minus the number required by the job, which is determined by the Dictionary of Occupational Titles or as subjectively reported by the worker; see "The Impact of Surplus Schooling on Productivity and Earnings," *Journal of Human Resources* vol. 22, no. 1 (1987). He as well as others then claim that over-education has occurred in the US, with Verdugo and Verdugo even claiming that the returns to overschooling are negative; see "The Impact of Surplus Schooling on Earnings: Some Additional Findings," *Journal of Human Resources* vol. 24, no. 4 (1989). Elchanan Cohn, George Psacharopoulos and Shahina Khan as well as others challenge this surplus schooling thesis. See Cohn, "The Impact of Surplus Schooling on Productivity and Earnings," *Journal of Human Resources* vol. 27, no. 4 (Fall 1992); Psacharopoulos, "Returns to Investment in Education: A Global Update," *World Development* vol. 22, no. 9 (1994) and Cohn and Khan's "The Wage Effects of Overschooling Revisited," *Labor Economics* no. 2 (1995). Even if the rate of return to schooling is below market

rates, if people are willing to invest in their education, they must be deriving some value above and beyond the purely monetary return. As long as they finance their own education, there is no added social cost and from a social welfare view, these people are not overeducated.

16 For example, if H = 25 people, L = 75 people, A_H = 200 I.Q. points, A_L = 100 I.Q. points, W_H = US$200, W_L = US$100, and p = US$1.00, then W = US$125. If education costs US$60, then the individuals who know that they are of higher ability will pay for schooling. As a result of the school's screening function, the market identifies those who are more able. Each more able individual gains US$15 (US$200 – US$60 – US$125), for a total group gain of US$375 (25 X US$15). The private return to education for these individuals is clearly positive. Each lower-ability individual, however, has a loss of US$25 (US$125 – US$100) for a total group loss of US$1,875 (75 X US$25). The social return to education is thus negative, as the population as a whole lost US$1,500 (US$1,875 – US$375).

Instead of just ranking students from most to least able on a unidimensional scale, the education industry may be helping students find their comparative advantages. If higher education is inexpensively screening individuals by providing them with credentials for a given type of job for which they are relatively best suited, then education is serving a productive function to the student and society as well. It is providing a positive kind of externality in the form of information.

For example, assume that there are two types of output produced by society, each valued at US$100 per unit, and two kinds of individuals. Individuals of characteristic A_x (plumbers, for example) can produce 100 units of output X and zero units of output Y. Individuals of characteristic A_y (lawyers, for example) can produce 100 units of output Y and zero units of output X. If the size of the population is 100, with 50 of each type of individual, then random assignments of jobs would imply an output for society (GNP) of US$5,000. On the average, half of society would be in the wrong occupation. With equal income distribution, however, all individuals share in the output, with each individual receiving US$50.

If higher education can assist individuals by assigning them to (or by helping them identify and select) their most productive jobs at a cost of less than US$5,000, then society and individuals can gain from screening. At an educational cost of US$1,000, for instance, society's net GNP would be US$9,000. All individuals would be in their most productive occupation. With the cost of education paid equally and with equal income distribution, each individual would receive US$90. The private and social return to education is clearly positive for this type of educational assessment even though there is no change in a person's abilities produced by the screening.

17 If self-financing is not an option then government financing may be justified but this does not require a subsidy. The availability of government financing is only required to correct market imperfections associated with the noncollateralization of the human capital.

18 Kingsley Amis, *Lucky Jim* (New York: Viking Press, 1958).

19 The screening hypothesis cannot be tested directly because innate ability is unknown. Cognitive skills, schooling and wages are usually observed together with self-selection, leading to the more able getting more education and higher pay. Little support for the screening hypothesis has been found in the few data sets that have enabled testing. To control for innate ability, Orley Ashenfelter

and Alan Krueger use data from a sample of twins raised apart in the United States and find a large and significant schooling effect; "Estimates of the Economic Return to Schooling from a New Sample of Twins," *American Economic Review* vol. 84, no. 5 (December 1994): 1157–73. Harold Alderman et al. find that cognitive achievement, and not school screening that is devoid of achievement, raises wages; see "The Returns to Endogenous Human Capital in Pakistan's Rural Labour Market," *The Oxford Bulletin of Economics* vol. 58, no. 1 (February 1996): 29–55.

20 Within developing countries there is concern that greater growth in the school age populations, with fixed educational budgets, is leading to falling expenditures per student and falling quality (increasing student/teacher ratios implying less teacher attention per student, lower teacher salaries and in turn poorer quality teachers, lower expenditure on materials per student implying less exposure to new technologies etc.). Lant Pritchett finds no relationship between population growth and schooling growth in LDCs but using Hanushek's work suggests that this is not a problem because the relationship between costs and test scores is not sufficiently tight that per pupil costs can reliably be used as indicators of quality; see *Population Growth, Factor Accumulation and Productivity*, Policy Research Working Paper 1567, The World Bank Policy Research Department, January 1996: 10–14. Again, this misses the point that test scores need not be the relevant measure of the educational output. As discussed later in this chapter, the absolute and growing divergence of LDC per capita gross domestic product from the per capita GDPs of developed countries may reflect the importance of school quality.

21 In the US, higher education is not centralized and there is no attempt to have "uniform quality." In France, on the other hand, degrees bear the imprimatur of the state, not the individual institution. These institutions do not have the administrative freedom to select students on alternative criteria or to respond flexibly to their students' varying abilities or needs. In Australia, attempts to maintain uniform standards with rapid expansion of institutions and enrollments have resulted in claims that universities other than the eight or ten established institutions have become "parking places" for the government to keep young people out of the unemployment statistics. Similarly, *The Economist* (October 4, 1997) reports that, "Arab universities are awash with students, only a fraction of whom graduate successfully." For universities to be more than parking places they must have incentives to respond to their students' needs. When they do, universities can be more than credentialing agents.

22 William E. Becker, "Teaching Economics to Undergraduates," *Journal of Economic Literature* vol. 35, no. 3 (September 1997): 1347–73.

23 Externalities are social benefits (or costs) that cannot be captured by the individual making the investment. They are benefits that spill over to others but they do not have a market value for which property rights can be assigned to the person making the decisions. The social benefit can be monetary, as in raising the earnings growth rate of everyone, or they can be nonmonetary, as in making for better conversation on a street corner. For example, for two identical individuals each with like educations, the one living in a country with a higher average education level likely enjoys better health care, less crime and other benefits associated with education for which his or her individual decision to invest in education has no

effect. As discussed later, the growth rate in the country with the higher education level is also likely higher but yet an individual investing in education cannot capture or has no property right to the added growth associated with his or her contribution to the average education level. The externalities of education can be negative (well-educated criminals or unwanted social unrest around college campuses) but on balance the externalities of education are considered to be positive.

24 If the cost of an additional year of schooling is US$100.00, and the expected differential earnings to accrue from this additional schooling over the next three years are US$110.00, US$121.00 and US$133.10, then the internal rate of return to this schooling is 10 percent. That is, r = 0.10 makes the cost equal to the present value of the expected differential earnings flow as represented in the following equation:

$$100 = [110/(1+r)] + [121/(1+r)^2] + [133.1/(1+r)^3]$$

Instead of calculating an internal rate of return investment decisions could also be made by comparing cost (US$100) with the present value of the expected differential earnings which is calculated by inserting a discount rate (r) that might be the rate at which funds may be borrowed. The internal rate of return approach and the net present value approach need not lead to the same decision regarding school choice; see William E. Becker, "Why Go To College? The Value of An Investment in Higher Education," in Becker and Lewis (eds) *The Economics of American Higher Education* (Boston, MA: Kluwer Academic Press, 1992), 105–6.

25 Anil Deolalikar, "Gender Differences in the Returns to Schooling and in School Enrollment Rates in Indonesia," *Journal of Human Resources* vol. 28, no. 4 (Fall 1993): 899–932.

26 The use of the semi-log earnings equation is justified on theoretical grounds by assuming that earnings increase by compounding raises over time. If starting earnings of the i-th person in year 0 are Y_{i0}, then annual raises at a rate of c implies earnings in year t of Y_{it}, where:

$$Y_{it} = (1 + c)^t Y_{i0}$$

with continuous compounding at rate c, earnings grow exponentially by:

$$Y_{it} = e^{ct} Y_{i0}$$

In practice, the natural log transformation required to scale earnings has a greater effect at higher earnings and a straight line sample relationship typically can be demonstrated between $\ln Y_i$ and any one of the explanatory variables

In cross-sectional age-earnings scatter plots, where there is higher variability in earnings at advanced ages, use of the semi-log specification is justified even without reference to the underlying time compounding process. McMahon, however, calls attention to the need for an adjustment for the time process in cross-sectional estimates of the return to schooling that ignore upward shifts in the age-earnings profiles; Walter W. McMahon, "Conceptual Framework for the Analysis of the Social Benefits of Lifelong Learning," *Education Economics* (Summer/Fall 1998). Ignoring the time process that tends to drive age-earnings profiles up results in a downward bias in the rate of return estimates obtained from Mincerian type estimates of the rate of return to education using cross-sectional data. See also Jacob Mincer, *Schooling, Experience, and Earnings* (New York and London: Columbia University Press, 1974), 83.

27 George Psacharaopoulos, "Returns to Investment in Education: A Global Update," *World Development* vol. 22, no. 9 (1994): 1325–43.

28 Education is not randomly assigned; individuals make their own schooling decisions. Depending on how choices are made, the schooling coefficient in a Mincerian earnings equation may be over- or underestimated. Although many social scientists believe the ordinary least squares estimator is biased upward, Card's review of sample selection problems and development of estimation methods designed to control for sample selection problems suggests that the cross-sectional correlation between education and earnings understates the true effect of schooling; David Card, "Earnings, Schooling, and Ability Revisited," *Research in Labor Economics* vol. 14 (1995): 23–48. Ashenfelter and Rouse, in their large sample study of identical twins, report a 10.8 percent real rate of return to education, where controlling for student ability and family background lowers this estimate by about 25 percent and adjusting for measurement error raises it by 30 percent; Orley Ashenfelter and Cecilia Rouse, "How Convincing is the Evidence Linking Education and Income?" in Ashenfelter and Rouse (eds) *Cracks in the Bell Curve: Schooling, Intelligence, and Income* (Washington, DC: Brookings Institute Press, 1997), 11.

29 Psacharopoulos, op. cit., 1326.

30 George Psacharopoulos and E. Velez, "Does Training Pay Independent of Education? Some Evidence from Columbia," *International Journal of Economic Research* vol. 17, no. 6 (1992): 581–91.

31 Walter McMahon (op. cit.) provides an excellent review of the non-market benefits and externalities associated with education. Wolfe and Zuvekas reconfirm Haverman and Wolfe's estimates that these non-market effects associated with years of schooling are approximately equal in value to the increments to earnings; Barbara Wolfe and Samuel Zuvekas, "Non-Market Outcomes of Schooling," *International Journal of Education Research* vol. 27, no. 7 (1997): 74–94 and Robert Haverman and Barbara Wolfe, "Schooling and Economic Well Being: The Role of Non-Market Effects," *Journal of Human Resources* vol. 19, no. 3 (1984).

32 William J. Baumol, Sue Anne Batey Blackman and Edward N. Wolff, *Productivity and American Leadership: The Long View* (Cambridge, MA: The MIT Press, 1989), Chapter 9.

33 John E. Kendrick, *Productivity Trends in the United States* (Princeton, NJ: Princeton University Press, 1961); Edward Denison, *The Sources of Economic Growth in the United States and the Alternatives Before Us*, Supplementary Paper No. 13 (New York: Committee for Economic Development, 1962) and *Why Growth Rates Differ* (Washington, DC: Brookings Institute, 1967).

34 Maddison, op. cit., 653.

35 Paul H. Douglas, "Are There Laws of Production?" *American Economic Review* vol. 38, no. 1 (1948): 1–41.

36 John Pencavel, "Higher Education, Productivity, and Earnings: A Review," *Journal of Economic Education* vol. 22, no. 4 (Fall 1991): 331–59.

37 Maddison, op. cit.

38 Robert J. Barro and Xavier Sala-i-Martin, *Economic Growth* (New York: McGraw-Hill, Inc., 1995), 352.

39 Gregory Mankiw, David Romer and David Weil, "A Contribution to the Empirics of Economic Growth," *Quarterly Journal of Economics* vol. 107, no. 2 (May 1992): 407–37.

40 Jess Benhabib and Mark M. Speigel, "The Role of Human Capital in Economic Development: Evidence from Aggregate Cross-Country Data," *Journal of Monetary Economics* vol. 24 (1994): 143–73.

41 Barro and Sala-i-Martin, op. cit.

42 Ibid., 431–3.

43 One of the "weak" conditional convergence mechanisms implies that total factor product growth is higher the lower the initial level of gross domestic product. A statistician will recognize this as regression to the mean; an econometrician will say it is simultaneity. In any regression, if the dependent variable is a change measure or percentage change, then using the base measure as a regressor implies an expected negative coefficient. This conditional convergence does not imply absolute convergence, as evidenced by less developed or poorer countries falling behind developed richer countries even though the former's growth rate has been higher than the latter's.

44 In contrast to Becker, Greene and Rosen's (1990) distinction between what markets are rewarding and what test scores are measuring, as condensed in note 12 of this chapter, Douglas North (1990) and Kevin Murphy et al. (1991) argue that entrepreneurs will pursue rent seeking activity if the returns to this activity are higher than alternatives even if the alternatives are more beneficial for society; see North's *Institutions, Institutional Change and Economic Performance* (Cambridge University Press, 1990); and Murphy et al., "The Allocation of Talent: Implications for Growth," *Quarterly Journal of Economics* vol. 106, no. 2 (1991). As North illustrates, if piracy on the high seas is rewarded more than chemical manufacturing, then entrepreneurs will gain the knowledge to be pirates even though it might not be socially beneficial. Murphy et al. find that there is a positive relationship between the fraction of tertiary students studying engineering and economic growth and a negative relationship between the study of law and growth. Although engineers and non-lawyers may find this empirical finding intuitively appealing, policy makers should be reminded that manpower studies have never been shown to outperform the market – i.e., bureaucrats are not good at identifying future manpower needs. What is true, as North writes, is that the personal incentives built into the institutional framework play a decisive role in shaping the types of skills and knowledge that are pursued and the economic development that may or may not follow. If the institutional framework is identifying the "wrong knowledge" and rewarding it in the "wrong way" then society may not benefit even if there is a lot of formal education. William Becker and Sherwin Rosen (1992) discuss the learning effect of alternative forms of assessment and evaluation in schools.

45 William E. Becker and Robert Toutkoushian, "The Measurement and Cost of Removing Unexplained Gender Differences in Faculty Salaries," *Economics of Education Review* vol. 14, no. 3 (September 1995).

46 El Erian et al. blindly follow Prichett in the construction of "human capital" stock measures for six Arab countries. They find no detectable relationship

between GDP and their contrived measure of human capital for Algeria, Egypt, Jordan, Kuwait, Syria and Tunisia for the period 1970–95. They do not, however, recognize the lack of validity in Prichett's or their own attempt to extract a measure of human capital from the present value of logarithmic differences in wages. See Mohamed El Erian, Thomas Helbling and John Page, "Human Resource Development and Economic Growth in the Arab Countries," mimeograph presented at the Joint Arab Monetary Fund/Arab Fund for Economic and Social Development Seminar on Human Resource Development and Economic Growth, Abu Dhabi, UAE (February 1998).

47 Romer (1990), op. cit.: S71–S102.

48 Paul Romer, *Human Capital and Growth: Theory and Evidence*, National Bureau of Economic Research, Working Paper Series, No. 3173 (November 1989): 8.

49 Ibid.: 9–10. Romer adds that technological advancements have not had an effect in the delivery of education: "School instruction today bears a remarkable resemblance to instruction 100 years ago . . . it is not through the school-house that science has its effect on output . . . it is through the introduction of new goods."

50 Julian Simon shocked gloom-meisters by observing that natural resources are not finite in any serious way because their value is derived from the human intellect, which is not limited. Coal, oil and uranium were not valued resources until human innovation created technologies for their use. Similarly, innovation can create new resource mixes that do not rely on these particular inputs. It is the unbounded nature of human knowledge that gives rise to unbounded growth. See Simon's *The Ultimate Resource* (Princeton, NJ: Princeton University Press, 1981) and *The Ultimate Resource Vol. 2* (Princeton, NJ: Princeton University Press, 1996).

51 Baumol et al., op. cit., 195–210.

52 McMahon, op. cit.

53 Donal O'Neill, "Education and Income Growth: Implications for Cross-Country Inequality," *Journal of Political Economy* vol. 103, no. 6 (1995): 1289–97.

54 Robert J. Barro and Jong-Wha Lee, "International Comparicons of Educational Attainment," *Journal of Monetary Economics* vol. 32, no. 3 (December 1993): 363–94.

55 Michael S. McPherson et al. (eds) *Paying the Piper: Productivity, Incentives, and Financing in US Higher Education* (Ann Arbor, MI: the University of Michigan Press, 1993).

2

PARTNERSHIP:
A THEME FOR EDUCATION AND COMMUNITIES IN THE
TWENTY-FIRST CENTURY

1 Jerome Bruner, "The Culture of Education," *The Annenberg Challenge Newsletter* (Fall/Winter 1996), 22–24.

2 Joyce L. Epstein, "Proposal to the Office of Educational Research and Development, US Department of Education" (Boston: Center on Families, Communities, Schools and Children's Learning, Boston University, 1990), 3–6.

3 Some of the major references on this topic are Uri Bronfenbrenner, *The Ecology and Human Development: Experiment by Nature and Design* (Cambridge, MA: Harvard University Press, 1986); Hope Leichter, *The Family as Educator* (New York: Teachers College Press, 1974); David S. Seeley, *Education through Partnership* (Washington, DC: American Enterprise Institute, 1981); Don Davies, *Family, Community and School Partnerships in the 1990's: The Good News and the Bad* (Boston, MA: Boston Institute for Responsive Education, 1996); James S. Coleman, "Families and Schools," *Educational Researcher* vol. 16, no. 6 (August–September 1987): 32–8; and Epstein, loc. cit.

4 The ideas of Durkeim and Tonnies are discussed by Leroy S. Rouner, "Building and Sustaining Community," *The World and I* vol. 5, no. 10, October 1990, 470.

5 William Schambra, "The Quest for Community in Twentieth Century America," *The World and I*, op. cit., 472.

6 Stephen Stoer and Luisa Cortisão, *Projects, Pathways, Synergies in the Field of Intercultural/Multicultural Education* (Lisbon: University of Oporto, 1997), 6.

7 Don Davies, op. cit., 6–7, based on Center for the Study of Social Policy, *Kids Count Data Book* (Washington, DC: Annie E. Casey Foundation, 1993).

8 Statement by the Bishop of Ripon Wisconsin, "Synthesis Paper" (Washington, DC: 21st. Century Learning Initiative, 1997), 13.

9 From a speech by Robert Kennedy, 1967, provided by the National Center for Service Integration, Des Moines, Iowa.

10 Reported by Khalled Al Maeena, senior columnist, *Arab News*, February 25, 1997, Saudi Arabia, from the "Arab View" on the Internet: www.arab.net/arabview/articles/maeena16.html.

11 Byron G. Massialis and Samir Ahmed Jarrad, *Education in the Arab World* (New York: Praeger, 1983), 14.

12 R. Freeman Butts, *A Cultural History of Western Education* (New York: McGraw-Hill, 1955), 430–511.

13 Ira Harkavy, "Progressing Beyond the Welfare State," *Universities and Community Schools* vol. 2, no. 1–2 (Spring–Summer 1991): 3–28.

14 Massialis, op. cit., 28.

15 John Abbott, "School is Not Enough: Learning for the 21st. Century," no. 2 (Summer 1997): 32.

16 Ibid., 29.

17 J. S. Coleman, op. cit.

18 Kettering Foundation, *Creating Citizens Through Public Deliberation* (Dayton, OH: Kettering Foundation, 1997), 1–16.

19 John Dewey, "School and Society," *The Child and the Curriculum* (Chicago, IL: University of Chicago Press, 1943), 6–7.

20 Alexis de Tocqueville, *Democracy in America*, ed. J. P. Maier, trans. George Lawrence (Garden City, NY: Anchor Books, 1969), 5–13.

21 Robert Putnam, *Making Democracy Work: Civic Traditions in Modern Italy* (Princeton, NJ: Princeton University Press, 1994).

22 "Bowling Alone: America's Declining Social Capital: An Interview with Robert Putnam," *Journal of Democracy* (on-line) http:jhupress.jhu.edu/demo/journal-of-democracy/vol6/6.iputnam.html

23 Saad Eddin Ibrahim, "Management and Mismanagement of Diversity, The Case of Ethnic Conflict and State Building in the Arab World," *Discussion Paper*

no. 10 (UNESCO – www.unesco.org/most/ibraeng.htm – August 15, 1997). Also see analysis of recent events in "Civil Society and Democratic Transformation," in *Arab World Newsletter*, April–August issues, 1994.

24 Chicago Innovations Forum. *A Primer for a School's Participation in the Development of Its Local Community* (Chicago, IL: Center for Urban Affairs and Policy Research, Northwestern University, undated, circa 1988), 1–11.

25 Putnam, loc. cit.

26 See, for example, C. Ames et al., *Teachers' School-to-Home Communications and Parent Involvement: The Role of Parent Perceptions and Beliefs* (Baltimore, MD: Center on Families, Communities, Schools and Children's Learning, 1995); J. L. Epstein, *School and Family Partnerships* no. 6 (Baltimore, MD: Center on Families, Communities, Schools and Children's Learning, 1992); and D. Davies, *Partnerships for Student Success* (Baltimore, MD: Center on Families, Communities, Schools, and Children's Learning, 1996).

27 Davies, op. cit., 1–5.

28 Epstein, "School and Family Partnerships," *Encyclopedia of Educational Research* (New York: Macmillan, 1992), 1143–6.

29 Theodore Davies, T. Ooms and S. Jara, *The Family-School Partnership: A Critical Component in School Reform* (Washington DC: Family Impact Seminar, American Association for Marriage and Family Therapy, 1991), 13–16 .

30 Abbott, loc. cit.

31 From an interview with Howard Gardner by Bill Allen, www.ed.psu.edu/dept/ae-insys-wfed/insyst/esd/Gardner, November 14, 1996.

32 Howard Gardner, "Intelligence in Seven Steps," *Creating the Future*, www.newhorizons.org/crgut_gardner.htm

33 Bruner, loc. cit.

34 Abbott, loc. cit., 29–32.

35 The Education 2000 Trust, Response to the White Paper, Broadway (Letchworth Garden City, Hertfordshire), 1, 3.

36 Twenty-First Century Learning Initiative, "Synthesis," *1997 Report of the Education 2000 Trust* (Washington, DC: Rothchild Natural Resources), 1–3.

37 Twenty-First Century Learning Initiative, op. cit., 7; *Education 2000 Trust*, op. cit., 12.

38 Harkavy, op. cit., 4–5.

39 Ameetha Palanki, unpublished, "Parent–Teacher Action Research in American Schools," prepared for the Center on Families, Communities, Schools and Children's Learning 1995, 1–2.

40 Ameetha Palanki and Patricia Burch, *In Our Hands: A Multi-Site Parent–Teacher Action Research Project* (Boston, MA: Center on Families, Communities, Schools, and Children's Learning, 1995), 1–185.

41 Dewey, loc. cit.

42 A final brief afterthought: I have learned that research and examples in one country and culture are useful to those in other countries and cultures who are seeking to improve educational policies and practices. This is what I call the "more distant mirror" phenomenon. Looking at one's problems and alternative solutions at a distance seems to give policy makers, planners, administrators and researchers different ways of thinking about close-to-home problems. Research and successful practice in one country offer support for those who want to act to improve education in another.

Some anthropologists who have studied the process of cultural change point out that "diffusion does not typically involve the replication in one society of some practice developed elsewhere; rather what is transposed is the basic idea, a model – one might even say a metaphor – which is then applied to the particular circumstances of the receiving society." [C. Renfrew, *Before Civilization* (Harmondsworth, UK: Penguin, 1976) quoted in G. Room, *Cross National Innovation in Social Policy: European Perspectives on the Evaluation of Action Research* (New York: St. Martin's, 1986), 10.] We should seize as many opportunities as we can in the years ahead to engage in cross-national and cross-cultural studies and conversation. That is one of the reasons why the ECSSR conference and this volume are so important.

3

INVESTMENT IN HUMAN CAPITAL:
A COST-BENEFIT APPROACH

1 See Maureen Woodhall, *Economic Aspects of Education: A Review of Research in Britain* (Windsor: NFER Publishing Company Ltd., 1972); Maureen Woodhall, "Economics of Education: A Review," in G. Psacharopoulos (ed.) *Economics of Education Research and Studies* (Oxford: Pergamon Press, 1987); and John Vaizey, *The Economics of Education* (London: Macmillan Press, 1973).

2 Adam Smith, *The Wealth of Nations* Book 1, ch. 10, part one (1916), quoted in Mark Blaug, *An Introduction to The Economics of Education* (Harmondsworth: Penguin Books, 1976), 2.

3 Alfred Marshall, *Principles of Economics* Book 6 , ch. 4, para 4 (1890), quoted in Mark Blaug, op. cit., 4.

4 Ibid.

5 T. W. Schultz, "Education and Economic Growth," his contribution to National Society for the Study of Education, in N. B. Henry (ed.) *Social Forces Influencing American Education* (Chicago, IL: University of Chicago Press, 1961).

6 T. W. Schultz, "Investment in Human Capital," *American Economic Review* vol. 51, no. 1 (1961); Edward F. Denison, "Measuring The Contribution of Education (And The Residual) To Economic Growth," OECD Conference on the Residual Factor and Economic Growth, Paris (May 1963), DAS /PD/63.2.

7 As the literature on economics of education in general, and on investment in education in particular is so remarkable in quantity and quality, to conserve space we cite a number of the most important works such as Gary S. Becker's "Investment in Human Capital: A Theoretical Analysis," *Journal of Political Economy* vol. 70, part 2 (October 1962); *Human Capital: A Theoretical and Empirical Analysis With Special Reference to Education* (New York: Columbia University Press, 1964); and *Human Capital* (Princeton, NJ: Princeton University Press, 1964). See also W. L. Hansen, "Total and Private Returns to Investment in Schooling," *Journal of Political Economy* vol. 7, no. 2 (April 1963); Jacob Mincer, "On-The-Job Training: Costs, Returns and Some Implications," *Journal of Political Economy* (supplement) (October 1962); H. P. Miller, "Annual and Life-time Income in Relation to Education: 1939–59," *American Economic*

Review vol. 50, no. 4 (December 1960); John Vaizey, *The Economics of Education* (London: Faber and Faber, 1962); M. F. Leite et al., *The Economics of Educational Costing* (Lisbon: Centro de Economia e Finanças, 1969); G. Psacharopoulos, *Returns to Education: An International Comparison* (Amsterdam: Elsevier Scientific Publishing Company, 1973) and *Earning and Education in OECD Countries* (Paris: OECD, 1975); Mark Blaug et al., *The Causes of Graduate Unemployment in India* (London: Allen Lane, The Penguin Press, 1969); M. Carnoy and H. Thias, *Cost-Benefit Analysis in Education: A Case Study of Kenya* (Baltimore, MD: IBRD, Johns Hopkins Press, 1972); and M. Bowman et al. (eds) *Reading in The Economics of Education* (Paris: UNESCO, 1968).

8 Lester Thurow, *Investment in Human Capital* (Belmont, CA; Wadsworth Publishing Company, 1970), 1.

9 Howard M. Wachtel, *Labor and the Economy* (Orlando, FL: Academic Press, Inc., 1984), 181.

10 Gian S. Sahota, "Theories of Personal Income Distribution: A Survey," *Journal of Economic Literature* vol. 16, no. 1 (March 1978): 10–11.

11 We deliberately avoid the controversy as to whether education is an investment, consumption or a combination of both; see E. Cohn, *The Economics of Education* (Cambridge, MA: Ballinger, 1979); also, Blaug, op. cit., ch. 1; John Vaizey, *The Economics of Education* (London: Faber and Faber, 1962), ch. 2

12 Blaug et al., op. cit., 169; also, H. S. Houthakker, "Education and Income," *Review of Economics and Statistics* vol. 50, no. 1 (January 1969): 24–8.

13 Zvi Griliches, "Estimating The Returns to Schooling: Some Econometric Problems," *Econometrica* vol. 45, no. 1 (January 1977): 1–22.

14 See Cohn, op. cit., 45.

15 Interested readers may consult Jacob Mincer, "Investment in Human Capital and Personal Income Distribution," *Journal of Political Economy* vol. LXVI, no. 4 (1958); E. F. Denison, "Measuring The Contribution of Education (And The Residual) To Economic Growth," OECD Conference on the Residual Factor and Economic Growth, Paris, DAS/PD/63.2 (May 1964); Y. Ben-Porath, "The Production of Human Capital and Life Cycle of Earnings," *Journal of Political Economy* vol. 75, no. 4, part I (August 1967); Z. Griliches and W. M. Mason, "Education, Income, and Ability," *Journal of Political Economy* vol. 80, no. 2 (1972): Supplement S74–103; B. R. Chiswick and J. Mincer, "Time Series Changes in Personal Income Inequality in the United States from 1939, with Projections to 1985," *Journal of Political Economy* vol. 80, no. 2 (1972): Supplement S34–66; James J. Heckman, "A Life Cycle Model of Earnings, Learning, and Consumption," *Journal of Political Economy* vol. 84, no. 4, part II (August 1976); Orley Ashenfelter, "Estimating the Effect of Training Programs on Earnings," *Review of Economics and Statistics* vol. LX, no. 1 (February 1978); Orley Ashenfelter and J. Ham, "Education, Employment and Earnings," *Journal of Political Economy* vol. 87, no. 5, part 2 (October 1979); and J. L. Medoff and K. G. Abraham, "Experience, Performance, and Earnings," *Quarterly Journal of Economics* vol. XCV, no. 4 (December 1980).

16 The inclusion of foregone output (earnings) in the economic cost of education received considerable attention; see, for example, John Vaizey, op. cit.; M. J. Bowman, "The Human Investment Revolution in Economic Thought," *Sociology of Education* vol. 39 (1966); L. C. Solmon, "Capital Formation by

Expenditures on Education, 1960," *Journal of Political Economy* vol. 79, no. 4 (November–December 1971); and D. O. Parsons, "The Cost of School Time, Foregone Earnings, and Human Capital Formation," *Journal of Political Economy* vol. 82, no. 1 (March–April 1974).

17 See G. J.Thuesen and N. V. Fabrycky, *Engineering Economy* (Englewood Cliffs, NJ: Prentice-Hall, Inc., 1984), 42.

18 R. S. Eckaus, "Economic Criteria for Education and Training," *Review of Economics and Statistics* vol. 46, no. 2 (May 1964): 181.

19 Wachtel, op. cit., 189.

20 Eckaus, op. cit., 182.

21 See Psacharopoulos, op. cit., 19–21; we added to Psacharopoulos' equation the allowance for risk and uncertainty.

22 For the data on the native and immigrant workers in the UAE, see Yousef Khalifeh Al-Yousef, "Economic Developments in the UAE 1975–1990," *The Economic and Administrative Sciences Review,* UAE University, no. 8 (September 1992): 23–78.

23 Jacob Mincer (1962) op. cit.: supplement.

24 See Becker, op. cit., 9–49.

25 For a lengthy exposition on general and specific training, see Don Bellante and Mark Jackson, *Labor Economics: Choice in Labor Markets* (New York: McGraw-Hill Book Company, 1983), 133–137; also C. R. McConnell and S. L. Brue, *Contemporary Labor Economics* (New York: McGraw-Hill Book Company, 1986), 89–92, 360–1.

26 Charles Brown, "Empirical Evidence on Private Training," *Research in Labor Economics,* vol. 11, JAI Press (1990); Robert J. Lalonde, "The Promise of Public Sector-Sponsored Training Programs," *Journal of Economic Perspectives* vol. 9, no. 2 (Spring 1995).

27 D. Al-Ali, "Education and Economic Growth," unpublished MA thesis, University of Jordan, Amman, 1976.

28 Monther Sharè, "Rates of Return to the Education of Jordanian Workers," unpublished PhD dissertation, University of Wales, UK, 1981.

29 A. Al-Khateeb and N. Shatnawy, "Cost-Benefit Analysis of Education in Jordanian Community Colleges 1989–1990," *Abhath Al-Yarmouk,* Humanities and Social Sciences Series vol. 10, no. 1 (1994).

4

HUMAN CAPITAL AND QUALITY MANAGEMENT:
STRATEGIES FOR AN ERA OF GLOBALIZATION

1 J. Delors, *Learning: The Treasure Within,* UNESCO International Commission on Education for the Twenty-First Century (UNESCO 1996).

2 Carnegie publication, *Year of Promise: A Comprehensive Learning Strategy for America's Children* (September 1996) emphasized the education of children aged 3 to 10.

5
EDUCATION IN THE TWENTY-FIRST CENTURY:
JUST-IN-TIME LEARNING OR LEARNING COMMUNITIES?

1 Jean Piaget, *The Origins of Intelligence in Children* (New York: Norton, 1952); J. Bruner, *The Process of Education* (Cambridge, MA: Harvard University Press, 1961).

2 Sam Stringfield, Steven M. Ross and Lana Smith (eds) *Bold Plans for Restructuring: The New American Schools Design* (Mahwah, NJ: Lawrence Erlbaum Associates, 1996); D. Meier, *The Power of Their Ideas: Lessons from a Small School in Harlem* (Boston, MA: Beaken Press, 1995); L. Darling-Hammond, *The Right to Learn: A Blueprint for Creating Schools that Work* (San Francisco, CA: Jossey-Bass, 1997); R. Ruopp, S. Gal, B. Drayton and M. Pfister, *LabNet: Toward A Community of Practice* (Hillsdale, NJ: Lawrence Erlbaum Associates, 1993).

3 Cohen and Jordan, "Audrey Cohen College System of Education: Purpose Centered Learning," in Stringfield et al. (eds) op. cit.; Beverly Hunter, "Learning and Teaching on the Internet: Contributing to Educational Reform," in B. Kahin and J. Keller (eds) *Public Access to the Internet* (Cambridge, MA: MIT Press, 1995); B. Goldberg and J. Richards, "The Co-NECT Design for School Change," in Stringfield et al. (eds) op. cit.; Campbell et. al., "The Expeditionary Learning Outward Bound Design," in Springfield et al. (eds) op. cit.

4 Ruopp et al., op. cit.; Math Learning Forums.

5 E. Hirsch, *The Schools We Need and Why We Don't Have Them* (New York: Doubleday, 1996); D. Ravitch and C. Finn, *What Do our Seventeen Year Olds Know? A Report on the First National Assessment of History and Literature* (New York, NY: Harper and Row, 1987).

6 L. Kohlberg and R. Mayer, "Development as the Aim of Education," *Harvard Educational Review* vol. 14 (1972): 449–96.

7 C. Twigg, "The Need for a National Learning Infrastructure," *Educom Review*, vol. 29 (1994) and available on-line at: http://educom.edu/program.nlii/keydocs/mongraph.html

8 M. Scardamalia and C. Bereiter, "Computer Support for Knowledge-Building Communities," *Journal of the Learning Sciences* vol. 3, no. 3 (1994): 219–25; M. Scardamalia and C. Bereiter, "Schools as Knowledge-building Organizations," in D. Keating and C. Hertzmann (eds) *Today's Children, Tomorrow's Society: The Developmental Health and Wealth of Nations* (New York, NY: Guilford Publications, 1998).

9 A. Neill, *Summerhill: For and Against* (New York, NY: Hart Publishing Company, 1970).

10 L. Cuban, *How Teachers Taught: Constancy and Change in American Classrooms, 1890–1990, 2nd edition* (New York, NY: Teachers College Press, 1993).

11 SCANS, Secretary's Commission on Achieving Necessary Skills, *What Work Requires of Schools: A SCANS Report for America 2000* (Washington, DC: US Department of Labor, 1991).

12 J. Oakes, *Keeping Track* (New Haven, CT: Yale University Press, 1986).

13 H. Mehan, I. Villanueva, L. Hubbard, and A. Linz, *Constructing School Success: The Consequences of Untracking Low-Achieving Students* (Cambridge: Cambridge University Press, 1996).

14 M. Cole, "The Zone of Proximal Development: Where Culture and Cognition Create Each Other," in J. V. Werstch (ed.) *Culture, Communication and Cognition: Vygotskian Perspectives* (Cambridge: Cambridge University Press, 1985).

15 J. Lave and E. Wenger, *Situated Learning: Legitimate Peripheral Participation* (Cambridge: Cambridge University Press, 1991); Ruopp et al., op. cit.; R. D. Pea and L. M. Gomez, "Distributed Multimedia Learning Environments: Why and How?", *Interactive Learning Environments* vol. 2, no. 2 (1994); K. Dunbar, "How Scientists Think: Online Creativity and Conceptual Change in Science," in T. B. Ward, S. M. Smith and S. Vaid (eds) *Conceptual Structures and Processes: Emergence, Discovery and* Change (Washington, DC: APA Press, 1996).

16 J. Levin, M. Riel, N. Miyake and M. Cohen, "Education on the Electronic Frontier: Teleapprenticeships in Globally Distributed Educational Contexts," *Contemporary Educational Psychology* vol. 12 (1987); A. L. Brown and J. C. Campione, "Guided Discovery in a Community of Learners," in K. McGilly (ed.) *Classroom Lessons: Integrating Cognitive Theory and Classroom Practice* (Cambridge, MA: MIT Press/Bradford Books, 1994); Pea and Gomez, op. cit.; R. Pea, "Seeing What we Build Together: Distributed Multimedia Learning Environments for Transformative Communications," *Journal of the Learning Sciences* vol. 3, no. 3 (1994); Dunbar, op. cit.; and Levin (1977).

17 Stringfield et al., op. cit.

18 M. Riel, "Learning in the Networlds of Tommorrow" (1997): http://www. iearn.org/webtour/2

19 Scardamalia and Bereiter, op. cit.

20 T. D. Koshmann, "Toward a Theory of Computer Support for Collaborative Network Technologies," *Journal of the Learning* Sciences vol. 3, no. 3 (1994); Pea, op. cit.

21 For more information on this project, see: http://summit.stanford.edu/creatures/

22 John Dewey, *Democracy and Education* (New York, NY: The Free Press, 1916), 9.

23 Clifford Stoll, *Silicon Snake Oil: Second Thoughts on the Information Superhighway* (Charlotte, NC: Anchor, 1996); T. Oppenheimer, "The Computer Delusion," *Atlantic Monthly*, July 1997.

24 The GLOBE project was created by Vice-President Al Gore to increase student understanding and participation in environmental issues. For more information on GLOBE, see: http://www.globe.gov.

25 B. Means, et al., *GLOBE Year 2 Evaluation: Implementation and Progress* (Menlo Park, CA: SRI International, 1997).

26 Pea and Gomez, op. cit.

27 Learning Circles are collaborative partnerships where students from many different regions design and participate in projects organized around a curriculum theme. These projects often involve extensive community and cultural research: http://www.iearn.org/circles

28 Margaret Riel, "Learning Circles: A Functional Analysis of Educational Tele-computing", *Interactive Learning Environments* vol. 2 (1992): 15–30.

29 Global Lab is project organized by TERC in which students share data on a tract of land near their school as a way to understand important issues in environmental science: http://hub.terc.edu/gl/gl118.html

30 W. J. Rohwedder and A. Alm, "Using Computers in Environmental Education: Interactive Multimedia and On-line Learning" (1997): http://www.eelink.umich.

edu/computers/pp.html#additionaltools Also, Onset Instruments, PO Box 3450, Pocasset, MA, USA 02559, Telephone: 001 508 563 9000.

31 For more information on using telescopes on the Internet, see: http://www.eia.brad.ac.uk/rti/automated.html

32 To view the telegarden and experiment with the telerobots for planting and watering the seeds, see: http://www.telegarden.aec.at/cgi-bin/knapsack/html/info.html Mag-Nify Virtual Science and Technology Centre hosts a research project for students on heating and cooling using a small-scale model of a house. From anywhere in the Networld, students can turn on different numbers of light bulbs and a fan. Students measure the heating and cooling effect. One of the goals of this site is to experiment with remote operation of tools: http://www.magnify.educ.monash.edu.au/measure/computer_house.htm

33 A list of these electronic field trips and adventure learning opportunities is now available on the Internet. See "Electronic Travel" in Riel (1997) op. cit. "Transportation for the Mind": http://www.att.com/edresources/wt/

34 Live from the Hubble Telescope was a Passport to Knowledge Project: http://www.quest.arc.nasa.gov/hst/index.html

35 The Monterey Bay Virtual Canyon Project is an NSF-funded partnership between schools, the Monterey Bay Aquarium and the Monterey Bay Research Institute: www.virtual-canyon.org The MayaQuest Project was one of a number of excellent projects sponsored by MECC: www.mecc.com/internet/maya/maya.html

36 See the last section, "Learning Spaces in the Networlds of Tomorrow" for more ideas on how this might be used as an educational activity: http://www.iearn.org/webtour/2/vision.html

37 ThinkQuest is an international contest that challenges students to work in teams creating teaching materials for other students: http://io.advanced.org/thinkquest/tq97.winners.html

38 For more information on the Holocaust project, see: http://www.iearn.org/iearn/hgp.html

39 CyberFair is a contest organized each year by the Global Schoolhouse Network: http://gsn.org

40 A list of these electronic field trips and adventure learning opportunities is now available on the Internet. See "Electronic Travel" in Riel, op. cit. (1997), "Transportation for the Mind": http://www.att.com/edresources/wt/travel.html

41 For a listing of different types of on-line mentoring programs and links to them, see: http://www.iearn.org/circles/mentors

42 R. D. Pea, "Seeing What We Build Together: Distributed Multimedia Learning Environments for Transformative Communities, *Journal of the Learning Sciences* vol. 3, no. 3 (1994): 219–225.

6

APPLICATIONS OF TOTAL QUALITY MANAGEMENT
IN EDUCATION AND TRAINING

1 Philip B. Crosby, *Quality Without Tears: The Art of Hassle-Free Management* (New York: McGraw-Hill Book Company, 1984); W. Edwards Deming, *Out of*

the Crisis (Cambridge, MA: Productivity Press or Washington, DC: The George Washington University, MIT-CAES, 1982); Joseph M. Juran, *Juran On Planning For Quality* (Cambridge, MA: Productivity Press, 1988).

2 Ibid.

3 Robert A. Cornesky, Sam McCool, Larry Byrnes and Robert Weber, *Implementing Total Quality Management in Institutions of Higher Education* (Madison, WI: Magna Publications, Inc., 1991).

4 Ray F. Boedecker, *Eleven Conditions for Excellence: The IBM Total Quality Improvement Process* (Boston, MA: American Institute of Management, 1989); Cornesky et al., op. cit.; Robert A. Cornesky, *Turning Continuous Quality Improvement into Institutional Practice: The Tools and Techniques* (Port Orange, FL: Cornesky and Associates, Inc., 1995); Stephen R. Covey, *The 7 Habits of Highly Effective People* (New York: Simon and Schuster, 1989); Masaaki Imai, *Kaizen: The Key to Japan's Competitive Success* (Cambridge, MA: Productivity Press, 1986); Tom Peters and Nancy Austin, *A Passion for Excellence* (New York: Random House, Inc., 1985); Keith Roberts and James B. Rieley, *Institutional Effectiveness* (Milwaukee, WI: The Center for Continuous Quality Improvement, Milwaukee Area Technical College, 1995); Peter M. Senge, *The Fifth Discipline: The Art & Practice of the Learning Organization* (New York: Currency Doubleday, 1990); Daniel Seymour, *Once Upon a Campus: Lessons for Improving Quality and Productivity in Higher Education* (Phoenix, AZ: the Oryx Press, 1995); Daniel Seymour, *The AQC Baldrige Report: Lessons Learned By Nine Colleges and Universities Undertaking Self-Study With the Malcolm Baldrige National Quality Award Criteria* (Washington, DC: Academic Quality Consortium, A Project of the American Association for Higher Education, 1996).

5 Robert A. Cornesky, *The Quality Professor: Implementing Total Quality Management in the College Classroom* (Madison, WI: Magna Publications, Inc., 1993); Robert A. Cornesky and William Lazarus, *Continuous Quality Improvement in the Classroom: A Collaborative Approach* (Port Orange, FL: Cornesky and Associates, Inc., 1995); Robert A. Cornesky, *Quality Indices: Self-Assessment Rating Instrument for Educational Institutions* (Port Orange, FL: Cornesky and Associates, Inc., 1995).

6 See Philip B. Crosby, *Let's Talk Quality* (New York: McGraw-Hill Book Company, 1989); Jay Conger and Rabindra Kanungo," The Empowerment Process: Integrating Theory and Practice," *Academy of Management Review*, July 1988; Robert A. Cornesky and Sam McCool, *Total Quality Improvement Guide for Institutions of Higher Education* (Madison, WI: Magna Publications, Inc., 1992); and Daniel Seymour (ed.) *The Malcolm Baldrige National Quality Award as a Framework for Improving Higher Education. Volume I: Theory and Concepts. Volume II: Case and Practice* (Maryville, MO: Prescott Publishing Company, 1996).

7 See Robert Levering, *A Great Place to Work* (New York: Random House, Inc., 1988); Robert H. Waterman, *Adhocracy: The Power to Change* (Knoxville, TN: Whittle Direct Books, 1990).

8 See J. S. Brown, A. Collins and P. Duguid, "Situated Cognition and the Culture of Learning," *Educational Researcher* vol. 18, no. 1 (1989); David W. Johnson and Roger T. Johnson, *Meaningful and Manageable Assessment Through Cooperative*

Learning (Edina, MN: Interaction, 1996); Barbara Millis and Philip G. Cottell, Jr., *Cooperative Learning for Higher Education Faculty* (Phoenix, AZ: American Council on Education Series on Higher Education, Oryx Press, 1997); Joseph Cuseo, *Cooperative Learning: A Pedagogy for Addressing Contemporary Challenges and Critical Issues in Higher Education* (Stillwater, OK: New Forums Press, Inc., 1996); and David W. Johnson, Roger T. Johnson and Karl A. Smith, "Cooperative Learning Returns to College: What Evidence Is There That It Works?", *Change* July/August 1998.

9 Waterman, op. cit.

10 Levering, op. cit.

11 Senge, op. cit.

12 Richard J. Light, *The Harvard Assessment Seminars: Exploration with Students and Faculty about Teaching, Learning, and Student Life* (Cambridge, MA: Harvard University Graduate School of Education, 1992).

13 Robert Cornesky, Ron Baker, Cathy Cavanaugh, William Etling, Michael Lukert, Sam McCool, Brian McKay, An-Sik Min, Charlotte Paul, Paul Thomas, David Wagner and John Darling, *Using Deming to Improve Quality in Colleges and Universities* (Madison, WI: Magna Publications, Inc., 1989).

14 R. Edgerton, Wingspread Report, "An American Imperative: Higher Expectations for Higher Education," in *An American Imperative: Report of the Wingspread Group on Higher Education* (Racine, WI: Johnson Foundation, 1993).

15 Ibid.

16 Ibid.

17 See Johnson, Johnson and Smith, op. cit. See also Steve Brigham (ed.) *CQI 101: A First Reader for Higher Education* (Washington, DC: AAHE CQI Project, 1994); Steve Brigham (ed.) *25 Snapshots of a Movement: Profiles of Campuses Implementing CQI* (Washington, DC: AAHE CQI Project, 1994); and Dean L. Hubbard (ed.) *Continuous Quality Improvement: Making the Transition to Education* (Maryville, MO: Prescott Publishing Company, 1993).

7

FUTURE SCHOOLS:
GETTING THE BALANCE RIGHT

1 Dr. Judy Codding, "Designing Highly Effective Programs for Successful Schools," Vice-President, Programs, National Center on Education and the Economy, Washington DC, Keynote Presentation, Successful Schools Conference, Melbourne, June 1997.

2 *Schools Under Scrutiny* (Paris: OECD, 1995).

3 S. Pascoe and R. Pascoe, "Education Reform in Australia: 1992–97: A Case Study," *The Education Reform and Management Series* vol. 1, no. 2 (1998): 19.

4 Quoted by Jack Kenny in "Clearing the Road to the Learning Society," *The Times Educational Supplement*, October 10, 1997.

5 J. Codding. op. cit.

6 Professor Peter Mortimore, *High Performing Schools and School Improvement*, Occasional Paper published by the Professional and Leadership Development Centre, Department of Education, Victoria, 1996.

7 Geoff Spring, "Is there a Crisis in Government Schools? Of Course Not!" address for Issues in Public Sector Change Lecture Series, Centre for Public Policy, University of Melbourne, Victoria, 1997.
8 Ibid.

8

EDUCATION IN MODERN JAPAN:
FORMAL SCHOOLING AND LEARNING ON THE JOB

I would like to thank Richard L. Petrick, Associate Vice-Chancellor of the Ohio Board of Regents for factual information and Ken Brevoort for able research assistance.

1 The study is published in Lisa Lynch, *Training and the Private Sector* (Chicago, IL: University of Chicago Press, 1994), chapter 4.
2 Alfred Marshall, *Principles of Economics, Book IV*, 8th Edition (London: Macmillan and Company Ltd., 1949), chapter VI.
3 See John Bishop, "The Productivity Consequence of What is Learned in High School," *Journal of Curriculum Studies* vol. 22 (Supplement 1990): 9–49. He finds that competence in science, language, arts and higher level mathematics indeed is associated with success in training and high performance in hands-on work sample tests.
4 It is fair to state that the Japanese want to have a homogeneous workforce that shares similar values and behavior.
5 For example, a recent international comparison of science achievement found that in a sample of young teenagers (mean age of 14.7 in Japan and 15.4 in the US), the mean science score (the coefficient of variation in parentheses) was 20.2 (24.8 percent) for Japan and 16.5 (30.3 percent) for the US. In the tabulations for other age groups as well as for separate scores for biology, chemistry and physics, the Japan–US differences in the mean and the coefficient of variation persist. See International Association for the Evaluation of Educational Achievement, *Science Achievement in Seventeen Countries: A Preliminary Report* (Oxford: Pergamon Press, 1988). John Bishop (op. cit.: 101–26) summarizes international comparisons of test scores in science and mathematics.
6 In the traditional US setting, such a practice was discouraged by the fear that the "teacher" may be displaced by a junior worker who becomes better than he/she.
7 James E. Rosenbaum and Takehiko Kariya, "From High School to Work: Market and Institutional Mechanisms in Japan," *American Journal of Sociology* vol. 94 (1989): 1334–65.
8 Masanori Hashimoto, "Employment-Based Training in Japanese Firms in Japan and in the United States: Experiences of Automobile Manufacturers," in Lisa Lynch (ed.) op. cit.
9 Ibid.
10 I hasten to add that vocational and technical schools do exist in Japan. See Ronald Dore and Mari Sako, *How the Japanese Learn to Work* (London: Routledge, 1989) for an informative discussion on Japanese schools, and

Solomon B. Levine and Hisashi Kawada, *Human Resources in Japanese Industrial Development* (Princeton, NJ: Princeton University Press, 1980) for an informative discussion on the role of industrial training in Japanese economic development.

11 For this discussion, I rely heavily on Dore and Sako, ibid. The readers are referred to this source for details.

12 Unless otherwise noted, the statistics reported here and subsequently are the author's computations based on various tables from *Gakko Kihon Chosa Hokoku Sho* (Report on the Survey of Schools), Japan Ministry of Education, 1996.

13 *Senshu* schools train most of the nurses and play-school teachers, however.

14 All states in the US promulgate compulsory school attendance for children, but the requirements are stated in terms of age brackets rather than years of schooling. The age bracket during which compulsory attendance is required ranges from as early as age 5 to as late as age 18. In practice, 12-year formal education had become the norm before World War Two. See Claudia Goldin and Lawrence Katz, "Why the United States Led in Education: Lessons from Secondary School Expansion, 1910 to 1940," Harvard University Working Paper (1997) for an informative historical account of US education history.

15 The progression rates to junior and four-year colleges were, respectively, 39 percent and 13 percent for Japan and 36 percent and 18 percent for the US. I thank Mr Petrick of the Ohio Board of Regents for supplying the underlying US data.

16 The ensuring discussion on employment-based training draws on the ideas discussed in Hashimoto (1994), op. cit.

17 John Bishop, op. cit. One possible reason for this phenomenon is that American school grades are not uniform in quality from school to school. In effect, grades contain too much "noise" to be useful to an employer. Since the Japanese education system is governed by the Ministry of Education, the contents of courses in Japan are much more uniform among schools than in the US. As a result, course grades are more informative in Japan.

18 A management level employee at Honda in Suzuka, Japan told me that Honda does, in fact, have such arrangements with several high schools. However, it also sends out recruiting brochures to other schools as well. Rosenbaum and Kariya (op. cit.) report that in an area near Tokyo a typical high school had semi-formal arrangements with about 77 employers, which is only a little over 11 percent of all employers who send job offer forms to this school. However, these 11 percent of firms hired almost half of all the work-bound graduates from each school.

19 This practice has an "experience rated" feature. Employers assign different size quotas to schools depending on their previous experiences with the school; see Rosenbaum and Kariya, op. cit.

20 Rosenbaum and Kariya, op. cit.

21 The emphasis on safety is ubiquitous in Japanese firms and transplants, perhaps underscoring the desire to protect investments in human capital.

22 See Arne L. Kalleberg and James R. Lincoln, "The Structure of Earnings Inequality in the US and Japan," *American Journal of Sociology* vol. 94 (1988): S121–S153.

23 Informal training in employment relations is also emphasized by a German-owned Siemens plant in North Carolina (National Public Radio News Transcript, January 20, 1998).

24 Job instruction, job methods (methods for improvement) and job relations (interpersonal relations) were the three components of the training within industry

(TWI) concept developed in the US during the war years to rapidly produce a skilled workforce. The TWI concept is synonymous with OTJ training. The GHQ's guidance was patterned on the US War Manpower Commission, which developed a comprehensive training approach based on TWI. The Commission is said to have trained about 2,000,000 supervisors during the war years. Japan also learned from the US how to conduct management training, quality control and interpersonal relations during these years. An important point, however, is that the GHQ provided only manuals, and that the Japanese had to interpret them and develop their own approach. See *Nihon Sangyo Kunren Kyokai* (Japan Industrial Training Association), *Sangyo Kunren Hyaku Nenshi* (A Hundred Year History of Industrial Training), Tokyo, 1971.

25 Marshall, op. cit.

9

THE SINGAPORE EDUCATION SYSTEM:
A QUALITY MODEL?

1 Organized, hosted by and held in Singapore, June 1–5, 1997.
2 As reported in *The Straits Times*, June 3, 1997, 29.
3 "Asian Economic Survey, 1997–1998" Supplement, *Asian Wall Street Journal*, October 20, 1997, S1.
4 The following data on education spending (as percentage of GDP) for 1993 is supplied by UNESCO: Australia (na), China (1.9 percent), Hong Kong (2.9 percent), India (3.7 percent), Indonesia (2.2 percent), Japan (4.7 percent), South Korea (4.2 percent), Laos (2.3 percent), Malaysia (5.1 percent), Pakistan (2.7 percent), Philippines (2.4 percent), Singapore (3.1 percent), Taiwan (7.1 percent), Thailand (4 percent), UK (5.2 percent) and US (5.3 percent).
5 Pennsylvania Governor Tom Ridge (Republican), as quoted in *USA Today*, reprinted in *The Straits Times*, November 26, 1997, 10.
6 As quoted in a report by Wang Hui Ling in *The Straits Times,* October 17, 1997, 29.
7 Brian Smith and David Smith (eds) *The Smith Guide to the Staff Development Jungle* (Brighton: Chatsworth Publications, 1993), p. 28.
8 Some of the more frequently used include the following.

- Operating indicators – e.g. staff–student ratio, staff teaching workload, range of available options, range of support services.
- Research indicators – e.g. research activities and publications, inventions and patents, consultancies.
- Teaching performance indicators – e.g. emphasis on excellence in teaching; innovation in curriculum/pedagogy; emphasis on practical training.
- Staff indicators – e.g. qualifications, staff development, service to the community.
- Student indicators – e.g. student calibre, success rate, employability.

9 Ronald Barnett, *Improving Higher Education: Total Quality Care* (Buckingham: Society for Research in Higher Education and Open University, 1992), 212.

10 "Agenda for Action: goals and changes," a Green Paper presented to Parliament by Goh Chok Tong outlining the goal of the nation, and the basis for nation-building and future government policy, 1988.

11 Primary education offered the following streams: gifted, normal bilingual, extended bilingual and monolingual. Secondary education includes these streams: gifted, special (for top 10 percent of cohort), express and normal (five instead of four years).

12 Physical education became a core subject in school while extra-curricular activities were emphasized to cultivate team spirit and civic consciousness; subjects such as moral education, aesthetic appreciation (Art/Music Elective Program) and computer appreciation were introduced.

13 Among other things, the Ministry of Education was restructured for greater coordination between departments, and a Schools Council was established to promote dialogue between the education ministry and schools. There was also a movement toward a decentralized system of school management.

14 According to findings of "Singapore Census of Population (1990)," the highest qualifications attained of resident non-student population aged 10 years and over were as follows.

Highest Qualification Attained	1980	1990
No formal education/incomplete primary	36 percent	31 percent
Completed primary/incomplete secondary	44 percent	30 percent
Secondary	13 percent	25 percent
Upper secondary	5 percent	10 percent
University	2 percent	4 percent

15 For instance, training for Principals and Heads of Departments was intensified. Some secondary schools were accorded independent status, and these were empowered to recruit staff in a competitive market to serve as benchmarks for all schools. Pastoral care and career guidance became more important on the agenda.

16 Some examples are:

• BEST (Basic Education for Skills Training program)
• MoST (Modular Skills Training program), and
• WISE (Worker Improvement Secondary Education).

17 Concerted efforts were made to improve:

• teaching: manpower development, curriculum review, upgrading of facilities
• research: graduate schools and programs were expanded, as also the pool of R&D personnel, research facilities and new research centers and facilities; the Innovation Centre and Industry and Technology Relations Office were set up to facilitate and enhance links with outside organizations through research collaboration and high-level joint research committees involving the Ministries of Trade and Industry and National Development.

18 A Department of Statistics survey in 1995 found that those with only primary education dropped from 58.5 percent in 1990 to 48.9 percent.

19 More scholarships/bursaries are made available. In 1995, 48,000 received S$9 million in Edusave Merit Bursaries; over the next 5 years, projections are for 300,000 such awards for lower-income students. The Ministry of Education has also introduced Good Progress Awards to reward those who are not top students but who are making significant improvements.

20 A pilot scheme involving 60 schools gives schools more say in how they are run. A group of 6 schools forms a cluster under the direction of a cluster head who will be empowered with funds and the authority to change their management and teaching methods without having to seek the Education Ministry's approval.

21 A major exercise costing S$200–300 million (US$115–173 million) was implemented in 1997 to revamp the career path of teachers and make the profession more rewarding.

22 The following table gives some indication of rate of growth.

Enrollment in the Existing Two Universities and Four Polytechnics						
1986	1991	1992	1993	1994	1995	1996
42,317	60,369	65,771	73,772	77,215	83,914	92,140

Source: *Singapore Yearbook of Statistics,* 1996.

23 The following enrollment/output statistics spanning last three decades give some idea of the rate of growth.

Year	Percentage of Primary 1 Cohort		Annual Output	
	Polytechnic	University	Polytechnic	University
1965	2	3	237	968
1975	6	5	2,581	1,459
1986	14	9	5,173	4,521
1996	38	22	12, 650	8,218

Source: *Singapore Statistical Highlights, 1996.*

24 *Singapore Yearbook of Statistics,* 1996, Section 18.1, "Enrolment in Educational Institutions."

25 The Prime Minister has indicated five challenges for the polytechnics:
- providing quality teaching
- encouraging more top polytechnic engineering students to pursue a university degree (in the dialogue with the Deputy Prime Minister, Lee Hsien Loong, during the recent Second Polytechnic Forum, students expressed their hope for greater recognition and more opportunities for university education)
- complementing universities in research relevant to industry
- producing well-rounded graduates (communication skills, politically aware etc), and
- becoming major centers of continuing education.

26 Mark Richmond, Lee Kuan Yew Distinguished Visitor, as reported in *The Straits Times*, November 24, 1995.

27 Professor David Newland, Head of Cambridge University's Engineering Department on a 4-day visit to NTU, was reported as saying: "It is already in a wonderful state of completion . . . What impressed me is the rate of change that must have taken place to establish NTU in 15 years." *The Straits Times*, December 15, 1997, 31.

28 NUS is currently planning to introduce a core curriculum for all its students comprising four identified areas: (i) history of Singapore; (ii) history/culture of regional countries; (iii) expository writing; and (iv) human relations.

29 The R&D base will also help to offset the expected decline in foreign technology transfer and help to sustain product innovation and internal efficiency gains. NUS spawned and currently hosts a number of research institutes (e.g. Molecular and Cell Biology, Manufacturing Technology, Materials Research and Engineering, Microelectronics).

30 For example, through the Lee Kuan Yew Fellowship Programme in Public Policy and NTU's Nanyang Fellowship program for Business Administration.

31 "Singapore's 9-year-olds among the world's best in maths and science," *The Straits Times,* July 11, 1997, 26.

32 Please see Figure 1:9 for a diagrammatic representation of the system.

33 According to the Third International Mathematics and Science Study (TIMSS) survey, Singapore pupils spend 4.6 hours a day doing homework, in comparison to the international average of 2–3 hours.

34 The December 8, 1997 issue of *Newsweek* carried a somber lesson: German universities, which used to be the best in the world, "are a wreck" because of lowering of admission requirement. Andrew Nagorski, "Germany: Bottom of the Class?" *Newsweek,* December 8, 1997, 30–31.

35 The findings of the survey for the TIMSS, led by a team of researchers at the Boston College Graduate School of Education and sponsored by Amsterdam-based International Association for the Evaluation of Educational Achievement, attribute scholastic achievement to many factors, notable among which are "home factors."

36 *Asiaweek* ranking of universities ("The Best Universities in Asia," May 23, 1997)

Overall	University	Academic Reputation	Faculty Resources	Student Selectivity
1	Tokyo	1	12	3
2	Kyoto	4	7	2
3	Hong Kong	6	2	6
4	Singapore	2	4	16
5	Chinese U Hong Kong	20	3	21
6	New South Wales	10	10	26
7	Peking	7	1	7
8	National Taiwan	13	22	5
9	Melbourne	3	21	27
10	Hong Kong University of Science & Technology	19	14	22

Note: Derived from three attributes: number of enrollees compared with offered places, ratio of 1997 sophomores to 1996 freshmen and graduation rate.

37 See Table 1:4 in chapter 4 of this volume, "Human Capital and Quality Management: Strategies for an Era of Globalization," by Adnan Badran.

38 A Singaporean 11-year old recently topped the list for the English test. These tests were introduced in Singapore and other Asia Pacific countries 4 years ago.

39 Conducted by Moo Swee Ngoh and Goh Swee Chiew (National Institute of Education lecturers) and Josephine Lau (teacher), and presented at the Educational Research Association 1997 conference.

40 "How to stay on top for the next 30 years," a speech given at the 31st Annual General Meeting of Institution of Engineers, Singapore, by Dy Ho Ching, Chairman of Economic Development Board (reported in *Sunday Times,* May 25, 1997, 6).

41 Rear-Admiral Teo was speaking at a news conference arranged for the American media while in Washington (reported in *The Straits Times*, May 23, 1997, 47).

42 Abstracted from Ministry of Education Strategic Planning Exercise, University Education: Final Report.

43 Prime Minister Goh Chok Tong, "PM spells out formula for Singapore to stay ahead," reported in *The Straits Times,* June 3, 1997, 1.

44 Ibid.

45 See, for instance, Howard Gardner, *Multiple Intelligences* (New York, NY: Basic Books, 1993) and Howard Gardner et al., *Intelligence: Multiple Perspectives* (Fort Worth, TX: Harcourt Brace College Publications, 1996).

46 See, for instance, Edward De Bono, *Lateral Thinking: A Textbook of Creativity* (Harmondsworth: Penguin Books, 1990) and Edward De Bono, *Teach Yourself to Think* (London: Viking, 1995).

47 Daniel Goleman, *Emotional Intelligence* (New York, NY: Bantam Books, 1995).

48 Robert Sternberg, *Beyond IQ: A Triarchic Theory of Human Intelligence* (New York: Cambridge University Press, 1985) and *The Triarchic Mind: A New Theory of Human Intelligence* (New York: Viking, 1988).

49 Prime Minister Goh Chok Tong, "PM spells out formula for Singapore to stay ahead," *The Straits Times* June 3, 1997, 1.

50 Ibid.

51 The present computer–pupil ratios are 1:6.6 for primary schools, 1:5 at secondary and tertiary levels, and the target is 1:2.2 by 2001.

52 Some examples are:

•   at the primary level, by 1997, the "Accelerating the use of IT in Primary Schools" (AITP) project will provide each school with 100 multi-media computers to ensure computer literacy

•   at the secondary level, several secondary schools are currently piloting the "Teachers and Students Workbench," a Ministry of Education IT2000 flagship project done in collaboration with the National Science and Technology Board, which aims to provide a complete and integrated teaching and learning environment in schools with access to a rich depository of multimedia courseware and electronic library, and

•   at tertiary level, the National University of Singapore has initiated a number of IT-supported projects such as lecture-on-demand, course materials on the Web, collaborative courses with overseas institutions using video-conferencing etc.

53 Deputy Prime Minister Lee Hsien Loong, *The Straits Times*, November 25, 1997, 36.

54 *The Straits Times*, May 20, 1997, 29.

55 Singapore, *Shared Values* (Singapore: National Printers, 1991).

56 George Cherian, "My View," *The Sunday Times*, March 9, 1997, 3.

57 Prime Minister Goh Chok Tong, "Vision for a total learning environment – PM spells out formula for Singapore to stay ahead," *The Straits Times*, June 3, 1997.

10

THE FUTURE OF EDUCATION AND WORK:
A PERSPECTIVE FROM CANADA

1 OECD, *OECD Economic Surveys: Canada 1996* (Paris: Organisation for Economic Co-operation and Development, 1996).

2 CMEC, *The Development of Education: Report of Canada* (Toronto, Canada: Council of Ministers of Education, 1996), http://www.cmec.ca/international/deveduc.eng.pdf and CMEC, *The Report on Education in Canada 1998* (Toronto, Canada: Council of Ministers of Education, 1998): http://www.cmec.ca/reports/rec98/

3 Statistics Canada, *Education in Canada, 1996* (Ottawa, Canada: Statistics Canada, 1997); OECD, *Education at a Glance: OECD Indicators* (Paris: Organisation for Economic Co-operation and Development, 1996).

4 HRDC, Applied Research Branch, "What is Happening to Canadian Youth?", unpublished working document, 1997; Gordon Betcherman and Graham S. Lowe, *The Future of Work in Canada: A Synthesis Report* (Ottawa, Canada: Canadian Policy Research Networks, 1997); Statistics Canada, *The Labor Force*, various issues; CMEC, *The World of Work*, reference document for the Third National Forum on Education: Education and Life-Transitions (Toronto, Canada: Council of Ministers of Education, 1998), document coordinated by the Canadian Labor Congress: http://www.cmec.ca/NaForEd/english/clc.stm

5 Betcherman and Lowe, op. cit.

6 Lars Osberg, Fred Wien and Jan Grude, *Vanishing Jobs: Canada's Changing Workplace* (Toronto, Canada: James Lorimer, 1995).

7 HRDC, Applied Research Branch, "What is Happening to Canadian Youth?", unpublished working document, 1997; Statistics Canada, *Labor Force Survey*.

8 Ibid.

9 Betcherman and Lowe, op. cit.

10 OECD, *Education at a Glance: OECD Indicators* (Paris: Organisation for Economic Co-operation and Development, 1996).

11 Marie Lavoie and Richard Roy, "Employment Trends in the Information Economy," *Applied Research Bulletin* (Human Resources Development Canada) vol. 3, no. 2 (1997).

12 HRDC, Applied Research Branch, op. cit.

13 Richard Marquardt, *Youth and Work in Troubled Times: A Report on Canada in the 1990s* (Ottawa, Canada: Canadian Policy Research Networks, 1996).

14 HRDC, Applied Research Branch, op. cit.; Statistics Canada, op. cit.

15 Ibid.

16 HRDC, Ministerial Task Force on Youth, *Take on the Future: Canadian Youth in the World of Work* (Hull: Human Resources Development Canada, 1996): http://youth-jeunesse.hrdc.drhc.gc.ca and HRDC, Applied Research Branch, op. cit.

17 HRDC, Applied Research Branch, op. cit.; HRDC and Statistics Canada, *The Class of '90 Revisited* (Ottawa: Statistics Canada, 1997): http://www.hrdc-drhc.gc.ca/hrdc/corp/stratpol

18 HRDC, Applied Research Branch, op. cit.

19 Scott Steele, "Changing Notions of Work," *Maclean's* (December 25/January 1, 1995); Robert Barner, "Seven Changes That Will Challenge Managers – And Workers," *The Futurist* vol. 30, no. 2 (1996); Angus Reid, *Shakedown: How the New Economy Is Changing Our Lives* (Toronto: Doubleday Canada, 1996); and Ray Marshall and Marc Tucker, *Thinking for a Living: Education and the Wealth of Nations* (New York: Basic Books, 1992).

20 CMEC, *Updating Essential Skills for the Workplace*, reference document for the Third National Forum on Education: Education and Life-Transitions (Toronto: Council of Ministers of Education, 1998), document coordinated by Human Resources Development, Canada: http://www.cmec.ca.NaForEd/english/HRDC.STM

21 Peter F. Drucker, *Post-Capitalist Society* (New York, NY: Harper Business, 1993); OECD, *Education and Employment* (Paris: Organisation for Economic Co-operation and Development, 1996); Benjamin Levin, "How Can Schools Respond to Changes in Work?", *Canadian Vocational Journal* vol. 30, no. 3 (1995); Alex Molner, "Why School Reform Is Not Enough to Mend our Civil Society," *Educational Leadership* vol. 54, no. 5 (1997); and Richard J. Murnane and Frank Levy, "A Civil Society Demands Education for Good Jobs," *Educational Leadership* vol. 54, no. 5 (1997).

22 Paul Anisef and Paul Axelrod, *Transitions: School and Employment in Canada* (Toronto: Thompson Educational Publishing, 1993); and OECD, *Education at a Glance* (Paris: Organisation for Economic Co-operation and Development, 1996).

23 Harvey Krahn, *School-Work Transitions: Changing Patterns and Research Needs,* Discussion Paper prepared for Applied Research Branch, Human Resources Development, Canada, 1996.

24 Michael Bloom, *Reaching for Success: Business and Education Working Together* (Ottawa: Conference Board of Canada, 1990). See also by Bloom, *Profiles of Partnerships: Business-Education Partnerships that Enhance Student Retention* (Ottawa: Conference Board of Canada, 1991).

25 Conference Board of Canada, *Employability Skills Profile* (Ottawa: Conference Board of Canada, 1993).

26 OECD, *Prepared for Life?* (Paris: Organisation for Economic Co-operation and Development, 1997).

27 OECD, *Literacy, Economy and Society – Results of the First International Adult Literacy Survey* (Paris: OECD and Ottawa: Statistics Canada, 1995); HRDC and Statistics Canada, *Reading the Future: A Portrait of Literacy in Canada* (Ottawa: Statistics Canada, 1996).

28 HRDC and Statistics Canada, *Leaving School* – Results from a national survey comparing school leavers and high school graduates 18–20 yeas of age (Ottawa:

Statistics Canada, 1993); HRDC and Statistics Canada, *School Leavers Follow-up Survey: Background Paper* (Ottawa: Statistics Canada, 1995); and HRDC and Statistics Canada, *After High School: The First Years* – The first report of the School Leavers Follow-up Survey (Ottawa: Statistics Canada, 1996).

29 Social Research and Demonstration Corporation, *Evaluating the Effectiveness of Employment-Related Programs and Services for Youth* – Report to Human Resources Development Canada, 1996.

30 Maude Barlow and Heather-Jane Robertson, *Class Warfare: The Assault on Canada's Schools* (Toronto: Key Porter Books, 1994); and Heather-Jane Robertson, *Traders and Travellers: Public Education in a Corporate-Dominated Culture* (Ottawa: Canadian Teachers' Federation, 1995).

31 Arthur G. Wirth, *Education and Work for the Year 2000: Choices We Face* (San Francisco, CA: Jossey-Bass, 1992); David Ashton and Francis Green, *Education, Training and the Global Economy* (Cheltenham, UK: Edward Elgar, 1996); "Training and Jobs: What works?", *The Economist*, April 6, 1996; and "Education and the Wealth of Nations," *The Economist*, March 29, 1997.

32 Ashton and Green, op. cit.

33 Jeremy Rifkin, *The End of Work: The Decline of the Global Labor Force and the Dawn of the Post-Market Era* (New York, NY: Putnam, 1995) and "Preparing Students for 'The End of Work,'" *Educational Leadership* vol. 54, no. 5 (1997); Jon Van Til, "Facing Inequality and the End of Work," *Educational Leadership* vol. 54, no. 6 (1997); Clinton E. Boutwell, "Profits Without People," *Phi Delta Kappan* vol. 79, no. 2 (1997); and Stan Karp, "Educating for a Civil Society: The Core Issue is Inequality," *Educational Leadership* vol. 54, no. 5 (1997).

34 Peter F. Drucker, *Post-Capitalist Society* (New York, NY: Harper Business, 1993); OECD, *Lifelong Learning for All* (Paris: Organisation for Economic Co-operation and Development, 1996); UNESCO, *Learning: The Treasure Within* (Paris: UNESCO, 1996); and Donna Uchida, Marvin J. Cetron and Floretta McKenzie, "What Students *Must* Know to Succeed in the Communication Age," *The Futurist* vol. 30, no. 4 (1996).

35 E. F. Schumacher, *Good Work* (New York, NY: Harper Colophon Books, 1979).

11

EDUCATION AND TRAINING IN GCC COUNTRIES:
SOME ISSUES OF CONCERN

1 HMSO Publication Centre, Department of Education and Science, *Education and Training for the 21st Century*, 1991, London: HMSO.

2 "Education Survey," *The Economist*, November 21, 1992, 3–18.

3 *Educational Annual Statistics*, Ministries of Education, GCC Countries, 1996–1997.

4 Ministry of Education, *The National Educational Report 1995–96* (in Arabic) (Kuwait, 1996).

5 *Information Power: Guidelines for School Library Media Program* (Chicago, Ill: American Library Association, 1988), 1.

6 OECD, *Education and Economy in a Changing Society* (Paris: OECD, 1989), 10.

7 Anne Henderson and Nancy Berla (eds), *A New Generation of Evidence: The Family Is Critical to Student Achievements* (Washington, DC: National Committee for Citizens in Education, 1994), 174.

8 T. H. Bell, "Reflections One Decade After A Nation at Risk," *Phi Delta Kappan* (Bloomington, IN: Bloomington University, April 1993): 596–7, 588–9.

9 R. Williams, "Sweeping Centered of Educational Decision-making Authority," *Phi Delta Kappan* (Bloomington, IN: Bloomington University, April 1997): 626.

10 F. M. Newman, M. Bruce King and Mark Rigdon, "Restructuring Schools," *Harvard Educational Review* vol. 67, no. 1 (Spring 1997) 41–70.

11 H. McRae, *The World in 2020* (Boston, MA: Harvard Business School Press, 1994), 12–13.

12
HUMAN DEVELOPMENT IN THE UNITED ARAB EMIRATES: INDICATORS AND CHALLENGES

1 *UNDP Human Development Report, 1990* (New York, NY: UNDP, 1990).

2 UAE ranked 62 in 1992 (0.771). *UNDP Human Development Report, 1997* (New York, NY: UNDP, 1997), 146–7.

3 Ibid., 158–9.

4 Adult literacy in the UAE is now approximately 84 percent.

5 The life expectancy at birth in 1992 was 70.8 years and the adult literacy rate was 65 percent.

6 *UNDP Human Development Report, 1997*, op. cit., 53–4.

7 See T. W. Schultz, "Investment in Human Capital," *American Economic Review* vol. 51, no. 1 (1961): 1–17; H. Harbison, *Human Resources as the Wealth of Nations* (New York, NY: Oxford University Press, 1973).

8 B. Wootton, *The Social Foundations of Wage Policy* (London: George Allen and Unwin, 1955).

9 Gary Becker, *Human Capital* (New York, NY: Columbia University Press, 1993).

10 Paul Ryan, "Segmentation, Duality and the Internal Labor Market," in F. Wilkenson (ed.) *The Dynamics of Labor Market Segmentation* (London: Academic Press, 1981), 3–20.

11 Abdullah Mograby, "Youth Unemployment and Government Intervention in the NSW Labor Market," unpublished PhD thesis, Macquarie University, Sydney, 1991.

12 J. Behrman and N. Birdsall, "The Quality of Schooling: Quantity Alone is Misleading," *American Economic Review* vol. 73 (1983).

13 Federal Law no. 1 on Ministerial Mandates, *Government Gazette* no. 1, vol. 1 (1972); Federal Law no. 11 on Mandatory Education, *Government Gazette* no. 5, vol. 1 (1972); and Federal Law no. 9 on Private Schools, *Government Gazette* no. 5, vol. 2 (1972).

14 Cabinet Decree no. 1/1987 on the Organizational Structure of the Ministry of Education, *Government Gazette* no. 171, vol. 14 (1987); Decree no. 2/480/1989

on Registration and Matriculation, *Government Gazette* no. 207, vol. 16; Decree no. 7/1991 on the Cabinet Education Committee, *Government Gazette* no. 221.

15 There are also four defense schools enrolling approximately 567 students in 1996/1997.

16 UNDP Report 1997, op. cit., 80.

17 The new Zayed University opened in Abu Dhabi in September 1998.

18 Ministry of Education sources argue that it reached 2.35 percent in 1990–91.

19 *UNDP Human Development Report*, op. cit., 180.

20 There are currently over 3,000 UAE students in the US, *Gulf News*, May, 13, 1998.

21 Ministry of Education and the Department of Technical Education, phase I report "Analysis of the Labor Market and the Present Technical Education," August 1995.

22 Ministry of Education, Annual Report 1990–1991, Documentation and Information Division, 25.

23 See UAE Ministry of Education, Education Development Program: A Source Text, 1990. See also Mahmoud Ahmed Ajawi, *Education in the United Arab Emirates* (Al-Ain, 1991); Abdul Rahim Shaheen, *Higher Education in the United Arab Emirates: Public and Private Institutions* (University of the United Arab Emirates Publications, 1997).

24 See W. Streeck, *Social Institutions and Economic Performance* (London: Sage, 1992).

25 Michael Piore, "Labor Standards and Business Strategies," in S. Herzenberg and J. Perez-Lopex (eds) *Labor Standards and Development in the Global Economy* (Washington, DC: US Department of Labor, 1990).

26 Major reforms include the apprenticeship system and the establishment of vocational competency standards, industry training boards, workplace relations and community education.

13
DEVELOPING THE UNITED ARAB EMIRATES
WORKFORCE FOR 2015

1 Commission on National Investment in Higher Education, 1997.

14
ZAYED UNIVERSITY:
A NEW MODEL FOR HIGHER EDUCATION IN THE UNITED ARAB EMIRATES

1 Preliminary internal report of the Ministry of Higher Education in the UAE, unpublished. The data contained in the report was taken from the UAE census.

2 Samuel Huntington, *The Clash of Civilizations and the Remaking of World Order* (New York, NY: Simon and Schuster, 1996).

Selected Bibliography

A Nation Learning: Vision for the 21st Century (Albany, NY: Commission for a Nation of Lifelong Learners, 1997).

Abbott, John. "School is Not Enough: Learning for the 21st Century" 21st Century Learning Initiative, paper no. 2 (Summer 1997); *Upside down and inside out: Why good schools will never be enough to meet the challenges of the 21st Century* (Washington, DC: Rothchild Natural Resources, 1996).

Ajawi, Mahmoud A. *Education in the United Arab Emirates* (Al-Ain: Emirates Library Al-Ain, 1991).

Al-Ali, D. "Education and Economic Growth." Unpublished MA thesis, University of Jordan, Amman (1976).

Alderman, Harold, Jere R. Behrman, David R. Ross and Richard Sabot. "The Returns to Endogenous Human Capital in Pakistan's Rural Labour Market." *The Oxford Bulletin of Economics and Statistics* vol. 58, no. 1 (February 1996).

Al-Fares, Abdul Razak. *Higher Education and the Labor Market in the UAE* (Dubai: Science and Culture Forum, 1996).

Al-Khateeb, A. and N. Shatnawy. "Cost-Benefit Analysis of Education in Jordanian Community Colleges 1989–1990." *Abhath Al-Yarmouk*, Humanities and Social Sciences Series vol. 10, no. 1 (1994).

Al-Maeena, Khalled. *Arab News*. "*Arab View*" on the Internet www.arab.net/arabview/articles/maeena16.htm (February 25, 1997, Jeddah, Saudi Arabia).

Al-Sahli, Nabil M. "Economic Development and Direction of Human Developments in the Emirates." *Social Affairs*, Al Sharjah Sociologist Association, Al Sharjah, no. 43.

Al-Yousef, Yousef Khalifeh. "Economic Developments in the UAE 1975–1990." *The Economic and Administrative Sciences Review*, UAE University, no. 8 (September 1992).

Ames, C. et al. *Teachers' School-to-Home Communications and Parent Involvement: The Role of Parent Perceptions and Beliefs* (Baltimore, MD: Center on Families, Communities, Schools and Children's Learning, 1995).

Amis, Kingsley. *Lucky Jim* (New York, NY: Viking Press, 1958).

Anisef, Paul and Paul Axelrod. *Transitions: School and Employment in Canada* (Toronto: Thompson Educational Publishing, 1993).

Ashenfelter, Orley. "Estimating the Effect of Training Programs on Earnings." *Review of Economics and Statistics* vol. LX, no. 1 (February 1978).

Ashenfelter, Orley and J. Ham. "Education, Employment and Earnings." *Journal of Political Economy* vol. 87, no. 5, part 2 (October 1979).

Ashenfelter, Orley and Alan Krueger. "Estimates of the Economic Return to Schooling from a New Sample of Twins." *American Economic Review* vol. 84, no. 5 (December 1994).

Ashenfelter, Orley and Cecilia Rouse (eds) *Cracks in the Bell Curve: Schooling, Intelligence, and Income* (Washington, DC: Brookings Institution Press, 1997).

Ashton, David and Francis Green. *Education, Training and the Global Economy* (Cheltenham, UK: Edward Elgar, 1996).

Association of Muslim Professionals. "Factors Affecting Malay/Muslim Pupils' Performance in Education." *Occasional Paper Series, 1–95* (December 1994).

Badran, Adnan. *At the Crossroads: Education in the Middle East* (New York: Paragon House, 1989).

Ball, Stephen J. *Politics and Policy Making in Education* (London: Routledge, 1990).

Barlow, Maude and Heather-Jane Robertson. *Class Warfare: The Assault on Canada's Schools* (Toronto: Key Porter Books, 1994).

Barner, Robert. "Seven Changes That Will Challenge Managers – And Workers." *The Futurist* vol. 30, no. 2 (1996).

Barnett, Ronald. *Improving Higher Education: Total Quality Care* (Buckingham: Society for Research in Higher Education and Open University, 1992).

Barro, Robert J. and Jong-Wha Lee. "International Comparisons of Educational Attainment." *Journal of Monetary Economics* vol. 32, no. 3 (December 1993).

Barro, Robert J. and Xavier Sala-i-Martin. *Economic Growth* (New York: McGraw-Hill, Inc., 1995).

Baumol, William J. "Multivariate Growth Processes: Contagion as Possible Source of Convergence." Mimeograph (November 7, 1991).

Baumol, William J., Sue Anne Batey Blackman and Edward N. Wolff. *Productivity and American Leadership: The Long View* (Cambridge, MA: The MIT Press, 1989).

Becker, Gary S. "Investment in Human Capital: A Theoretical Analysis." *Journal of Political Economy* vol. 70, part 2 (October 1962); *Human Capital: A Theoretical and Empirical Analysis With Special Reference to Education* (New York: Columbia University Press, 1964); *Human Capital* (Princeton, NJ: Princeton University Press, 1964); "A Note on This Issue." *Educational Researcher* vol. 18 (1989).

Becker, William E. "Teaching Economics to Undergraduates." *Journal of Economic Literature* vol. 35, no. 3 (September 1997).

Becker, William E. and William Baumol (eds) *Assessing Educational Practices: The Contribution of Economics* (Cambridge, MA: The MIT Press, 1996).

Becker, William E., William Greene and Sherwin Rosen. "Research on High School Economic Education." *American Economic Review* vol. 80, no. 2 (May 1990); "Research on High School Economic Education." (expanded version) *Journal of Economic Education* vol. 21, no. 3 (Summer 1990).

Becker, William E. and Darrell Lewis (eds) *The Economics of American Higher Education* (Boston, MA: Kluwer Academic Press, 1992).

Becker, William E. and Sherwin Rosen. "The Learning Effect of Assessment and Evaluation in High School." *Economics of Education Review* (June 1992).

Becker, William E. and Robert Toutkoushian. "The Measurement and Cost of Removing Unexplained Gender Differences in Faculty Salaries." *Economics of Education Review* vol. 14, no. 3 (September 1995).

Behrman, Jere and Nancy Birdsall. "The Quality of Schooling: Quantity Alone is Misleading." *American Economic Review* vol. 73 (1983).

Bellante, Don and Mark Jackson. *Labor Economics: Choice in Labor Markets* (New York: McGraw-Hill Book Company, 1983).

Benhabib, Jess and Mark M. Speigel. "The Role of Human Capital in Economic Development: Evidence from Aggregate Cross-Country Data." *Journal of Monetary Economics* vol. 34 (1994).

Ben-Porath, Y. "The Production of Human Capital and Life Cycle of Earnings." *Journal of Political Economy* vol. 75, no. 4, part I (August 1967).

Betcherman, Gordon and Norm Leckie. *Youth Employment and Education Trends in the 1980s and 1990s* (Ottawa: Canadian Policy Research Networks, 1997).

Betcherman, Gordon and Graham S. Lowe. *The Future of Work in Canada: A Synthesis Report* (Ottawa: Canadian Policy Research Networks, 1997).

Bishop, John. "The Productivity Consequence of What is Learned in High School." *Journal of Curriculum Studies* vol. 22 (1990).

Blaug, Mark. *An Introduction to The Economics of Education* (Harmondsworth: Penguin Books, 1976); "The Empirical Status of Human Capital Theory, A Slightly Jaundiced Survey." *Journal of Economic Literature* vol. 4, no. 1 (September 1976).

Blaug, Mark et al. *The Causes of Graduate Unemployment in India* (London: Allen Lane, The Penguin Press, 1969).

Blinder, Alan S. (ed.) *Paying for Productivity: A Look at the Evidence* (Washington, DC: Brookings Institution, 1990).

Bloom, Michael. *Reaching for Success: Business and Education Working Together* (Ottawa: Conference Board of Canada, 1990); *Profiles of Partnerships: Business-Education Partnerships that Enhance Student Retention* (Ottawa: Conference Board of Canada, 1991).

Boedecker, Ray F. *Eleven Conditions for Excellence: The IBM Total Quality Improvement Process* (Boston, MA: American Institute of Management, 1989).

Boutwell, Clinton E. "Profits Without People." *Phi Delta Kappan* vol. 79, no. 2 (1997).

Bowman, M. J. "The Human Investment Revolution in Economic Thought." *Sociology of Education* vol. 39 (1966).

Bowman, M. J. et al. (eds) *Reading in the Economics of Education* (Paris: UNESCO, 1968).

Brigham, Steve (ed.) *CQI 101: A First Reader for Higher Education* (Washington, DC: AAHE CQI Project, 1994); *25 Snapshots of a Movement: Profiles of Campuses Implementing CQI* (Washington, DC: AAHE CQI Project, 1994).

Bronfenbrenner, Uri. *The Ecology of Human Development: Experiment by Nature and Design* (Cambridge, MA: Harvard University Press, 1986).

Brown, Charles. "Empirical Evidence on Private Training." *Research in Labor Economics* vol. 11, JAI Press (1990).

Brown, J. S., A. Collins and P. Duguid. "Situated Cognition and the Culture of Learning." *Educational Researcher* vol. 18, no. 1 (1989).

Bruner, Jerome. *The Process of Education* (Cambridge, MA: Harvard University Press, 1961); *The Culture of Education* (Cambridge, MA: Harvard University Press, 1996).

Butts, R. Freeman. *A Cultural History of Western Education* (New York: McGraw-Hill, 1955).

Caillods, Françoise and Gabriele G. Duret. *Science Education and Development: Planning and Policy Issues at Secondary Level* (Oxford: Published for the International Institute for Educational Planning by Pergamon, 1997).

Callaghan, J. *Times and Change* (London: Collins, 1987).

Canada Communication Group. *Education and Training in Canada* (Ottawa: Minister of Supply and Services, 1992).

Card, David. "Earnings, Schooling, and Ability Revisited." *Research in Labor Economics* vol. 14 (1995).

Carnoy, M. and H. Thias. *Cost-Benefit Analysis in Education: A Case Study of Kenya* (Baltimore, MD: IBRD, Johns Hopkins Press, 1972).

Cary, Rita. "Work in the 21st Century: A Series of Trapezes?" *Futures Research Quarterly* vol. 13, no. 3 (Fall 1997).

Chicago Innovations Forum. *A Primer for a School's Participation in the Development of Its Local Community* (Chicago, IL: Center for Urban Affairs and Policy Research, Northwestern University, undated, circa 1988).

Chiswick, B. R. and J. Mincer. "Time Series Changes in Personal Income Inequality in the United States from 1939, with Projections to 1985." *Journal of Political Economy* vol. 80, no. 2 (1972).

CMEC. *The Development of Education: Report of Canada* (Toronto: Council of Ministers of Education, Canada, 1996): http://www.cmec.ca/international/deveduc.eng.pdf; *The Report on Education in Canada 1998* (Toronto: Council of Ministers of Education, Canada, 1998a): http://www.cmec.ca/reports/rec98/; *The World of Work*. Reference document for the Third National Forum on Education: Education and Life-Transitions (Toronto: Council of Ministers of Education, Canada, 1998), (document coordinated by the Canadian Labor Congress): http://www.cmec.ca/NaForEd/english/clc.stm; *Updating Essential Skills for the Workplace*. Reference document for the Third National Forum on Education: Education Life-Transitions. (Toronto: Council of Ministers of Education, Canada, 1998), (document coordinated by Human Resources Development, Canada): http://www.cmec.ca/NaForEd/english/HRDC.STM

Cohn, Elchanan. *The Economics of Education* (Cambridge, MA: Ballinger, 1979); "The Impact of Surplus Schooling on Earnings." *Journal of Human Resources* vol. 27, no. 4 (Fall 1992).

Cohn, Elchanan and Shahina Khan. "The Wage Effects of Overschooling Revisited." *Labor Economics* no. 2 (1995).

Cole, Robert E. *Strategies for Learning* (Berkeley, CA: The University of California Press, 1989).

Coleman, James S. *Foundations Social Theory* (Cambridge, MA: Harvard University Press, 1990); "Families and Schools." *Educational Researcher* vol. 16, no. 6 (August–September 1987).

Commission on National Investment in Higher Education. *Breaking the Social Contract: The Fiscal Crisis in Higher Education* (New York, NY: Council for Aid to Education, CAE-100, May 1997).

Conference Board of Canada. *Employability Skills Profile* (Ottawa: Conference Board of Canada, 1993).

Conger, Jay and Rabindra Kanungo. "The Empowerment Process: Integrating Theory and Practice." *Academy of Management Review* (July 1988).

Cornesky, Robert A. *Continuous Quality Improvement Tools for Effective Teaching* (Port Orange, FL: Cornesky & Associates, Inc., 1995); *Quality Indices: Self-Assessment Rating Instrument for Educational Institutions* (Port Orange, FL: Cornesky and Associates, Inc., 1995); *The Quality Professor: Implementing Total Quality Management in the College Classroom* (Madison, WI: Magna Publications,

Inc., 1993); *Turning Continuous Quality Improvement into Institutional Practice: The Tools and Techniques* (Port Orange, FL: Cornesky and Associates, Inc., 1995).

Cornesky, Robert A., Ron Baker, Cathy Cavanaugh, William Etling, Michael Lukert, Sam McCool, Brian McKay, An-Sik Min, Charlotte Paul, Paul Thomas, David Wagner and John Darling. *Using Deming to Improve Quality in Colleges and Universities* (Madison, WI: Magna Publications, Inc., 1989).

Cornesky, Robert A. and William Lazarus. *Continuous Quality Improvement in the Classroom: A Collaborative Approach* (Port Orange, FL: Cornesky and Associates, Inc., 1995).

Cornesky, Robert A. and Sam McCool. *Total Quality Improvement Guide for Institutions of Higher Education* (Madison, WI: Magna Publications, Inc., 1992).

Cornesky, Robert A., Sam McCool, Larry Byrnes and Robert Weber. *Implementing Total Quality Management in Institutions of Higher Education* (Madison, WI: Magna Publications, Inc., 1991).

Corson, David and Stephen B. Lawton (eds) *Education and Work* (2 volumes). Proceedings of the International Conference Linking Research and Practice (Toronto: Ontario Institute for Studies in Education, 1993).

Covey, Stephen R. *The 7 Habits of Highly Effective People* (New York, NY: Simon and Schuster, 1989).

Cox, R. W. (ed.) *The New Realism: Perspectives on Multilateralism and World Order* (Tokyo, Paris: United Nations University Press, 1997).

Crane, David. *The Next Canadian Century: Building a Competitive Economy* (Toronto: Stoddart, 1992).

Crosby, Philip B. *Quality Without Tears: The Art of Hassle-Free Management* (New York: McGraw-Hill Book Company, 1984); *Let's Talk Quality* (New York: McGraw-Hill Book Company, 1989).

Cuban, L. *How Teachers Taught: Constancy and Change in American Classrooms, 1890–1990, 2nd Edition* (New York, NY: Teachers College Press, 1993).

Cuseo, Joseph. *Cooperative Learning: A Pedagogy for Addressing Contemporary Challenges and Critical Issues in Higher Education* (Stillwater, OK: New Forums Press, Inc., 1996).

Darling-Hammond, L. *The Right to Learn: A Blueprint for Creating Schools that Work* (San Francisco, CA: Jossey-Bass, 1997).

Davies, Don. *Communities and Their Schools* (New York, NY: McGraw-Hill, 1981); *Family, Community, and School Partnerships in the 1990's: The Good News and the Bad* (Boston, MA: Institute for Responsive Education, 1996.); *Partnership for Student Success* (Baltimore, MD: Center on Families, Communities, Schools and Children's Learning, 1996).

De Bono, Edward. *Lateral Thinking; A Textbook of Creativity* (Harmondsworth: Penguin Books, 1990); *Teach Yourself to Think* (London: Viking, 1995).

Delors, J. *Learning: The Treasure Within* (UNESCO International Commission on Education for the 21st Century, UNESCO, 1996).

Deming, W. Edwards. *Out of the Crisis* (Cambridge, MA: Productivity Press or Washington, DC: The George Washington University, MIT-CAES, 1982).

Denison, Edward F. "Measuring The Contribution of Education (And The Residual) To Economic Growth" OECD Conference on the Residual Factor and Economic Growth, Paris, DAS/PD/63.2 (May 1964).

Denison, Edward. *The Sources of Economic Growth in the United States and the Alternatives Before Us.* Supplementary Paper no. 13 (New York: Committee for Economic Development, 1962); *Why Growth Rates Differ* (Washington, DC: Brookings Institution, 1967).

Deolalikar, Anil. "Gender Differences in the Returns to Schooling and in School Enrollment Rates in Indonesia." *Journal of Human Resources* vol. 28, no. 4 (Fall 1993).

Department of Statistics. *Yearbook of Statistics* (Singapore: 1996).

de Tocqueville, A. *Democracy in America*, ed. J. P. Maier, trans. George Lawrence (Garden City, NY: Anchor Books, 1969).

Dewey, John. *The Child and the Curriculum* (Chicago, IL: University of Chicago Press, 1943); *Democracy and Education* (New York, NY: The Free Press, 1916).

Dore, Ronald and Mari Sako. *How the Japanese Learn to Work* (London: Routledge, 1989).

Douglas, Paul H. "Are There Laws of Production?" *American Economic Review* vol. 38, no. 1 (1948).

Drucker, Peter F. *Post-Capitalist Society* (New York: Harper Business, 1993).

Eckaus, R. S. "Economic Criteria for Education and Training." *Review of Economics and Statistics* vol. 46, no. 2 (May 1964).

Economic Council of Canada. *A Lot To Learn: Education and Training in Canada* (Ottawa: Minister of Supply and Services, 1992).

Edgerton, R. *An American Imperative: Report of the Wingspread Group on Higher Education* (Racine, WI: Johnson Foundation, 1993).

"Educational Innovation and Information." No. 81 (Geneva: International Bureau of Education, December 1994).

Eicher, Theo. "Interaction Between Endogenous Human Capital and Technological Change." *Review of Economic Studies* vol. 63 (1996).

El Erian, Mohamed, Thomas Helbling and John Page. "Human Resource Development and Economic Growth in the Arab Countries." Mimeograph presented at the Joint Arab Monetary Fund/Arab Fund for Economic and Social Development Seminar on Human Resource Development and Economic Growth. Abu Dhabi, United Arab Emirates (February 1998).

El Hikmi, Ali. "Prospects for the Human Development Plans in the GCC." *Al Iqtissadi Magazine*, Al Sharjah, UAE, no. 40 (November 1996).

Epstein, Joyce L. "Proposal to the Office of Educational Research and Development." (Baltimore, MD: Center on Families, Communities, Schools and Children's Learning, 1990); *School and Family Partnerships* (Baltimore, MD: Center on Families, Communities, Schools and Children's Learning, The Johns Hopkins University, 1992); "School and Family Partnerships." *Encyclopedia of Educational Research* (New York, NY: Macmillan, 1992).

Emirates Center for Strategic Studies and Research (ECSSR). *The Future of the Labor Market in the UAE,* Internal Report (Abu Dhabi: ECSSR, July 1997).

Foot, David K. with Daniel Stoffman. *Boom, Bust & Echo: How to Profit from the Coming Demographic Shift* (Toronto: Macfarlane Walter & Ross, 1996).

Freeman, Richard B. *The Overeducated American* (New York: Academic Press, 1976).

Gardner, Howard. *Multiple Intelligences* (New York: Basic Books, 1993); *Frames of Mind: The Theory of Multiple Intelligences* (New York: Basic Books, 1993); "Intelligence in Seven Steps." *Creating the Future.* www.newhorizons.org/ crgut_gardner.htm

Knight, Frank H. *Freedom and Reform: Essays in Economics and Social Philosophy* (New York: Harper & Brothers, [1947] 1982).

Kohlberg, L. and R. Mayer. "Development as the Aim of Education." *Harvard Educational Review* vol. 14 (1972).

Koshmann, T. D. "Toward a Theory of Computer Support for Collaborative Network Technologies." *Journal of the Learning Sciences* vol. 3, no. 3 (1994).

Krahn, Harvey. *School-Work Transitions: Changing Patterns and Research Needs.* Discussion Paper prepared for Applied Research Branch, Human Resources Development Canada, 1996.

Lalonde, Robert J. "The Promise of Public Sector-Sponsored Training Programs." *Journal of Economic Perspectives* vol. 9, no. 2 (Spring 1995).

Lave, J. and E. Wegner. *Situated Learning: Legitimate Peripheral Participation* (Cambridge: Cambridge University Press, 1991).

Lavoie, Claude. *Youth Employment: Some Explanations and Future Prospects* (1996): http://www.hrdcdrhc.gc.ca/hrdc/corp/stratpol/arbsite/publish/bulletin/vol2n2/ v2n2a2_e.html

Lavoie, Marie and Richard Roy. "Employment Trends in the Information Economy." *Applied Research Bulletin* (Human Resources Development Canada) vol. 3, no. 2 (1997).

Leckie, Norman. *On Skill Requirements Trends in Canada, 1971–1991* (Ottawa: Canadian Policy Research Networks, 1996).

Leichter, Hope. *The Family as Educator* (New York: Teachers College Press, 1974).

Leite, M. F. et al. *The Economics of Educational Costing* (Lisbon: Centro de Economia e Finanças, 1969).

Levering, Robert. *A Great Place to Work* (New York: Random House, Inc., 1988).

Levin, Benjamin. "How Can Schools Respond to Changes in Work?" *Canadian Vocational Journal* vol. 30, no. 3 (1995).

Levin, J., M. Riel, N. Miyake and M. Cohen. "Education on the Electronic Frontier: Teleapprenticeships in Globally Distributed Educational Contexts." *Contemporary Educational Psychology* vol. 12 (1987).

Levine, Solomon B. and Hisashi Kawada. *Human Resources in Japanese Industrial Development* (Princeton, NJ: Princeton University Press, 1980).

Light, Richard J. *The Harvard Assessment Seminars: Exploration with Students and Faculty about Teaching, Learning, and Student Life* (Cambridge, MA: Harvard University Graduate School of Education, 1992).

Lucas, Robert. "On the Mechanics of Economic Development." *Journal of Monetary Economics* vol. 22, no. 1 (July 1988).

Lynch, Lisa. *Training and the Private Sector* (Chicago, IL: University of Chicago Press, 1994).

Maddison, Angus. "Growth and Slowdown in Advanced Capitalist Economies: Techniques of Quantitative Assessment." *Journal of Economic Literature* vol. 25, no. 2 (June 1987).

Manasse, A. Lori. "From Organizations to Relationships: New Ways of Working and Their Implications for Learning." *Futures Research Quarterly* vol. 13, no. 3 (Fall 1997).

Mankiw, Gregory, David Romer and David Weil. "A Contribution to the Empirics of Economic Growth." *Quarterly Journal of Economics* vol. 107, no. 2 (May 1992).

Marquardt, Richard. *Youth and Work in Troubled Times: A Report on Canada in the 1990s* (Ottawa: Canadian Policy Research Networks, 1996).

Marshall, Alfred. *Principles of Economics, Book IV, 8th Edition* (London: Macmillan and Company Ltd., 1949).

Marshall, Ray and Marc Tucker. *Thinking for a Living: Education and the Wealth of Nations* (New York: Basic Books, 1992).

Massialas, Byron G. and Samir Ahmed Jarrad. *Education in the Arab World* (New York: Praeger, 1983).

McCloskey, Donald. "Writing as a Responsibility of Science: A Reply." *Economic Inquiry* vol. 30, no. 4 (October 1992).

McConnell, C. R. and S. L. Brue. *Contemporary Labor Economics* (New York: McGraw-Hill Book Company, 1986).

McGilly, K. (ed.) *Classroom Lessons: Integrating Cognitive Theory and Classroom Practice* (Cambridge, MA: MIT Press/Bradford Books, 1994).

McMahon, Walter W. "Conceptual Framework for the Analysis of the Social Benefits of Lifelong Learning." *Education Economics* (Summer/Fall 1998).

McPherson, Michael S., Morton Owen Schapiro and Gordon C. Winston (eds) *Paying the Piper: Productivity, Incentives, and Financing in US Higher Education* (Ann Arbor, MI: The University of Michigan Press, 1993).

McRae, H. *The World in 2020* (Boston, MA: Harvard Business School Press, 1994).

Means, B. et al. *GLOBE Year 2 Evaluation: Implementation and Progress* (Menlo Park, CA: SRI International, 1997).

Medoff, J. L. and K. G. Abraham. "Experience, Performance, and Earnings." *Quarterly Journal of Economics* vol. XCV, no. 4 (December 1980).

Mehan, H., I. Villanueva, L. Hubbard and A. Linz. *Constructing School Success: The Consequences of Untracking Low-Achieving Students* (Cambridge: Cambridge University Press, 1996).

Meier, D. *The Power of Their Ideas: Lessons from a Small School in Harlem* (Boston, MA: Beaken Press, 1995).

Miller, H. P. "Annual and Life-time Income in Relation to Education: 1939–59." *American Economic Review* vol. 50, no. 4 (December 1960).

Millis, Barbara and Philip G. Cottell, Jr. *Cooperative Learning for Higher Education Faculty* (Phoenix, AZ: American Council on Education Series on Higher Education, Oryx Press, 1997).

Mincer, Jacob. "Investment in Human Capital and Personal Income Distribution." *Journal of Political Economy* vol. LXVI, no. 4 (1958); "On-The-Job Training: Costs, Returns and Some Implications." *Journal of Political Economy* (supplement) (October 1962); *Schooling, Experience, and Earnings* (New York and London: Columbia University Press, 1974).

Ministry of Education. *New Education System (Primary Level), Implementation Guidelines.* (Singapore: MOE, 1979); *Improving Primary School Education, Report of the Review Committee* (Singapore: MOE, 1991); "Building a Firm Foundation." A Report to the Minister for Education on the Study Team's visit to Japan and Taiwan (Singapore: 1990); "Looking back, looking ahead: reflections and renewal in education." Proceedings of the Principals' Conference, September 4–6, 1995, Singapore.

Mograby, Abdullah. "Youth Unemployment and Government Intervention in the NSW Labor Market." Unpublished PhD thesis, Macquarie University, Sydney, 1991.

Thurow, Lester. *Investment in Human Capital* (Belmont, CA: Wadsworth Publishing Company, 1970).

Tibawi, A. L. *Islamic Education: Its Traditions and Modernizations into the Arab Nation System* (London: Luzak, 1972).

Twenty-First Century Learning Initiative. "Synthesis."*1997 Report of the Education 2000 Trust* (Washington, DC: Rothchild Natural Resources, 1997); "Response to the White Paper." From L. G. C. Heritage Foundation Offices, Broadway Letchworth Garden City, Hertfordshire SG6 3AB.

Twigg, C. "The Need for a National Learning Infrastructure." *Educom Review* vol. 29; online at: http://www.educom.edu/program/nlii/keydocs/mongraph.html

Uchida, Donna, Marvin J. Cetron and Floretta McKenzie. "What Students *Must* Know to Succeed in the Communication Age." *The Futurist* vol. 30, no. 4 (1996).

UNESCO. *World Education Report 1995* (Paris: UNESCO, 1995); *World Summit for Social Development Report* (Paris: UNESCO, 1996); *Learning: The Treasure Within* (Paris: UNESCO, 1996); *Report: R&D Indicators for the Arab States* (Cairo: UNESCO, 1997); *Thinking Ahead: UNESCO and the Challenges of Today and Tomorrow* (Paris: UNESCO, 1997); *World Development Report 1997* (New York: UNDP, 1997); *World Science Report, 1998* (Paris: UNESCO, 1998).

UNESCO Prospects. "New Technologies in Education." *Quarterly Review of Comparative Education* vol. XXVII, no. 3 (September 1997).

Vaizey, John. *The Economics of Education* (London: Faber and Faber, 1962); *The Economics of Education* (London: Macmillan Press, 1973).

Van Til, Jon. "Facing Inequality and the End of Work." *Educational Leadership* vol. 54, no. 6 (1997).

Verdugo, Richard, and Naomi Verdugo. "The Impact of Surplus Schooling on Earnings: Some Additional Findings." *Journal of Human Resources* vol. 24, no. 4 (1989).

Wachtel, Howard M. *Labor and the Economy* (Orlando, FL: Academic Press Inc., 1984).

Walberg, H. (ed.) *Educational Environments and Effects* (Berkeley, CA: McCutchan, 1979).

Ward, T. B., S. M. Smith and S. Vaid (eds) *Conceptual Structures and Processes: Emergence, Discovery and Change* (Washington, DC: APA Press, 1996).

Waterman, Robert H. *Adhocracy: The Power to Change* (Knoxville, TN: Whittle Direct Books, 1990).

Weiss, Andrew. "High School Graduation, Performance, and Wages." *Journal of Political Economy* vol. 96 (1988).

Werstch, J. V. (ed.) *Culture, Communication and Cognition: Vygotskian Perspectives* (Cambridge: Cambridge University Press, 1985).

Wilkinson, Frank (ed.) *The Dynamics of Labor Market Segmentation* (London: Academic Press, 1981).

Winokur, Jon. *The Portable Curmudgeon* (New York: Nal Books, 1987).

Wirth, Arthur G. *Education and Work for the Year 2000: Choices We Face* (San Francisco, CA: Jossey-Bass, 1992).

Wolfe, Barbara and Samuel Zuvekas. "Non-Market Outcomes of Schooling." *International Journal of Education Research* vol. 27, no. 7 (1997).

Womack, James P., Daniel T. Jones and Daniel Roos. *The Machine That Changed the World* (New York: Rawson Associates, 1990).

Woodhall, Maureen. *Economic Aspects of Education: A Review of Research in Britain* (Windsor: NFER Publishing Company Ltd., 1972).